Postcard History Series

Butler County

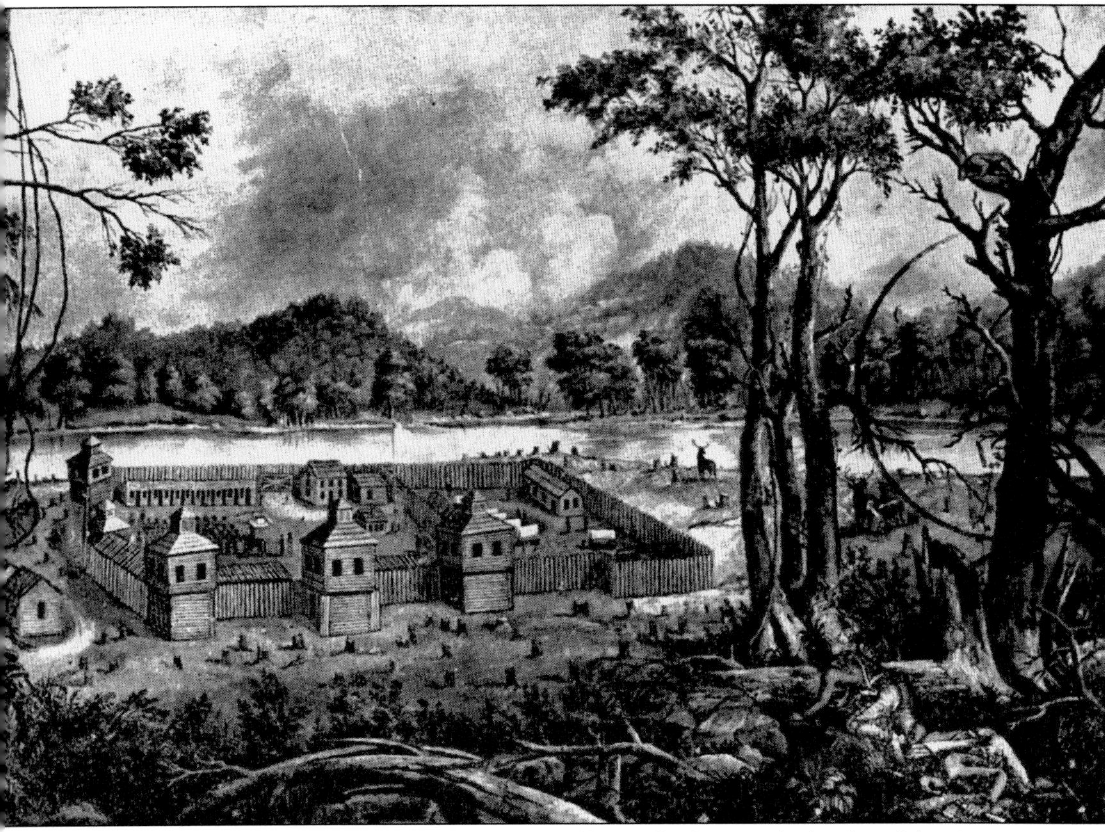

Butler County essentially began with the building of a fort on the banks of the Great Miami River in 1791. The fort, completed on September 31, housed supplies and soldiers for Gen. Arthur St. Clair's campaign against Native Americans in the region. Four blockhouses, a barracks, guardrooms, two storerooms, and a magazine made up the fort that was named for Alexander Hamilton, then secretary of the treasury. Tools were so scarce at the time that some of the soldiers lent their own to complete the fort in just a few weeks. Native Americans killed 31 people, mostly travelers, in the vicinity of the fort before the complex was abandoned in the summer of 1796.

On the front cover: Please see page 67. (Authors' collection.)

On the back cover: Please see page 53. (Authors' collection.)

POSTCARD HISTORY SERIES

Butler County

Cheryl Bauer and Randy McNutt

ARCADIA
PUBLISHING

ISBN 978-0-7385-4100-6

Published by Arcadia Publishing
Charleston, South Carolina

Printed in the United States of America

Library of Congress Catalog Card Number: 2006927304

For all general information contact Arcadia Publishing at:
Telephone 843-853-2070
Fax 843-853-0044
E-mail sales@arcadiapublishing.com
For customer service and orders:
Toll-Free 1-888-313-2665

Visit us on the Internet at www.arcadiapublishing.com

To the memory of Kay and Bill McNutt.

Contents

ACKNOWLEDGMENTS

Through vintage postcards, this book depicts life in Butler County from the days of Fort Hamilton through the 1950s and beyond. Most of the cards come from our personal collection. A few were provided by the Butler County Historical Society, which also worked with us on *Hamilton* in the Images of America series.

The cards would be far less informative without the history that goes with them. As a result, we wish to thank the local historians whose work has been invaluable to researchers through the years. Long after they are gone, their work will live on and inform other Butler County residents of the way of life in the 19th and 20th centuries.

Specifically, we are grateful to the following historians for their significant contributions to Butler County's past. James Blount, a Hamilton newspaper editor and teacher, has tirelessly written and spoken about historic Hamilton and Butler County. He has served on many community boards and helped improve life in the county. Jim is a good friend to many and an award-winning writer and historian who is respected throughout the county. The late Esther Benzing, a onetime county archivist and newspaper columnist from Fairfield, wrote books about the Soldiers, Sailors, and Pioneers Monument and the city of Fairfield. Her books have been helpful to everyone from city leaders to citizens interested in history. Esther was a kind and personable woman who touched many lives. The late George Crout, a Middletown historian and author, penned books about his county, city, and state. He donated much of his personal library to the Middletown Public Library, allowing other historians to use the books for their own research.

We also thank other area historians—too numerous to mention but certainly not forgotten—for their contributions. Through their work, they have made Butler County a more interesting and lively place to live.

Introduction

When settlers began arriving in the forested place that is now Butler County in the early 1790s, the frontier was protected by Fort Hamilton, named for founding father Alexander Hamilton. The wooden stockade sprawled alongside the Great Miami River about 25 miles northwest of Cincinnati, then the site of Fort Washington on the Ohio River.

Although Fort Hamilton did not see any battles, it provided security for the settlers and supplied the frontier army during the Ohio Country's American Indian wars of 1791–1794. After Gen. Anthony Wayne defeated the Native Americans in the Battle of Fallen Timbers in what is now Lucas County in northwest Ohio, a temporary peace encouraged settlers to head west for a new start. Soon a small town grew around the fort. In the late 1790s, soldiers turned Fort Hamilton over to the public. The community continued to expand but the memory of the frontier remained. Until 1913, the fort's old powder magazine stood next to the bridge on High Street, serving as a reminder of Butler County's pioneer past.

When photography became popular and picture postcards the craze in the early 1900s, other architectural gems crossed into the viewfinders of local photographers. Imagine the excitement they must have felt with this new medium. People actually wanted to buy their photographs! Never mind that the images were printed on postcards. All the photographers had to do was aim and shoot to capture a city stocked with Victorian architecture such as the magnificent sandstone Butler County Courthouse, the Butler County Children's Home, and the storefronts of Hamilton's High Street. Eager postcard buyers did not seem to mind what was on the front of the card, so long as it showed life as they lived it.

On July 4, 1906, Butler County citizens dedicated their Soldiers, Sailors, and Pioneers Monument along the Great Miami on the site where Fort Hamilton once stood. The new building was inspired by Civil War veterans but soon became a shrine to all pioneers and veterans. Immediately, the memorial became a favorite subject of postcard publishers. The building remains a popular subject to this day.

Of course, many other familiar buildings were celebrated on picture postcards, including workplaces all across the county. After Ohio statehood and the formation of Butler County in 1803, the county became a bastion of education and industry. Factories lined the streets of the larger communities. When the 20th century both started and ended, the county prided itself on its fine education, performing arts, and varied jobs. All were acknowledged on postcards.

Many Hamilton postcards celebrated factories—Mosler Safe, Beckett Paper, Champion Coated Paper, Estate Stove, and others. Meanwhile, Middletown photographers published images of their city's industries, including the Sorg Paper Company. It was as though a friendly competition existed between the photographers to see who could create the most postcards of their growing cities.

Throughout the last half of the 19th and first half of the 20th centuries, Hamilton was known as the greatest small industrial city in America, producing everything from paper to safes for national markets. Residents bought postcards of factories to show their friends and families where they worked. During this general era, Hamilton was also the home of important figures in the arts and in sports, including authors Fannie Hurst and William Dean Howells, music composer Johnnie Black, and Cincinnati Reds baseball legend Joe Nuxhall. But it was the factories that made Hamilton special.

Middletown also continued to thrive as an industrial city, serving as a global supplier of steel through the Armco Steel Corporation (later AK Steel). It was a town dominated by the steel factory and men of steel.

Through the years, postcards have also depicted the other sides of life in Butler County—more relaxed and cerebral times. For example, Hamilton and Middletown share a rich musical heritage with various symphonies, choral groups, and orchestras gaining regional fame. They also share a wealth of picturesque Federal and Victorian architecture, which is prominently illustrated by the postcard collection that appears in this book.

Oxford, the smallest of the county's three major communities, has gained the most national notoriety as the home of Confederate spies Lottie and Ginny Moon, pioneering textbook editor William Holmes McGuffey, and Miami University. As Miami plans its bicentennial in 2009, alumni can recall the earlier days by viewing the cards in the chapter devoted to the university and its pleasing brick architecture.

Early-20th-century photographers captured both the serene and tragic events of Butler County. They roamed the county looking for the familiar and the unfamiliar, from bridges to undiscovered small patches of green where people went to play and relax. But these photographers—most of them anonymous—also serve as visual historians through their work during the hard times. Their images of the county's devastating 1913 flood show a much different Hamilton—a place where water covers most of the downtown and threatens the lives of people across the parts of the county where the Great Miami flows. These postcards include some rare and dramatic shots that have never been published before in book form.

While the rains came in torrents in March 1913, photographers like C. S. Jacobi jumped in rowboats and paddled around town, finding people and animals trapped in unusual situations. The photographers also climbed to the highest buildings to take dramatic views of Hamilton's flooded streets and businesses. If it were not for the work of these dedicated photographers, we would not know what the great flood felt like—or even what it looked like—in the cold days of 1913.

Fortunately most of the cards in this book depict a more pleasantly remembered time and place, one that modern observers would expect to see—people going to church, playing games, walking along the sidewalks, boating, and meeting friends at a lodge. For us, vintage postcards reaffirm the image of Butler County's rural as well as its industrial heritage. It is a time long past but not forgotten.

One

Icons and Landmarks

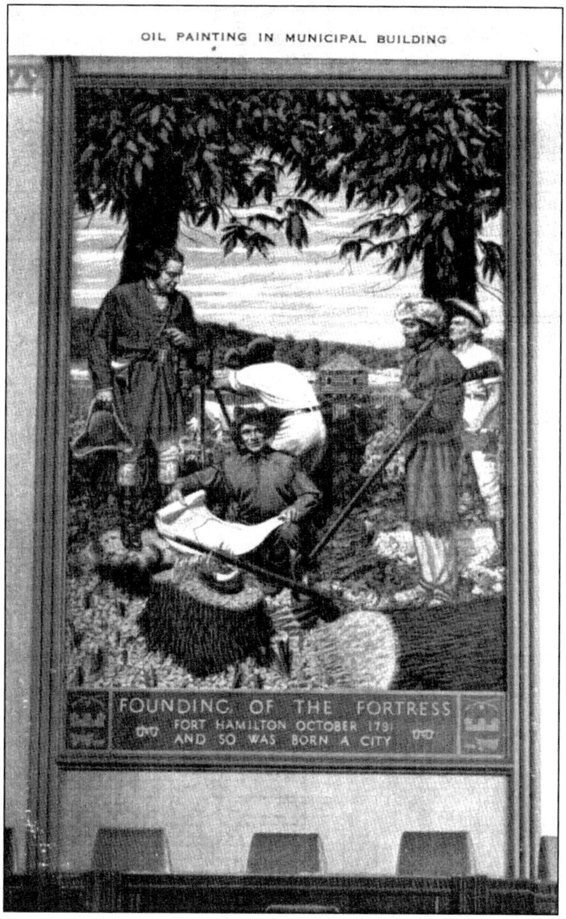

Maj. Gen. Richard Butler (left), for whom the new county was named, was the superintendent of Indian Affairs for the Northern United States District before serving as second in command to Gen. Arthur St. Clair. Israel Ludlow (center) laid out a town adjacent to Fort Hamilton in December 1794. He first called the town Fairfield in honor of the meadow that once existed there but soon changed the name to Hamilton. Ludlow's agent, Darious C. Orcutt, began selling lots to settlers soon after. The man to the right is William Wells. The two soldiers in the background are unidentified. Hamilton artist Jack Willard painted this mural of Hamilton's founding for the city council chamber in the old municipal building on the west end of High Street.

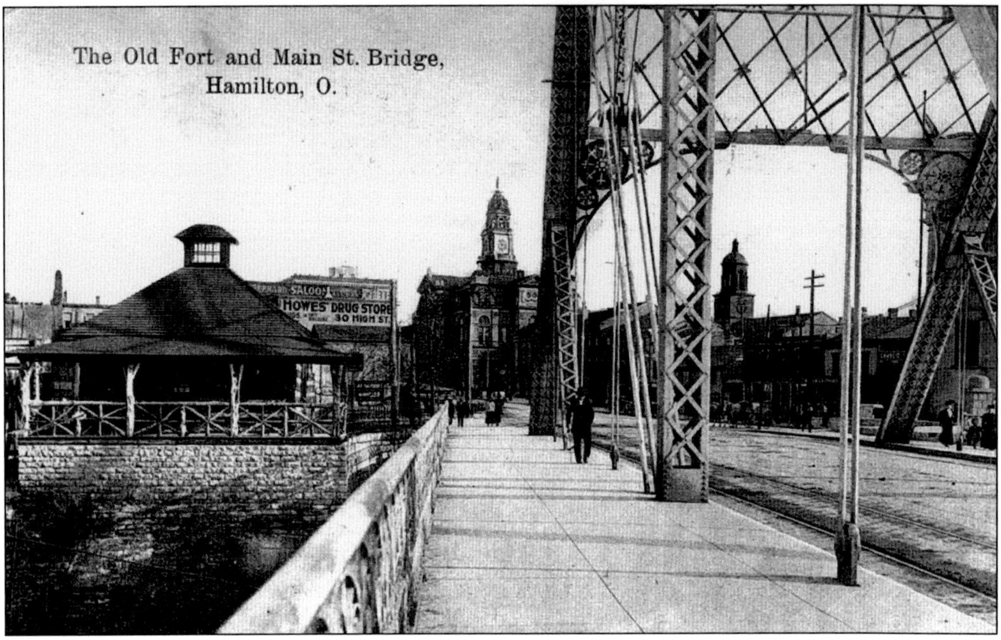

The old magazine of Fort Hamilton was the last major remnant of the fortress remaining when this card was mailed in 1908. City leaders were too busy planning for the future to think of historic preservation. They were focused on progress, represented by the stately courthouse in the background and by the Main Street Bridge. Note the span's ornate steelwork. The bridge, completed in 1895, connected Hamilton proper with the community of Rossville. The bridge and the magazine were subsequently destroyed by the 1913 flood.

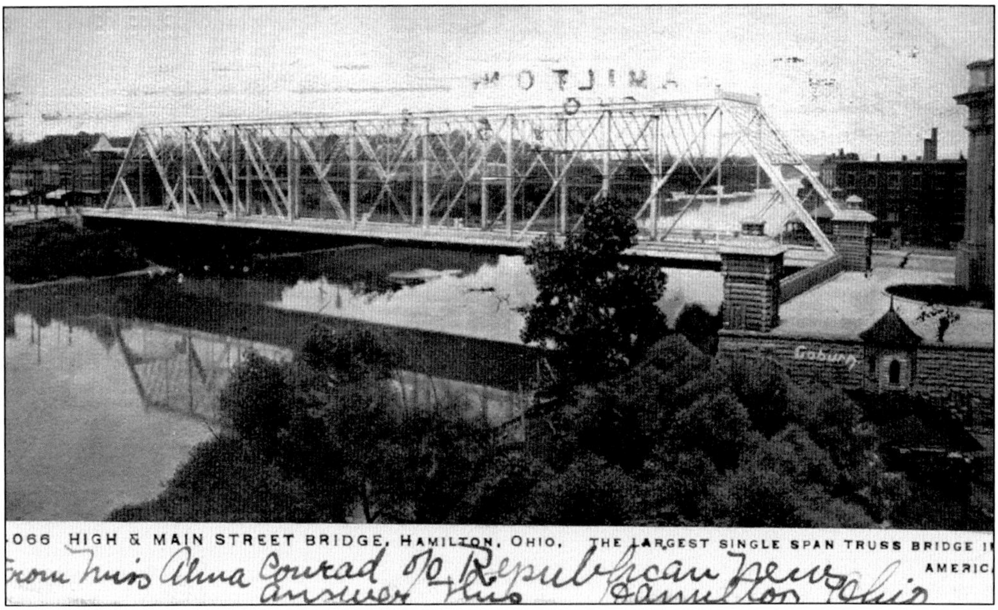

This view of Hamilton's Main Street Bridge shows the replica blockhouses, made of sandstone, at the east end of the bridge. The bridge was reportedly the largest single-span truss bridge in the country when this card was mailed in June 1906. The rear of the newly completed Soldiers, Sailors, and Pioneers Monument is visible on the far right.

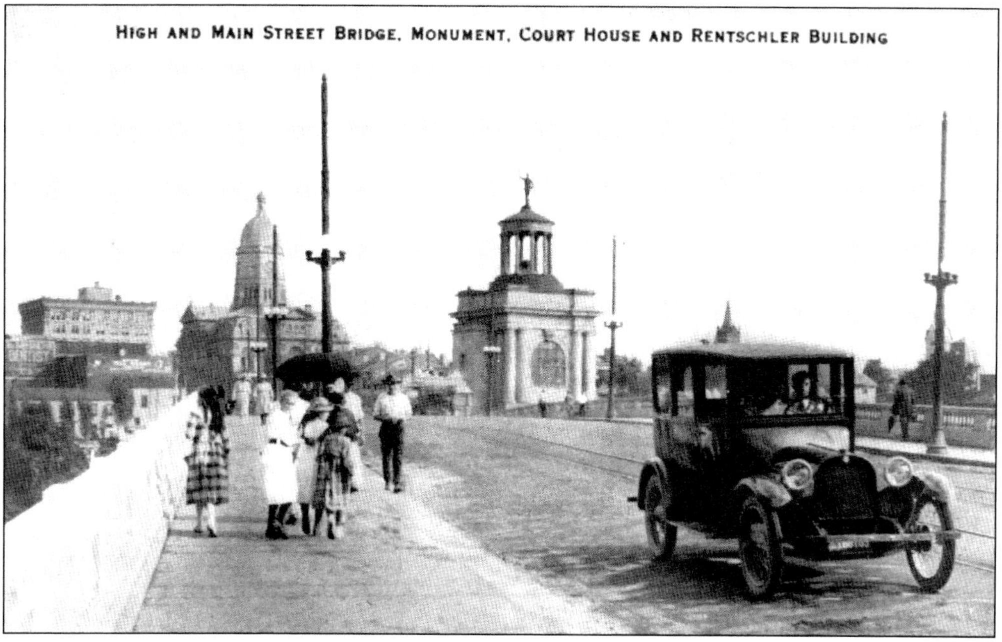

These cards depict Hamilton's ornamental High Street Bridge. The new bridge, completed in 1914, boasted wide pedestrian sidewalks and state-of-the-art concrete construction. Three prominent Hamilton landmarks are visible in both cards: the Rentschler Building (left), the city's tallest office building at the time; the courthouse (center); and the Soldiers, Sailors, and Pioneers Monument and Memorial Building.

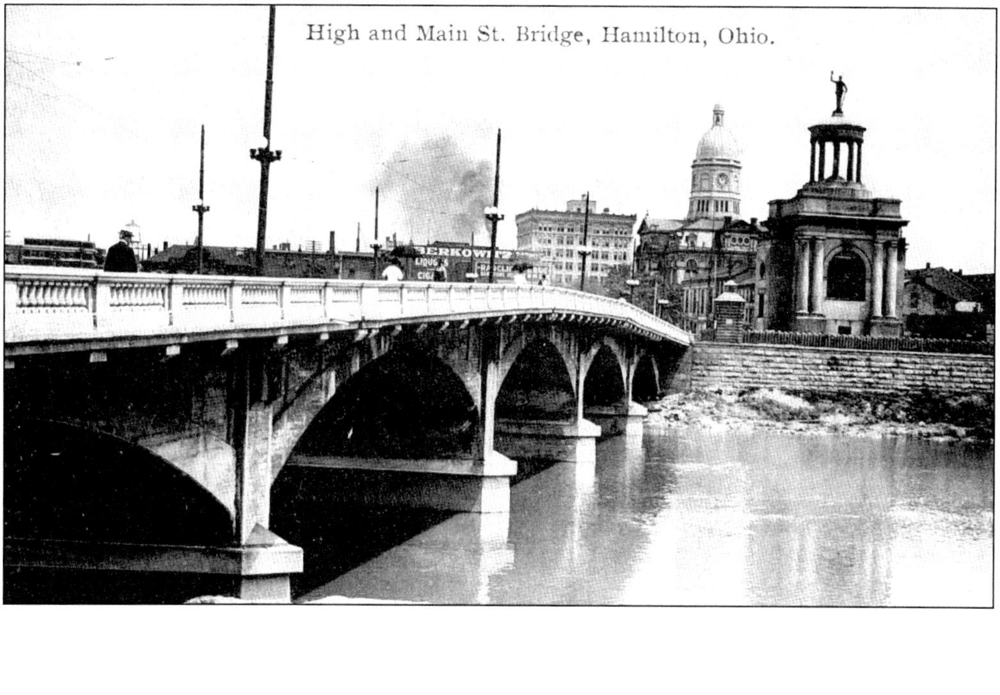

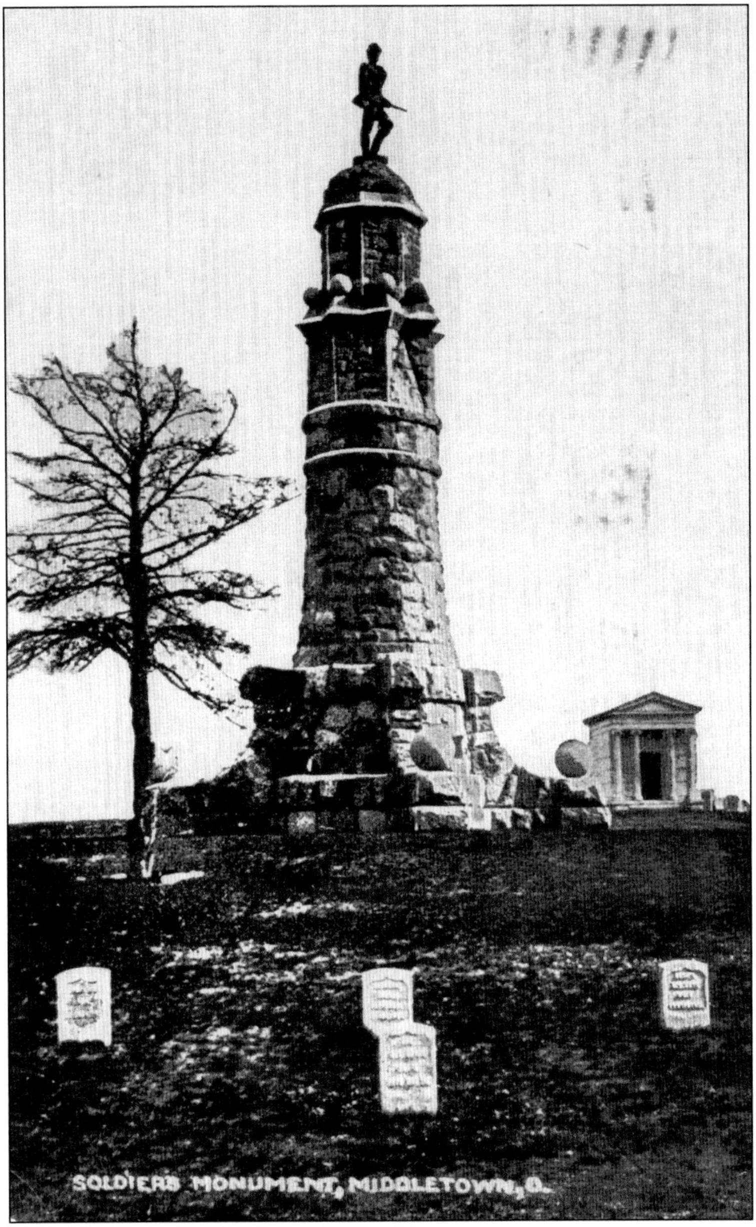

Middletown schoolchildren first proposed a memorial to Civil War soldiers in 1895. Businessman and philanthropist Paul J. Sorg was so moved that he promised to commission a statue of a soldier if children in Middletown and Lemon Township each contributed a stone to create the monument's base. A county levy passed in 1899 provided some funds. The Middletown committee, led by W. H. Todhunter, hired Dayton architect F. M. Andrews to draw the plans for a statue to be erected in Woodside Cemetery. C. L. Thiely of Dayton built the base of native boulders at a cost of $7,358; the bronze statue itself cost $3,000. Fallen heroes, members of the Grand Army of the Republic (GAR), and current soldiers were honored at a December 17, 1902, dedication service at Middletown's Sorg Opera House. The 3rd Regiment Band led citizens to the monument for the actual dedication. Sorg kept his promise to pay for the statue but did not live to see it completed. The Sorg Mausoleum is seen to the right of the memorial.

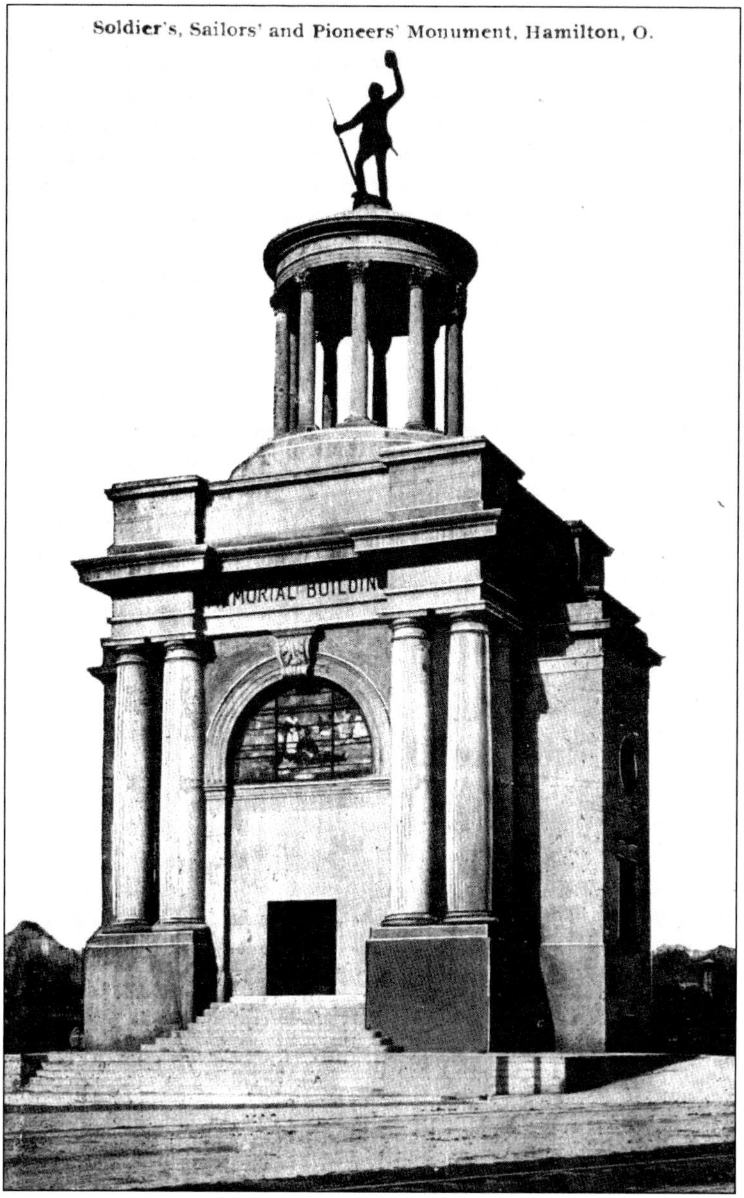

The 1899 tax levy that contributed to the Middletown monument also helped build the Butler County Soldiers, Sailors, and Pioneers Monument in Hamilton. Architect Frederich Noonan and engineer John C. Weaver, both local residents, designed the three-story steel and limestone building. Hamilton artist Rudolph Thiem created the bronze figure of Billy Yank to represent the average enlisted Union soldier in the Civil War. The total cost of the monument was a little over $71,000. The arched, art-glass window visible above the entrance is one of two beautiful windows that honor women's contributions during the Civil War. This one, facing High Street, shows two nurses tending to a wounded soldier on the battlefield. The one facing the Great Miami River depicts women in a home preparing bandages for the wounded. Two smaller windows show the seal of Ohio and the seal of the GAR. The names of more than 4,300 Butler County pioneers and heroes are carved on the interior white-marble walls. The monument was dedicated on July 4, 1906.

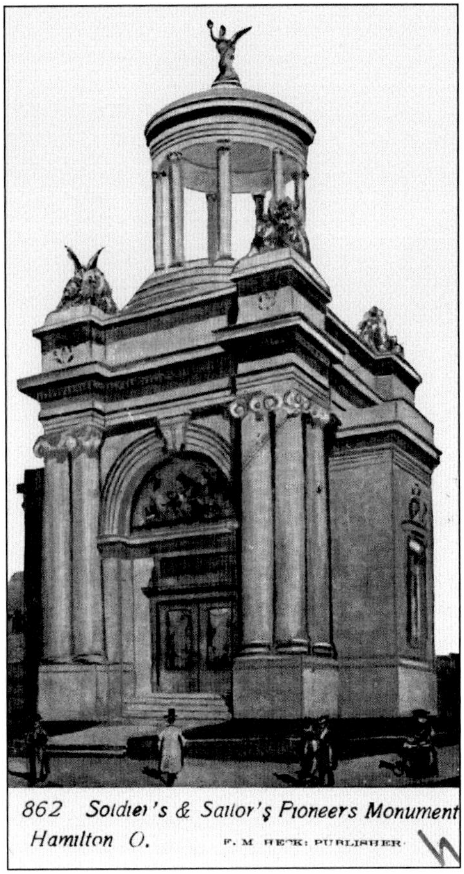

The Middletown and Butler County monuments have been popular topics for postcards over the years. This fanciful artist's drawing of the Soldiers, Sailors, and Pioneers Monument (left) shows gargoyle-type creatures on the four corners. The indistinct figure on top looks more like a winged god than the everyman Billy Yank. Inside the monument are many artifacts of Butler County's history and military heritage, as well as changing special exhibits. A county-wide celebration on July 4, 2006, marked the memorial's centennial. The Middletown monument (below), in its parklike setting, remains a spot for quiet contemplation.

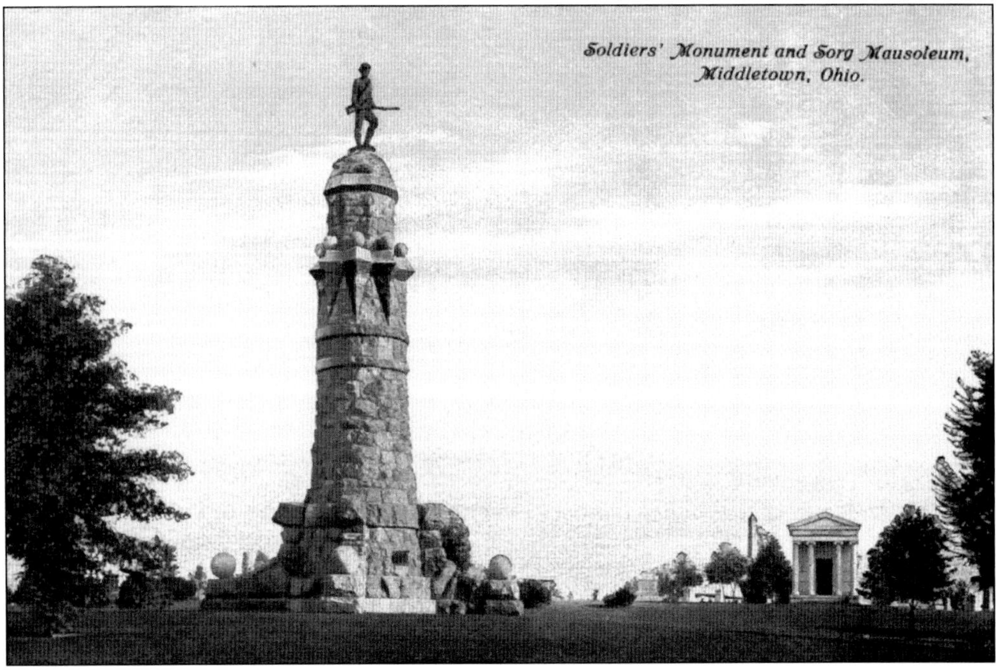

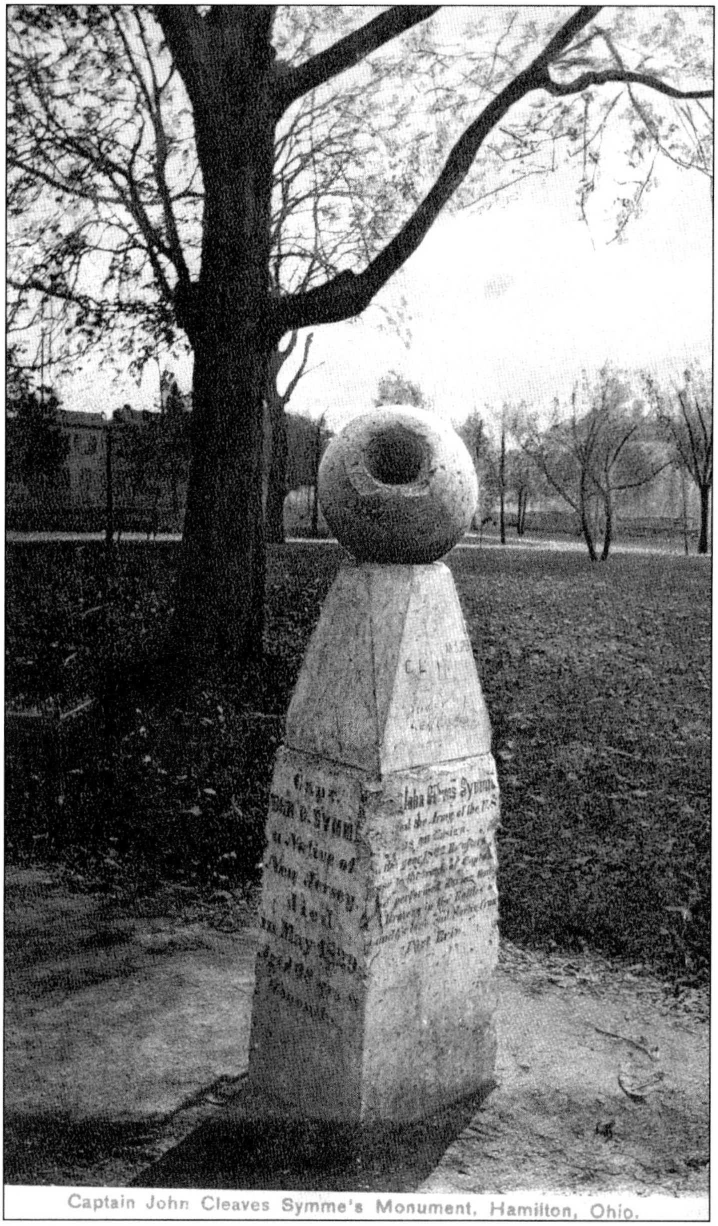

One of the strangest spots in Butler County is the grave and monument of Capt. John Cleves Symmes on Third Street in Hamilton. Symmes was a 19th-century soldier, scholar, philosopher, and originator of the Symmes Theory of Concentric Spheres and Polar Voids, otherwise known as the Hollow Earth Theory. Symmes theorized that the earth is hollow and inhabited by a different race of people. His dream was to lead an exploration party there. His lectures and writings on the subject nearly launched a federal expedition, inspired a fantasy novel, and attracted the interest of Edgar Allan Poe. After Symmes's death in Hamilton in 1829, his son Americus Vespucius Symmes erected a 5.5-foot stone marker topped by a 20-inch, 80-pound globe on his father's grave. The burying park on Third was abandoned after the larger Greenwood Cemetery was started in the mid-1800s, but Symmes's monument remains there, restored in 1991 through the efforts of Historic Hamilton.

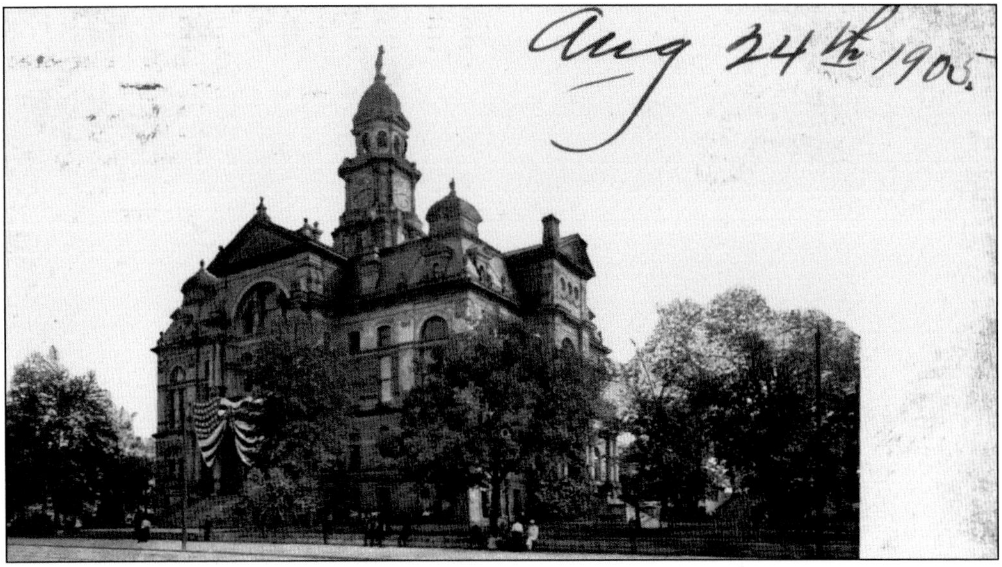

Butler County's fourth courthouse, shown in this 1905 postcard, was completed in 1889 for roughly $304,000. The first county court sessions had been held in John Torrance's tavern at Dayton and Water Streets in Hamilton in May 1803. Court moved to the former officers' mess at Fort Hamilton in 1804. A proper courthouse was built in 1818 at the current site on High Street in Hamilton. The new sandstone courthouse was constructed in the Victorian Second Empire style and graced with numerous dormers, porticos, and Corinthian columns.

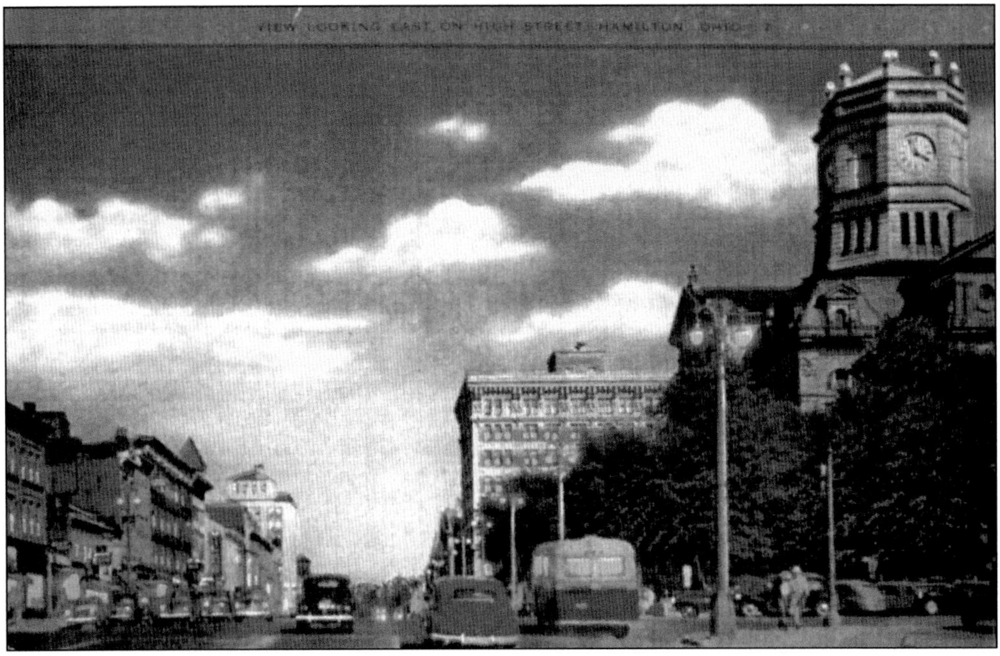

A tragic 1912 fire that claimed three firefighters changed the courthouse's summit. The graceful top tower seen in the 1905 card collapsed into the rotunda. When the courthouse was repaired, the clock tower became the highest point. The courthouse was placed on the National Register of Historic Places after an extensive 1980 restoration led by county archivist Esther Benzing and others.

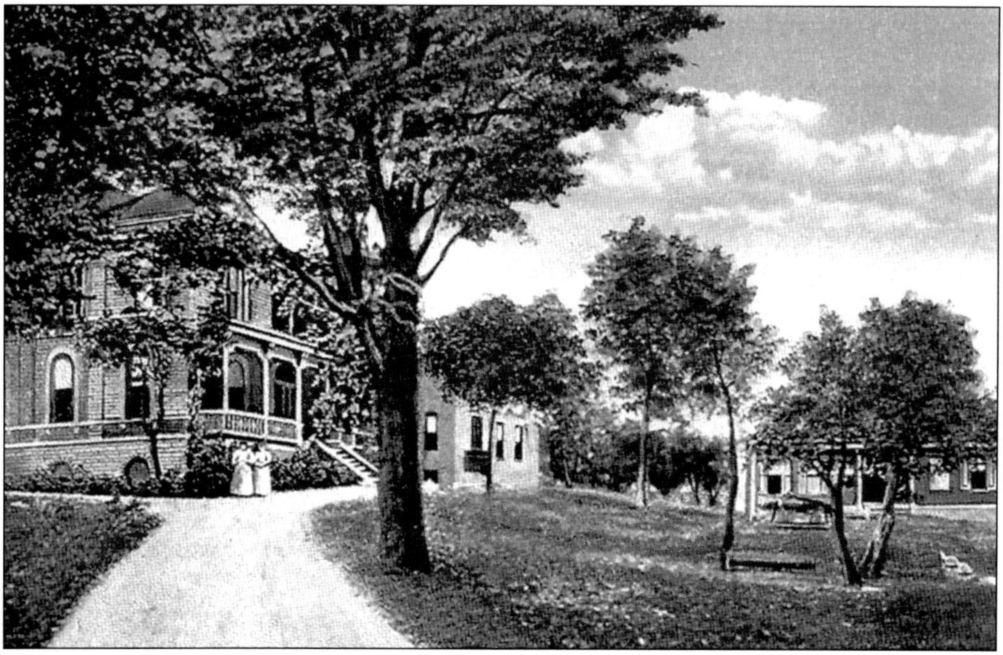

Many children orphaned by the Civil War were left desolate, prompting local governments to begin planning institutional care. The Butler County Children's Home opened at 425 South D Street, Hamilton, in September 1875. County commissioners obtained a large Italianate-style home built in 1850 by Clark Lane and E. J. Dyer to shelter the children.

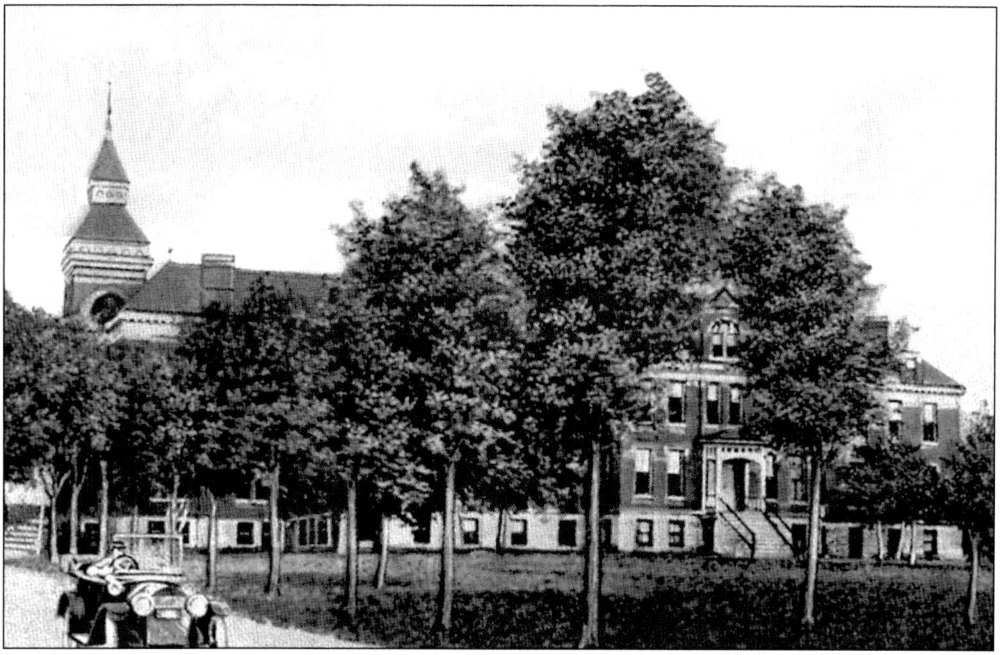

Commissioners began to plan a poorhouse in 1831, and the first board of directors, led by Richard Easton, was appointed in 1836. Residents raised their own food. Surplus produce, hogs, and stone gathered from a quarry on the property were sold to help pay expenses. The name was later changed to the Butler County Infirmary and Tuberculosis Hospital.

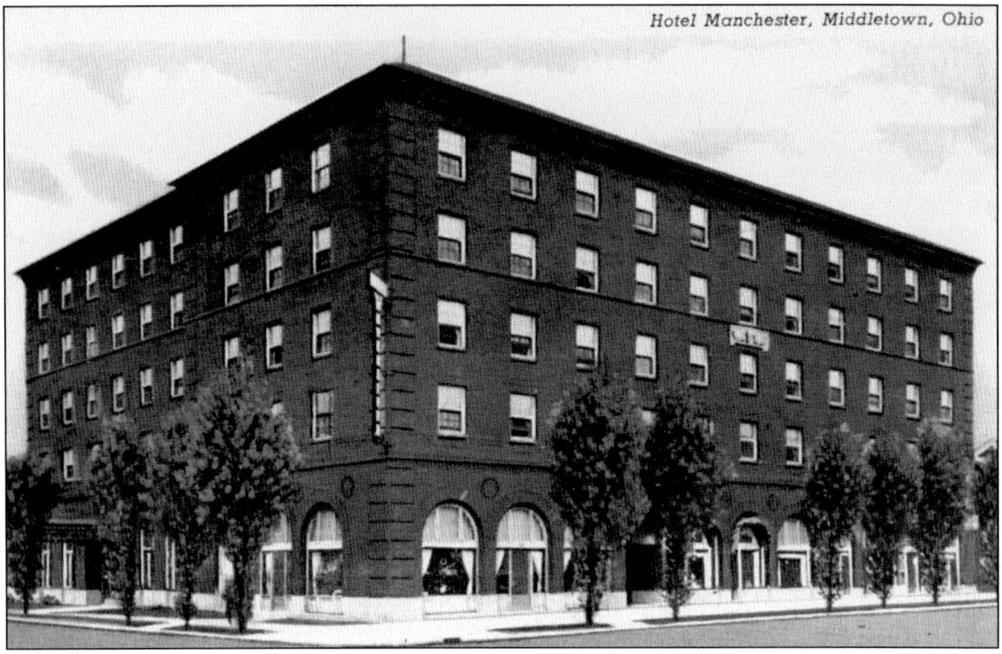

By the early 1920s, Middletown was bustling with business travelers visiting the city's steel mills, paper plants, and numerous other industries. The Middletown Chamber of Commerce formed a committee to secure funds to build a modern hotel for visitors. The Middletown Hotel Company was formed, and after securing $265,000 worth of stock, construction of a hotel on Manchester Avenue began in 1922.

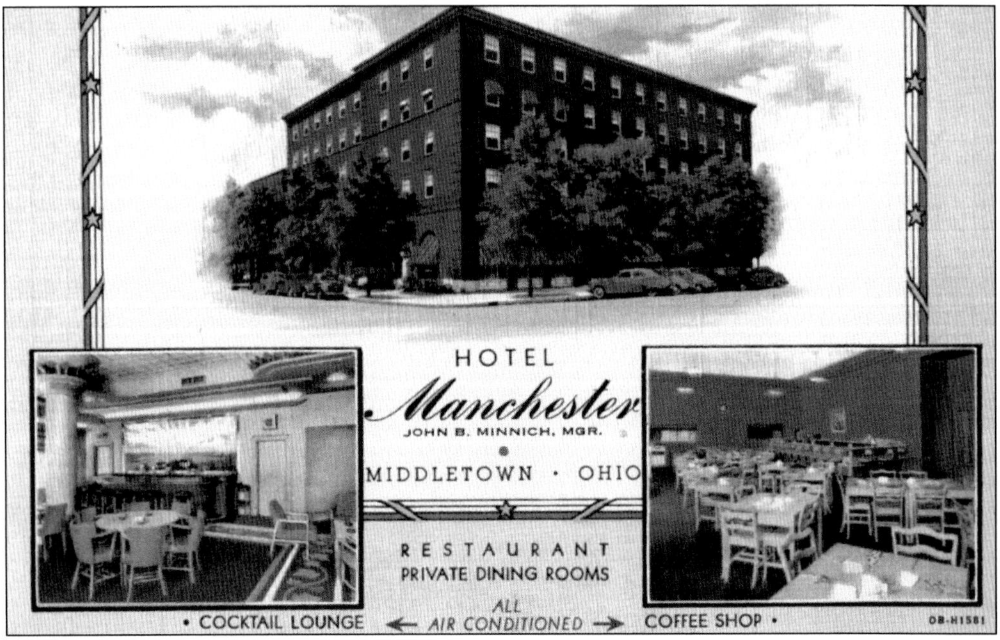

The five-story brick Hotel Manchester boasted air-conditioned private dining rooms, a restaurant, a coffee shop, a cocktail lounge, and a banquet hall that could seat 800 guests. The hotel included 110 guest rooms. As ownership changed over the decades, it became the Manchester Inn.

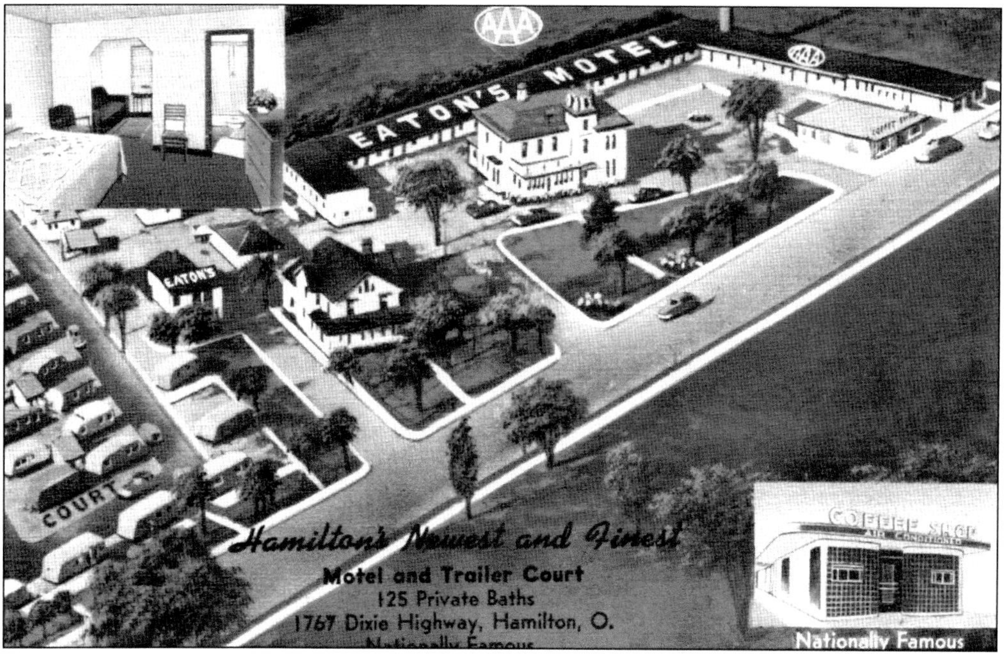

By 1920, Dixie Highway led travelers from Michigan to Florida, with thousands stopping along the way at Mr. and Mrs. John Eaton's motel and trailer park in Hamilton. The travel trailers shown at left in this *c.* 1950s card illustrate America's love of road travel. Paving of the Butler County section of the national route began in 1917, just north of the Winton Road intersection in modern Fairfield.

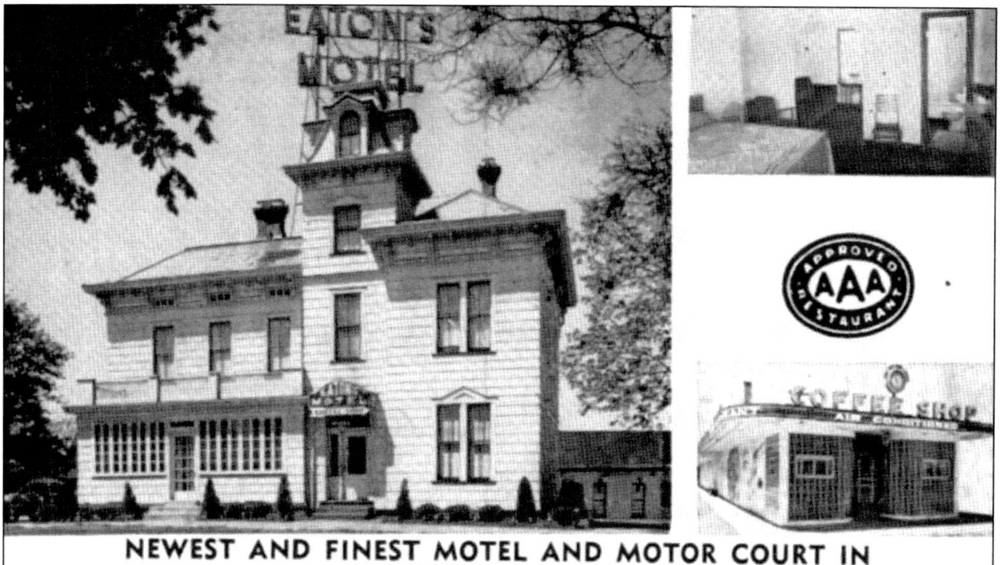

Eaton's Motel had 125 up-to-date rooms with private baths at its most successful point in the 1950s. Amenities included the security of fireproof rooms, the warmth of radiant heat, and the luxury of an air-conditioned coffee shop.

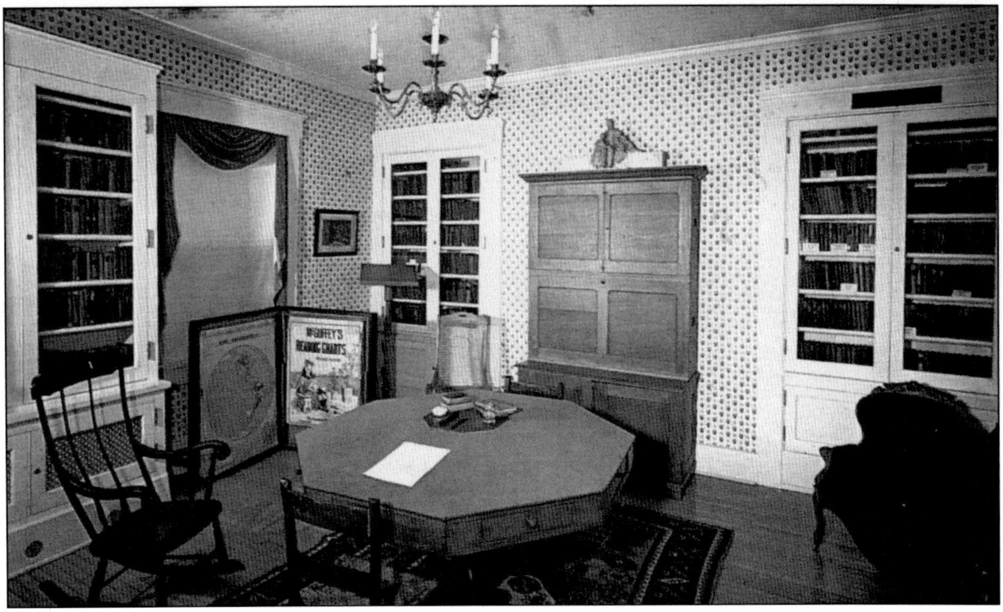

William Holmes McGuffey sat at this octagonal table as he created the famous McGuffey Readers series that taught several generations of youngsters to read. McGuffey taught at Miami University in Oxford from 1826 to 1836. The McGuffey Museum, located on the Oxford campus, contains the most complete collection of McGuffey Readers, Spellers, and Rhetorics in existence.

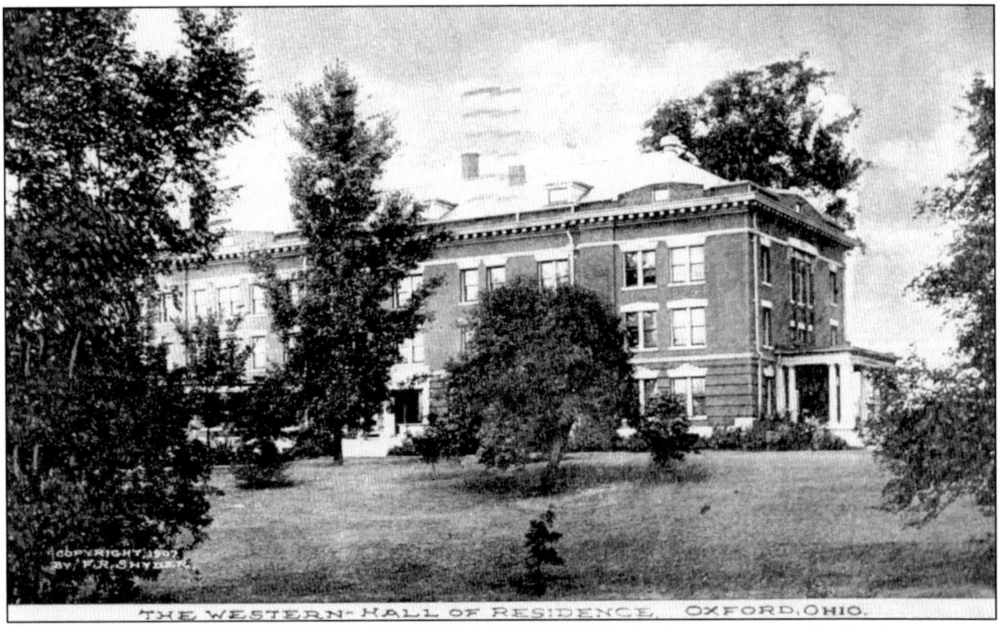

Miami University was the first of several institutions for higher learning in Oxford. The Western Female Seminary was chartered in 1853 to train teachers and missionaries. With a broadened curriculum, the name changed to the Western College for Women in 1904. The dormitory shown in this 1908-postmarked card was built in 1904 and later called McKee Hall. Miami acquired Western College in 1974.

Two

The Works

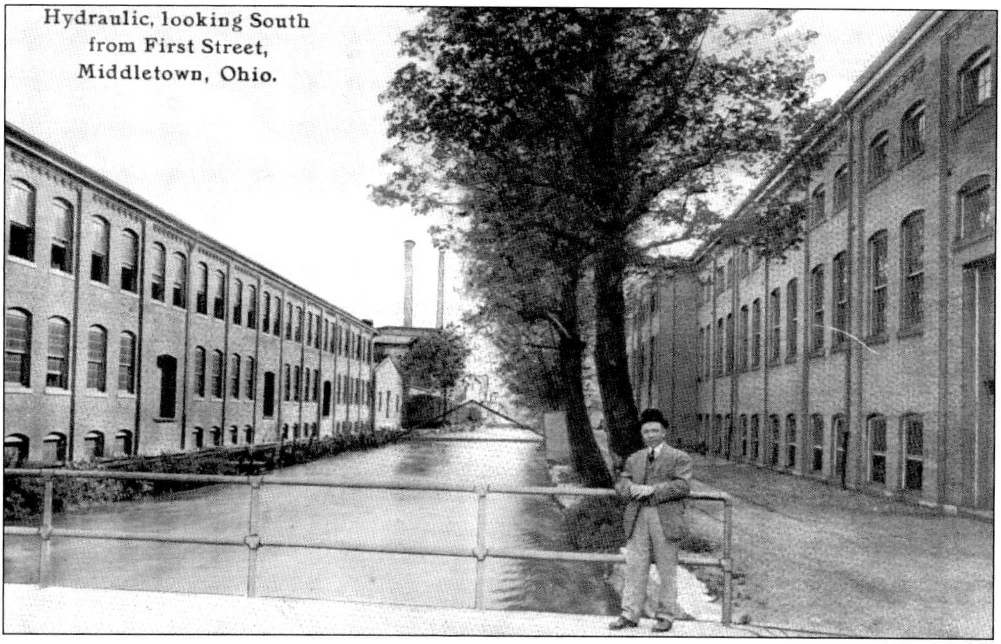

Middletown's hydraulic canal, engineered by John W. Erwin, opened in 1852 after nearly a decade of planning. Drawing from the Miami and Erie Canal, it provided waterpower for local factories. Scores of Irish laborers nicknamed "the Hydraulic Boys" built the feeder canal. The man in this *c.* 1910 postcard is unidentified.

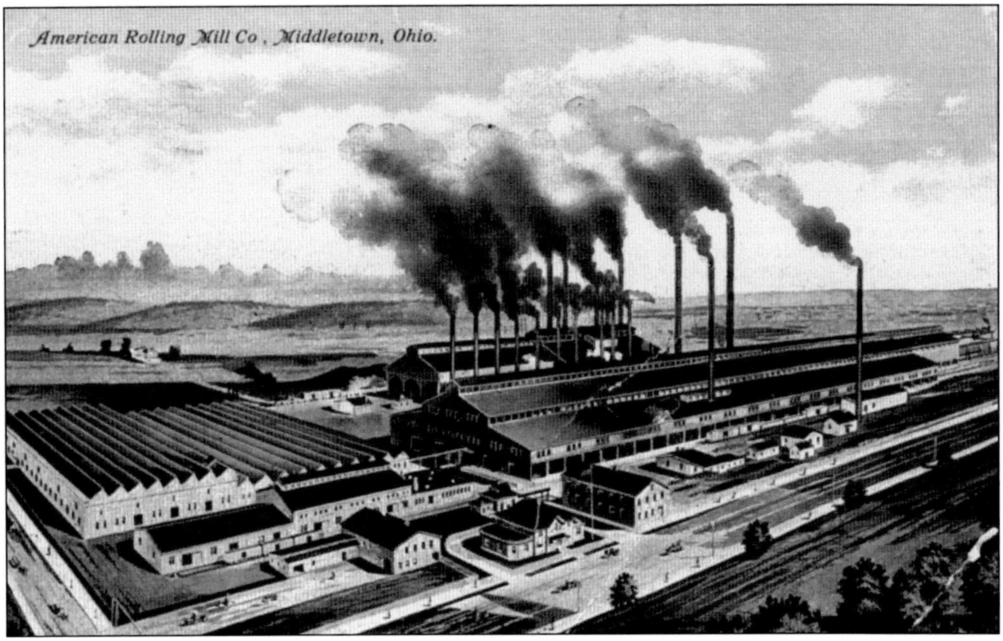

George M. Verity began in the steel business in Cincinnati in the 1890s after graduating from Nelson's Business College. By 1900, he was planning his own company to produce steel and roll it into sheets under one roof. Middletown's canal system drew him to the city. Middletown officials courted Verity and threw a huge parade on July 12, 1900, to welcome his American Rolling Mill Company (Armco) to town. The plant began operations in March 1901. This card, postmarked February 21, 1913, shows Armco's rapid growth. The firm became one of America's largest steel producers and one of Butler County's major employers. Verity later became a leading philanthropist to the city that had welcomed him.

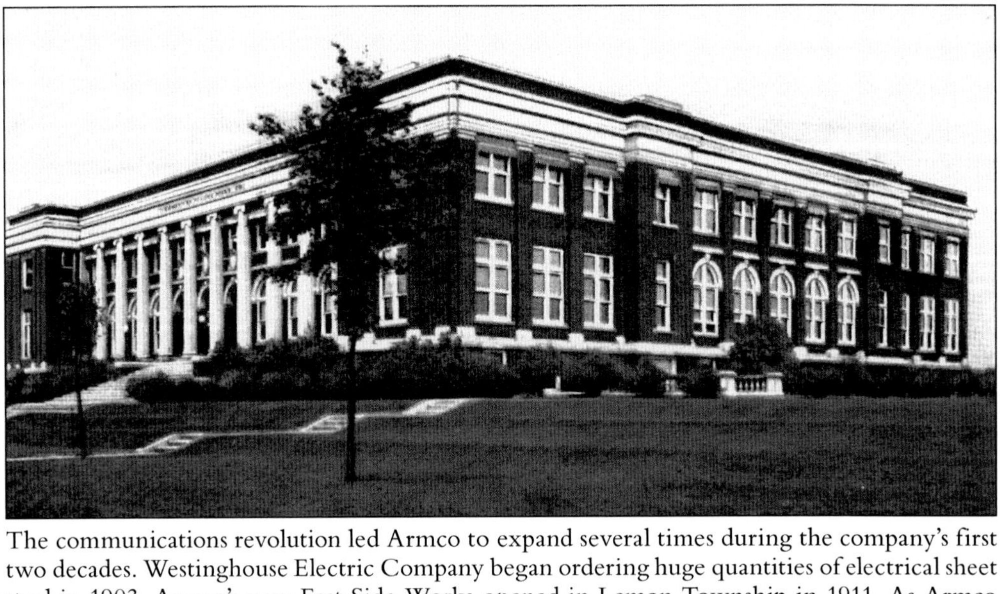

The communications revolution led Armco to expand several times during the company's first two decades. Westinghouse Electric Company began ordering huge quantities of electrical sheet steel in 1903. Armco's new East Side Works opened in Lemon Township in 1911. As Armco became one of the region's leading employees, thousands of workers passed through the brick headquarters shown on this card.

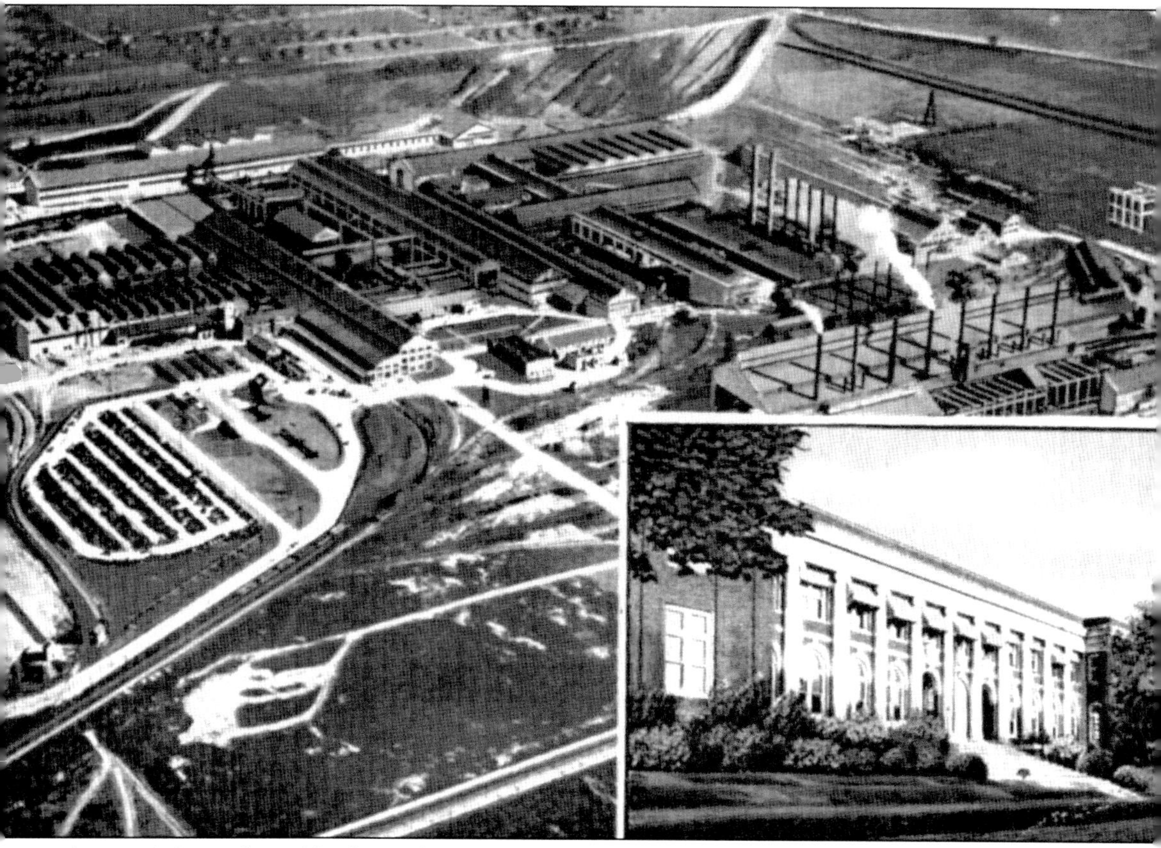

The East Side Works and landscaped general offices are pictured on this card, postmarked May 19, 1942. "This is just part of this enormous works," wrote the correspondent, who worked in the factory. After work, he noted, he walked down to the Great Miami River to cool off before returning to his rented room for the night. The demand for steel during World War II pushed workers to produce more than ever before.

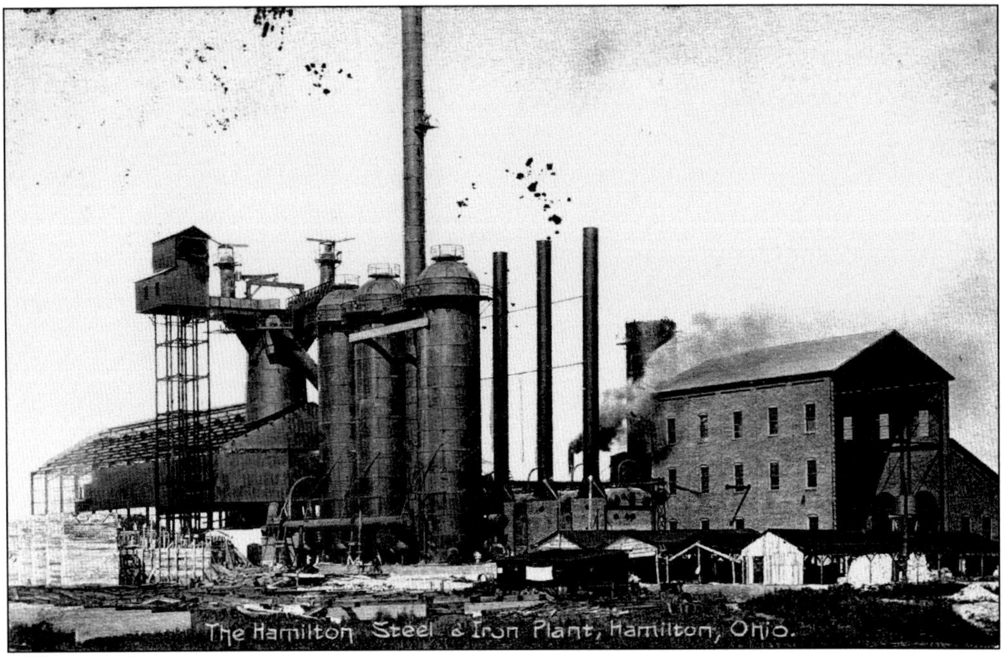

Lula Ernerick, an employee of the Hamilton Steel and Iron plant, sent this card to Julie Collins in New Lexington in 1918. Workers like Ernerick were establishing a strong economic base for Butler County and building the region's reputation as an industrial power.

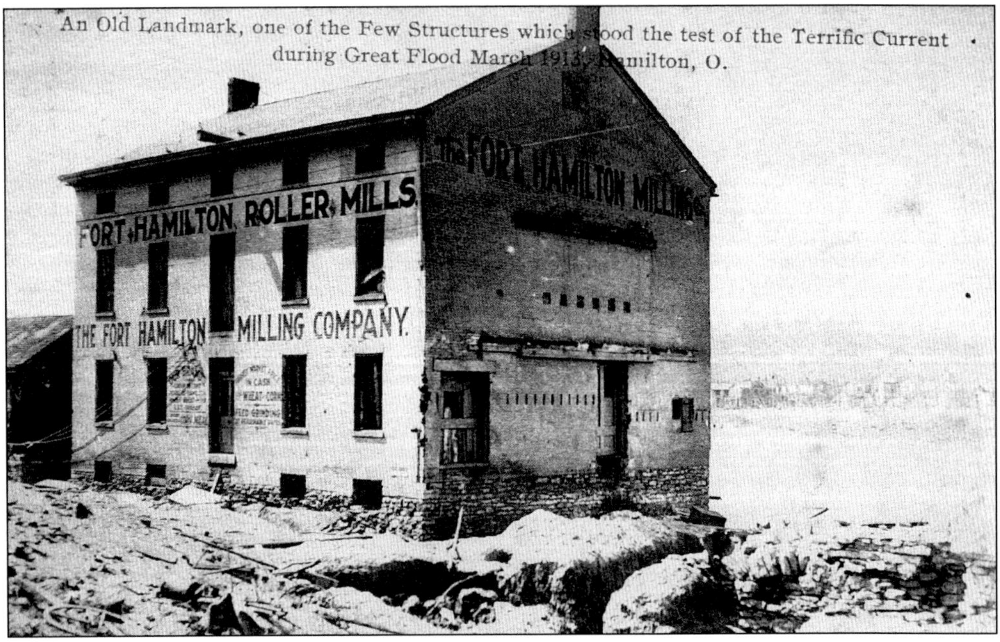

The Fort Hamilton Roller Mills and Milling Company was located at 11 South Monument Street in Hamilton. Incorporated in 1893, the firm held capital stock of $12,000 in 1907 when Charles Howald was president. The caption on the front of the card calls the building "an old landmark, one of the few structures which stood the test of the terrific current" during the March 1913 flood.

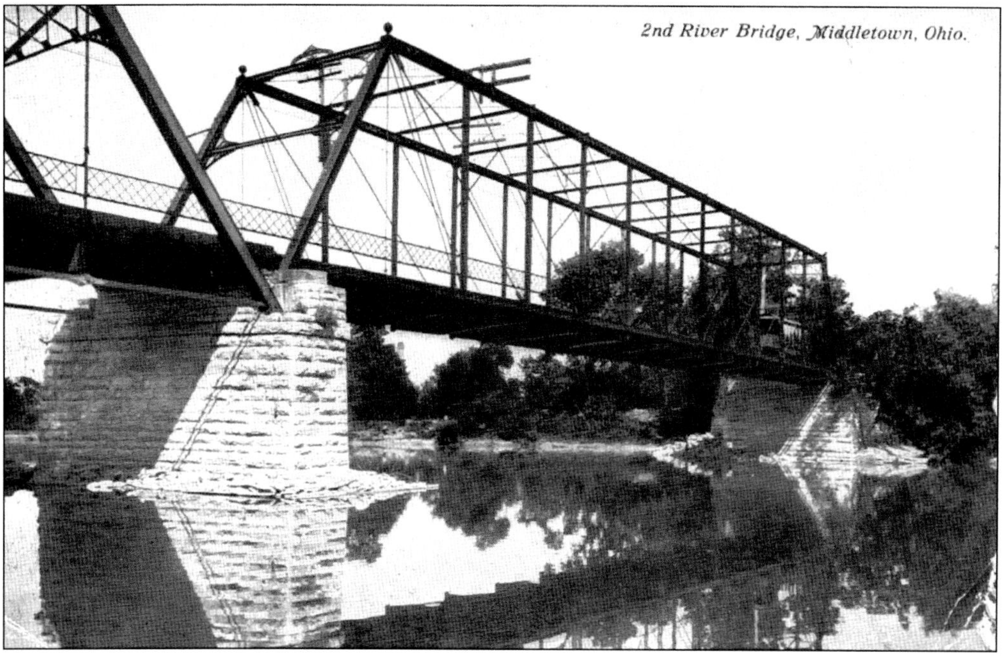

This card, depicting the Second River Bridge of Middletown, was postmarked August 30, 1912.

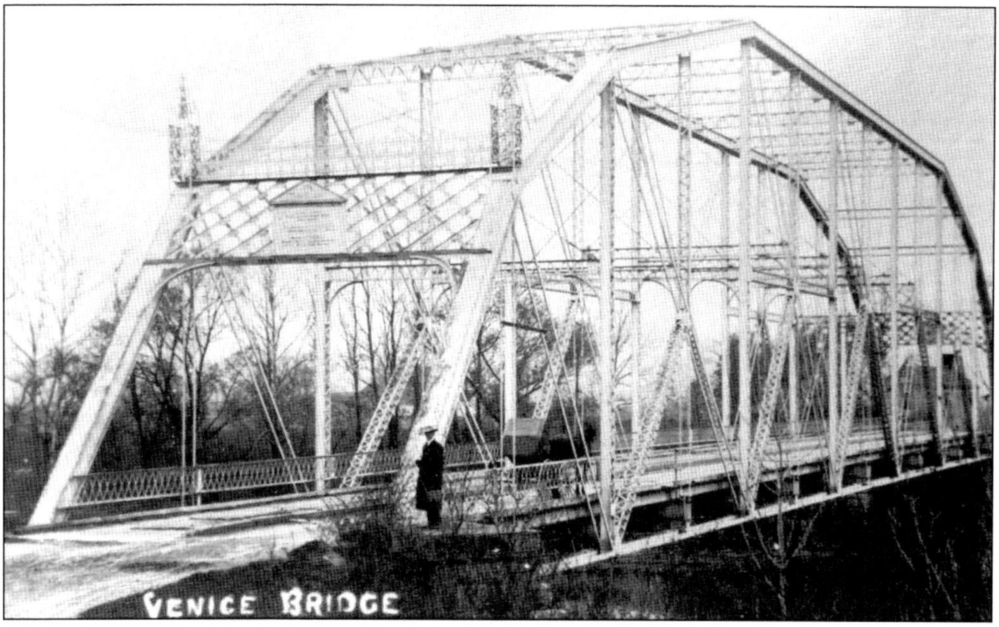

Brass bands and crowds of people greeted the opening of the Colerain and Venice Bridge in May 1895. Previous spans at the site had been wooden covered bridges. The span was a toll site until 1867, when county commissioners made it a free bridge. (Courtesy of the Butler County Historical Society.)

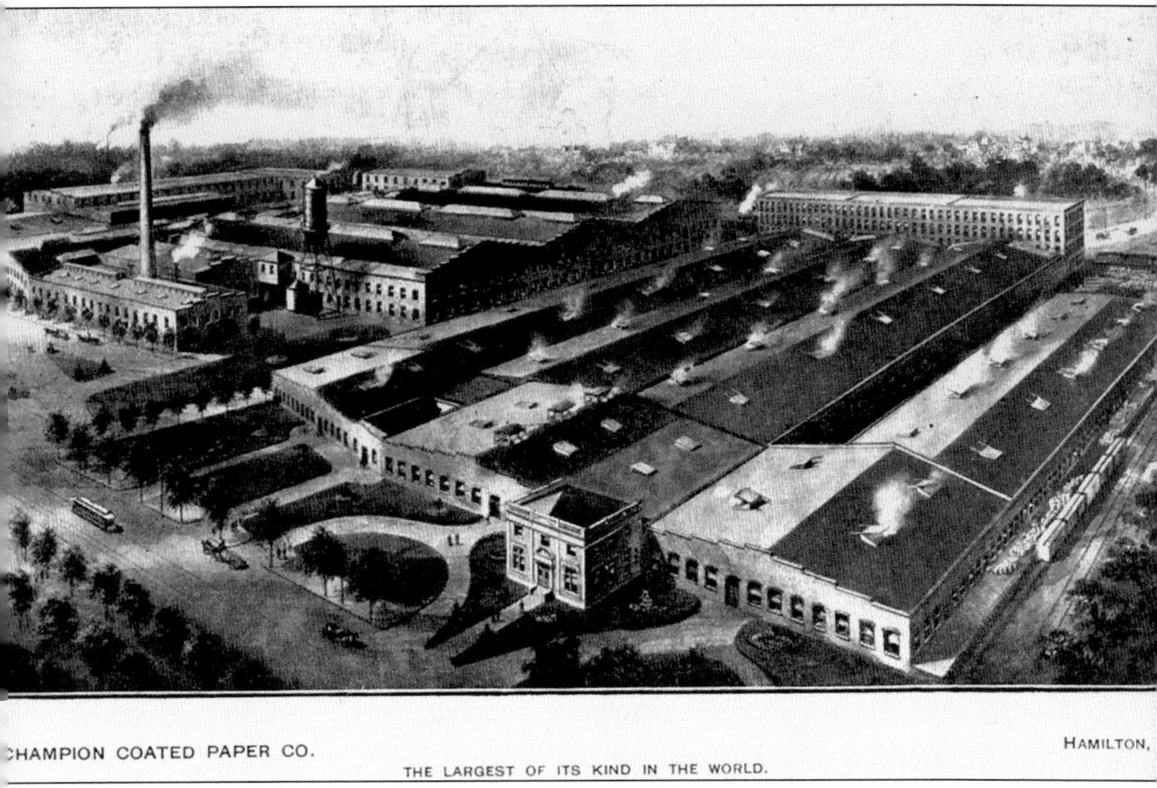

Champion Coated Paper Company, located on B Street in Hamilton, claimed to be the largest of its kind on this *c.* 1910 postcard. Paper production started in earnest in Butler County in 1848, when William Beckett founded his mill on Hamilton's D Street. Multiple paper mills operated in the region—primarily in Hamilton and Middletown—through the last half of the 19th century. Champion (founded in 1894) and Beckett remained industry giants into the next century. Champion founder Peter G. Thomson and his wife, Laura Thomson (née Gamble), first got involved with paper when they started a bookstore and printing business in Cincinnati in the 1870s. They even wrote and published some of the Valentine cards and children's books that they sold. Peter opened Champion as a mill to coat paper, buying from Hamilton's Fordham Paper Mill and Franklin Mill before deciding to produce his own paper too. By 1935, some 20 percent of Hamilton's wage earners worked for Champion.

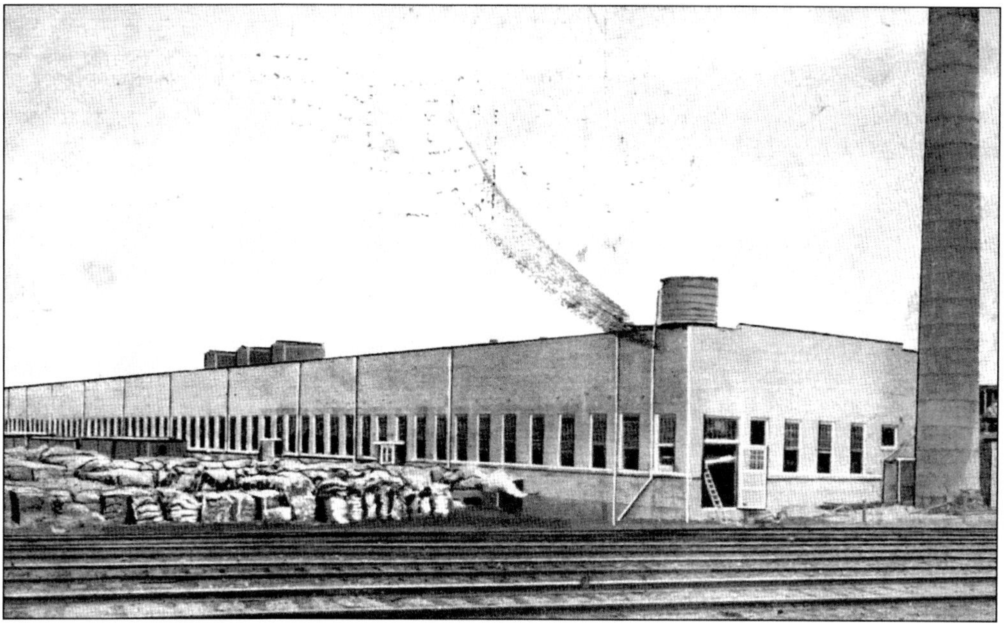

Middletown's Gardner Harvey Paper Company is shown on this 1911 card. Paper production flourished in Middletown and Hamilton due to the availability of waterpower, reliable transportation, and abundant material resources. The region became so renowned for paper making that Miami University began offering a major in paper science.

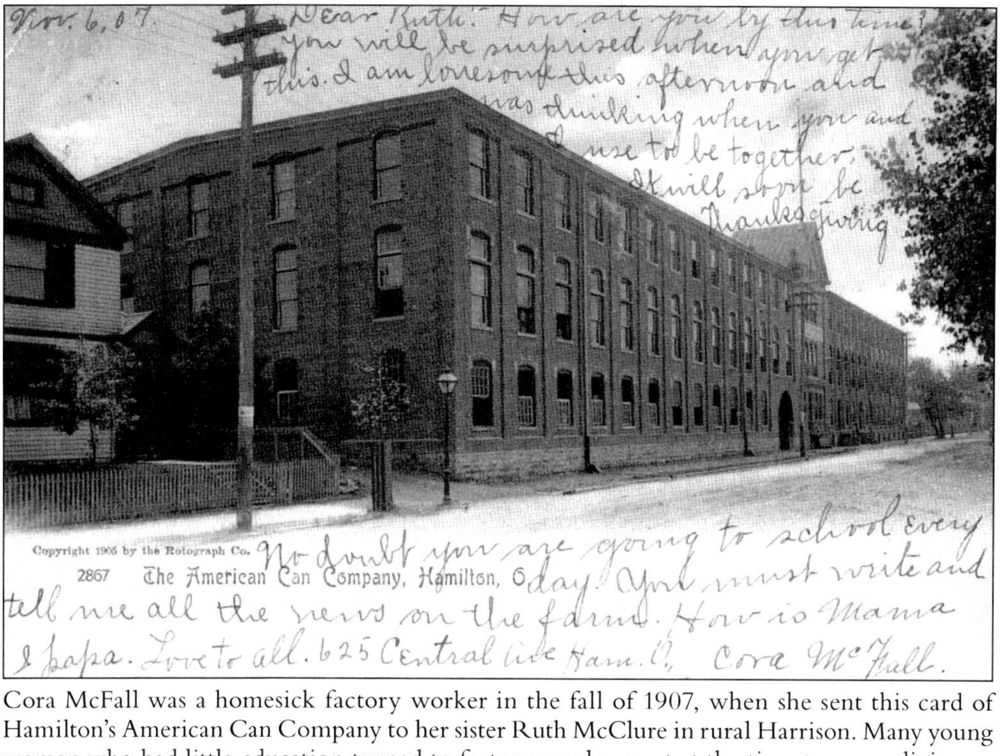

Cora McFall was a homesick factory worker in the fall of 1907, when she sent this card of Hamilton's American Can Company to her sister Ruth McClure in rural Harrison. Many young women who had little education turned to factory employment at the time to earn a living or help out their families.

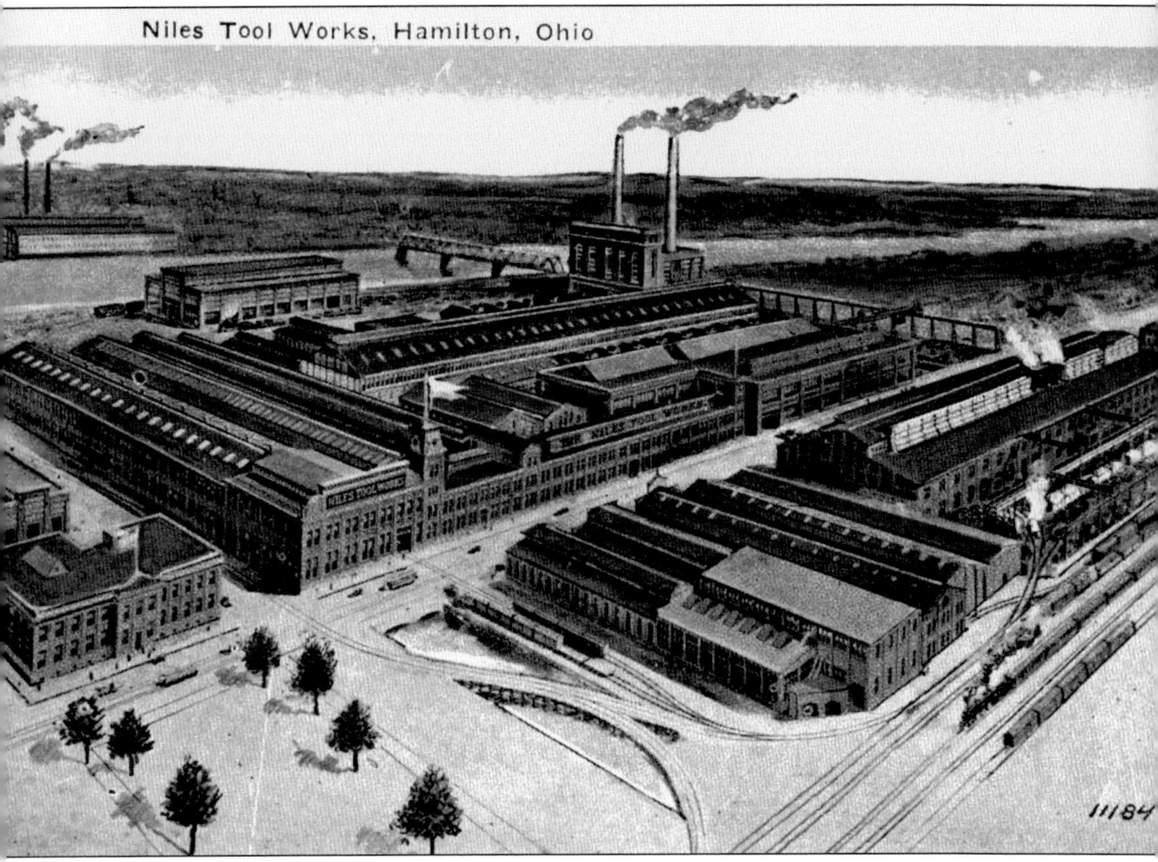

Niles Tool Works, pictured on this *c.* 1910 postcard, was another homegrown business that put Hamilton on the international industrial map. It began in 1834 in Cincinnati as a manufacturer of sugar mills, rolling mills, and stationary engines. When company officials decided to expand the business in the 1870s, Hamilton city leaders courted Niles vigorously. Hamilton donated the plant site at North Third and Mill Streets, along with construction materials. The Water Power Company also provided free power for a short time. Niles, which now manufactured large production machine tools, soon filled an entire block. It produced large planers and boring mills used by military arsenals and the railroad industry. By the first decade of the 20th century, federal government contracts for navy yards and arsenals were calling for products to be built according to the "Niles Standard." Company officers in 1910 were James K. Cullen, president; George T. Reiss, vice president; Charles L. Cornell, treasurer; Joseph L. Blair, secretary; and Lucius B. Potter, assistant treasurer.

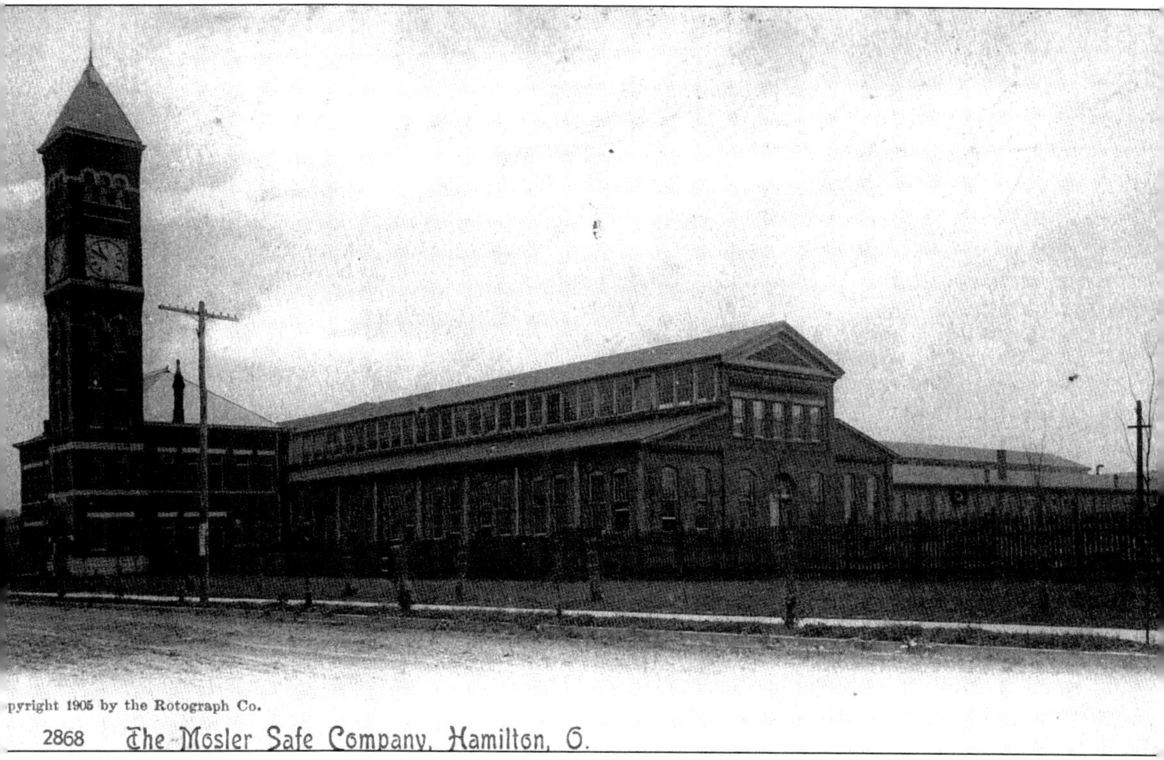

Featured on this 1905 card, Mosler Safe Company was another Cincinnati firm that Hamilton wooed. William Mosler engaged a special 12-coach train to bring 200 employees and their families to Hamilton in 1890 to examine the prospects. Hamilton treated the visitors to a full day of dancing, music, and refreshments, and Mosler said yes to the city's proposal. In 1907, Pres. Moses Mosler and Vice Pres. William Mosler listed capital of $1.3 million. The main office and Plant No. 1 operated on Grand Boulevard for nearly a century. Mosler safes were known around the world. During World War II, the company collaborated with Middletown's Armco Steel on the Cyclotron magnet used in atomic research. The firm also designed and constructed a special safe that now holds original copies of the Declaration of Independence and the Bill of Rights at the National Archives Building in Washington, D.C.

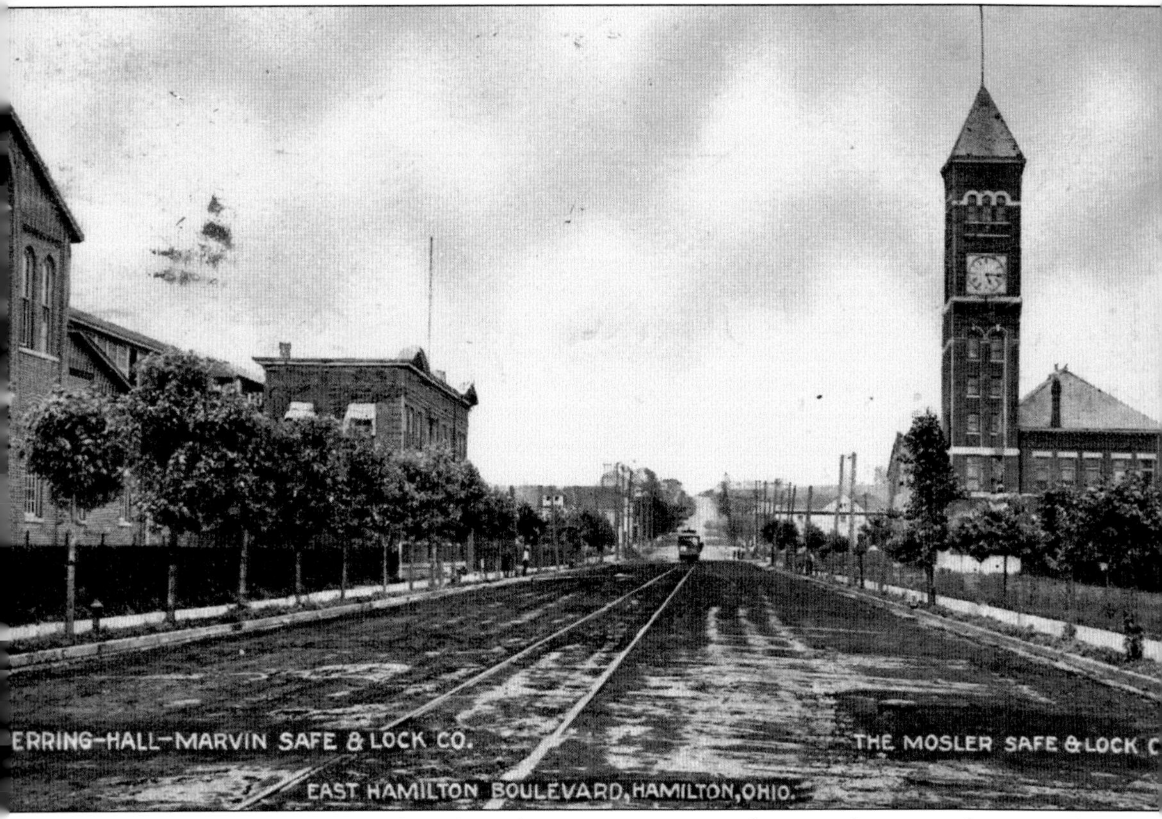

Herring-Hall-Marvin Safe and Lock Company operated across the street from Mosler Safe Company in Hamilton, inspiring the city's nickname of "Safe Capital of the World." Herring-Hall-Marvin predated Mosler in the city. After the infamous fire of 1871 devastated much of Chicago's business district, more than 400 Herring-Hall-Marvin safes were recovered intact, proving the firm's claim of making truly fireproof safes. This card, postmarked 1911, shows the local trolley line. During the 1940s, some Herring-Hall-Marvin employees assisted with grinding uranium bars for the Manhattan Project. Although the employees did not realize what exactly they were working on, they noticed their floor was sealed off from other workers and that armed guards watched over their scraps. A Treasurgard chest made by the firm was used in 1945 to hold the first United Nations charter as it was transported from San Francisco to Washington, D.C., to be presented to the United States Senate.

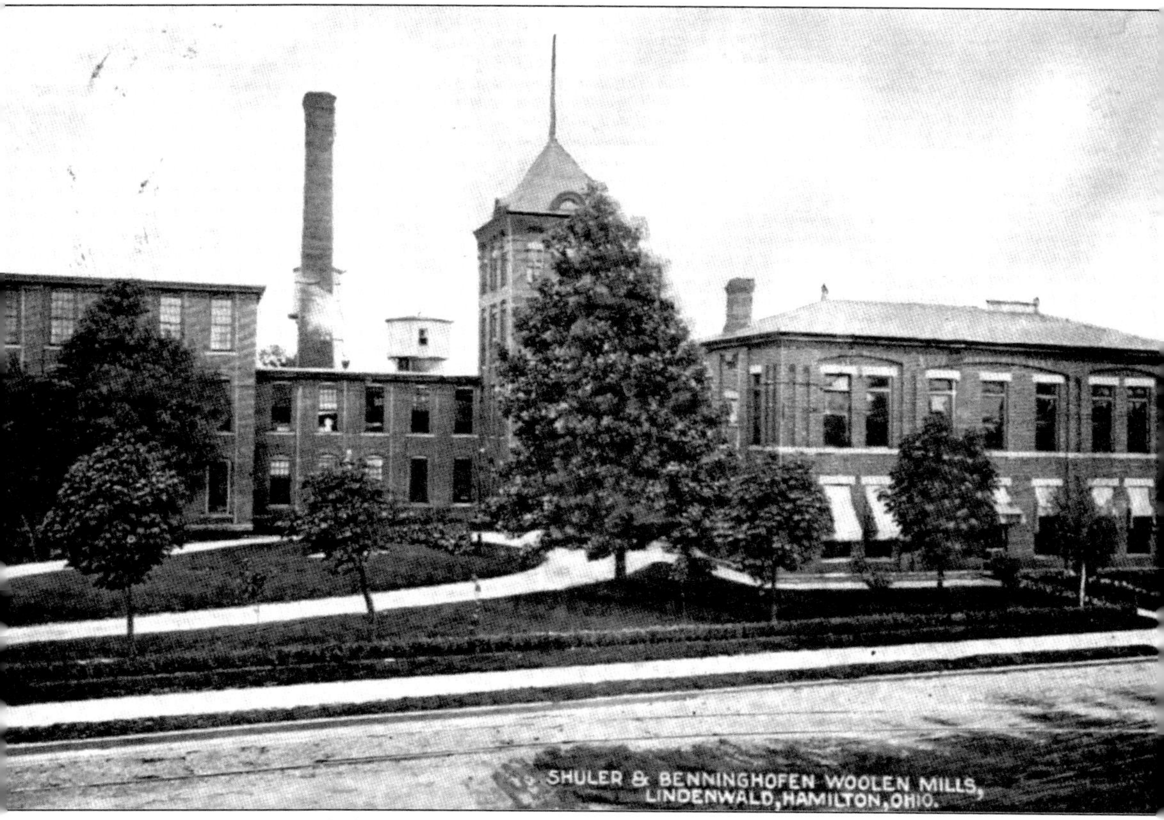

This 1912 card shows the Shuler and Benninghofen Woolen Mills in south Hamilton's Lindenwald neighborhood. The business started in 1858, when Asa Shuler and J. W. Benninghofen went into business together, producing blankets, clothing, and flannels in a mill at Heaton and Lowell Streets in Hamilton. A specialty was creating felts used by paper makers. By 1890, the company was doing business across the country, as well as in Mexico and Japan.

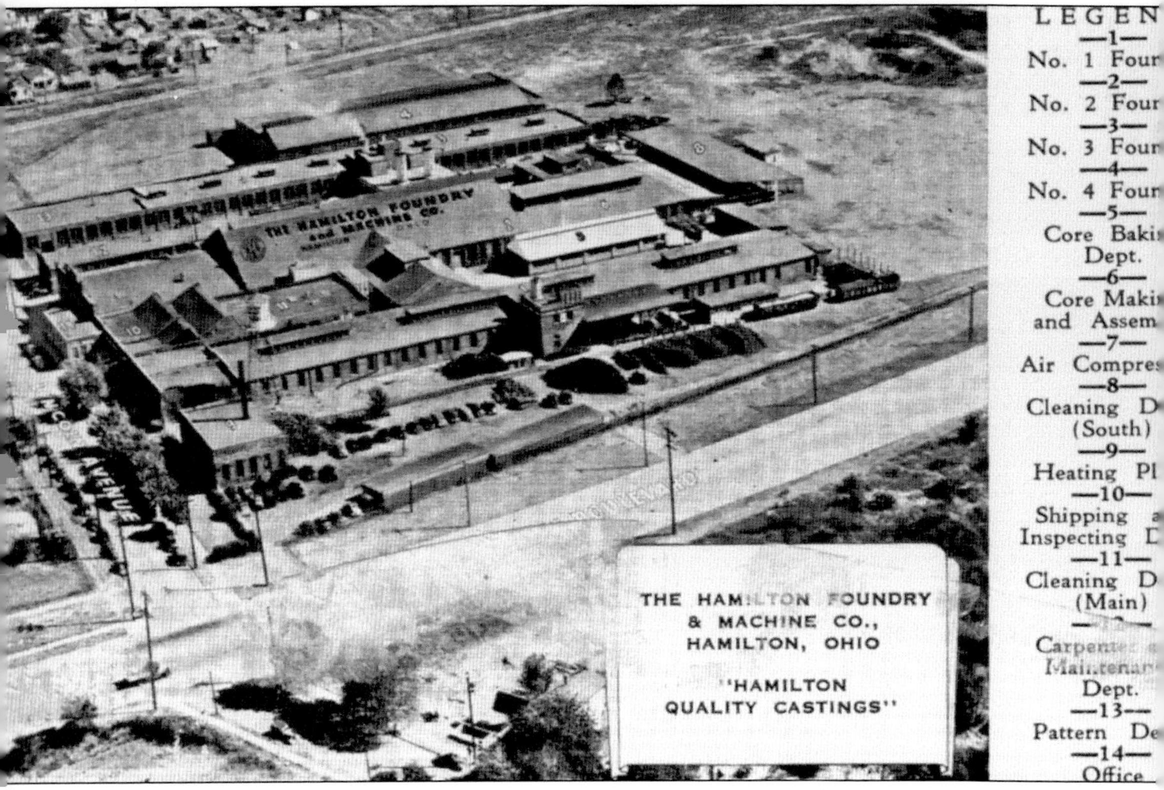

The Hamilton Foundry and Machine Company was one of industrialist George A. Rentschler's many Hamilton success stories. This *c.* 1910 postcard view reveals the variety of operations at the company, located at Lincoln Avenue and Erie Boulevard. The Pennsylvania Railroad, as well as the Baltimore and Ohio and Erie Railroads, served the 22-acre complex. The plant produced light and medium iron castings. Rentschler, who had learned metalworking at the Variety Iron Works in Indianapolis, moved to Hamilton with the company in 1873 as a foreman. In 1875, Rentschler started his first business, the Ohio Iron Works, with partners Henry C. Sohn and John V. Balle. From there, Rentschler's hard work and business savvy led him to become one of the county's leading industrialists. His other firms included the Phoenix Caster Company and the Hooven, Owens, and Rentschler Company, which manufactured machine tools.

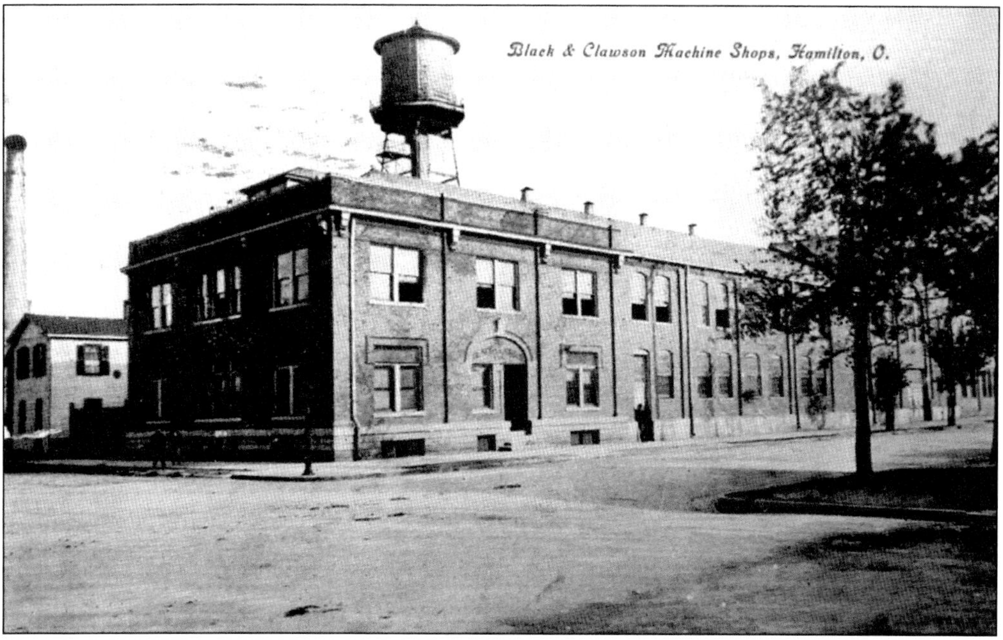

In 1878, Frank X. Black and Linus P. Clawson founded the Black and Clawson Machine Shops in Hamilton. The firm, located at Second and Vine Streets, manufactured machinery used in paper mills. (Courtesy of the Butler County Historical Society.)

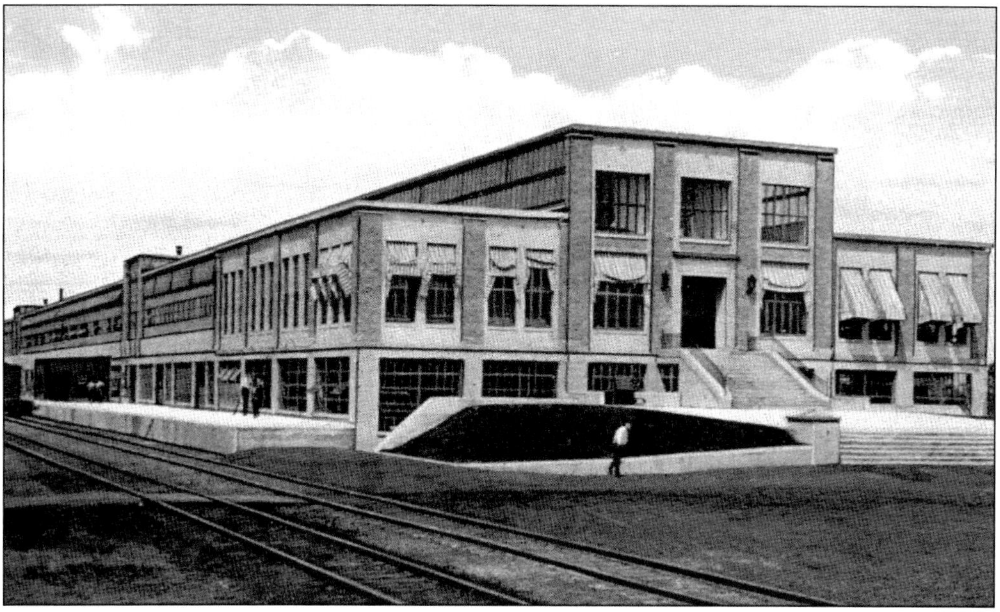

Hamilton's Fordson Heights subdivision owes its name to the Ford Motor Company's tractor plant that opened in 1920 in the city's north end. The factory was built to manufacture Fordson trucks, but after six months, it was retooled to produce wheels for Ford's popular Model T automobile. At the time, a Fordson truck cost approximately $700, and a Model T cost $600.

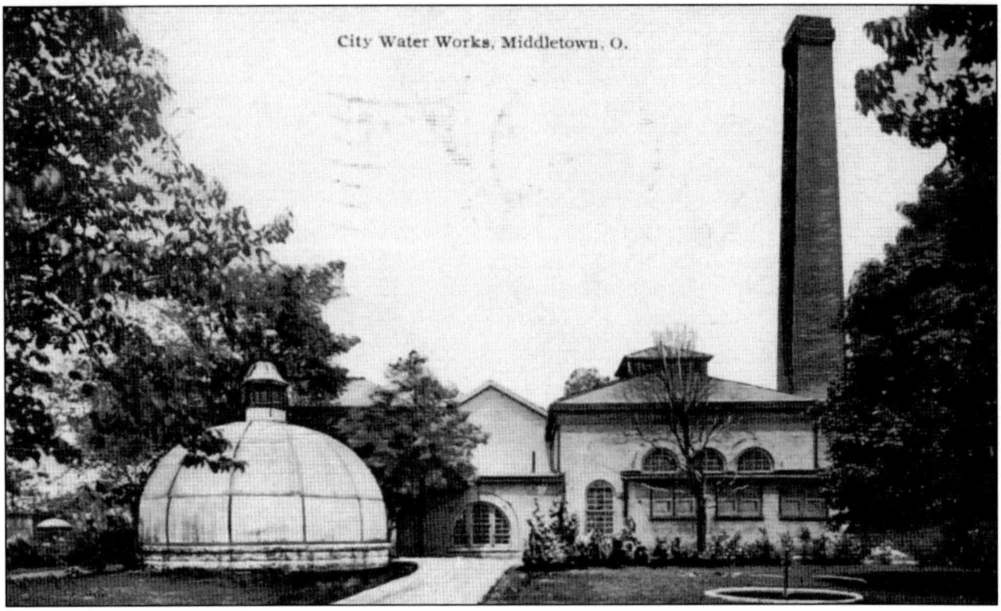

Middletown's new waterworks facility, shown in this *c.* 1920 card, served a population of 23,594 that year. Sixty-three percent of the population owned their own homes in 1920. Twelve public and parochial schools served the growing community.

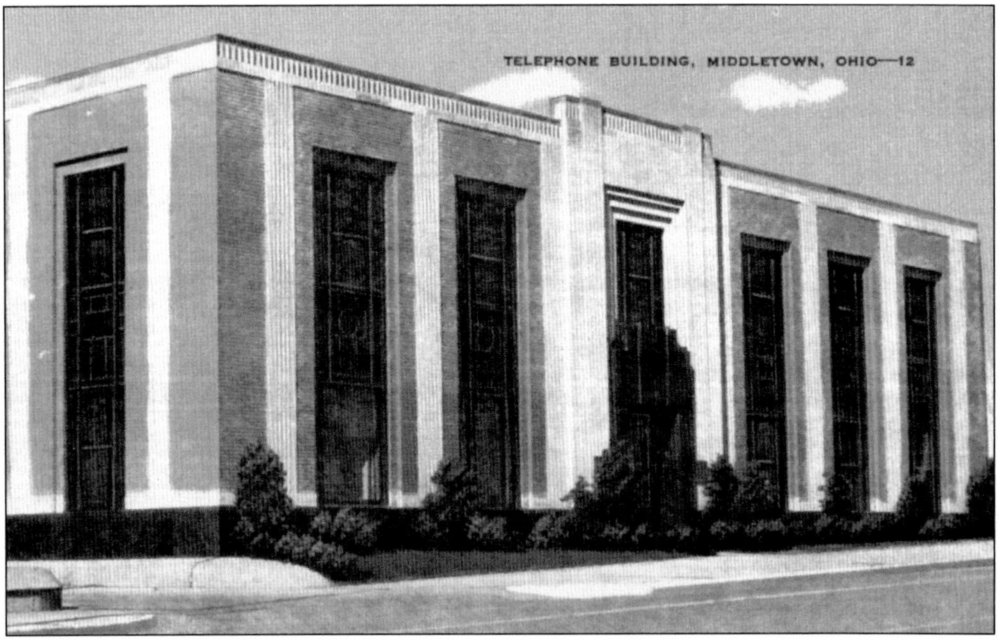

In 1916, the Middletown Telephone Company was located on Fourth Street, with Dr. D. B. Bundy serving as president and H. E. Allen as vice president. The Ohio Bell Telephone Company was operating from offices on First Avenue by the early 1920s. At the time, a private business line could be maintained for $4.25 per month. A private residential line was $2.75 a month. Rural residential customers paid $22 a year.

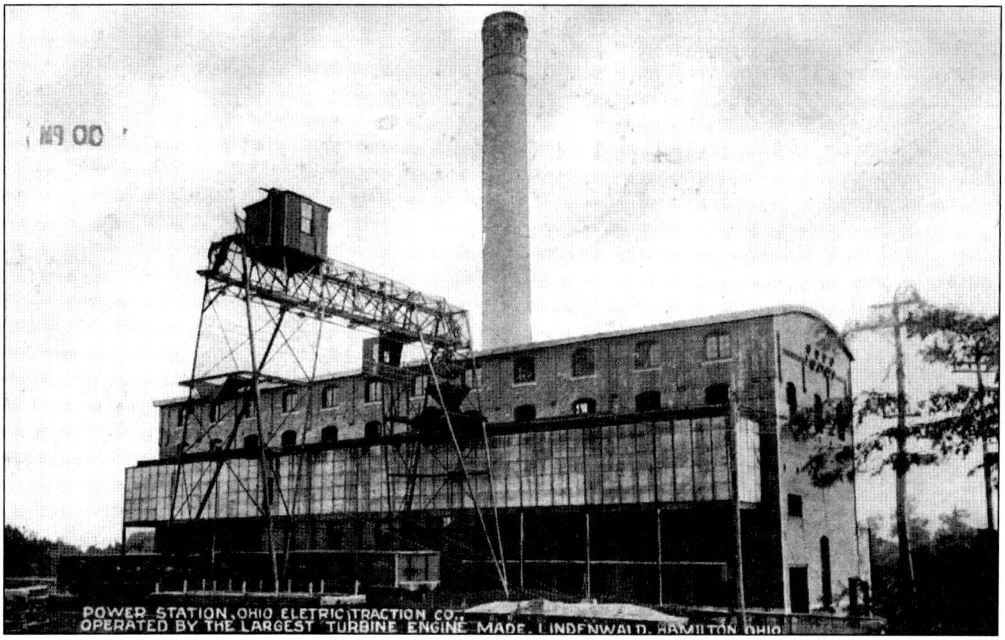

Laura and Marie Silipher lived just two blocks west of the Lindenwald Power Plant at Williams and Fairview Avenues in Hamilton when they mailed this card to Marie Armstrong of Eaton on February 4, 1913. The plant, nicknamed "the Power House," produced power to run the Ohio Electric Traction Company's interurban cars. Today only a concrete tower stands, and the property is commonly called Power House Park.

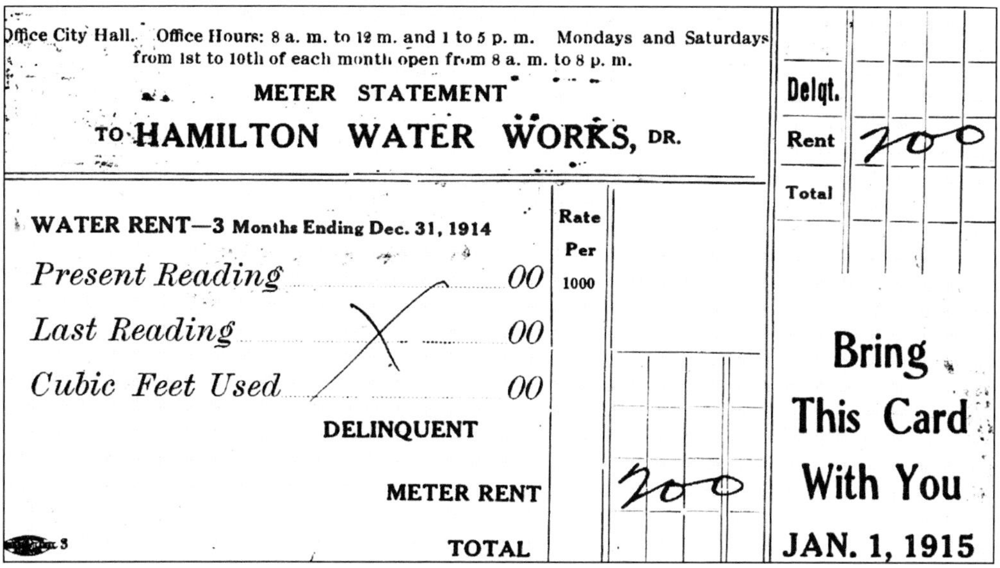

Office City Hall. Office Hours: 8 a. m. to 12 m. and 1 to 5 p. m. Mondays and Saturdays from 1st to 10th of each month open from 8 a. m. to 8 p. m.

METER STATEMENT

TO HAMILTON WATER WORKS, DR.

WATER RENT—3 Months Ending Dec. 31, 1914

		Rate Per 1000	
Present Reading	00		
Last Reading	00		
Cubic Feet Used	00		
DELINQUENT			
METER RENT			200
TOTAL			

Delqt.	
Rent	200
Total	

Bring This Card With You

JAN. 1, 1915

Hamilton Water Works mailed this bill to Anna Owens at 225 North Second Street, Hamilton, on December 31, 1914, instructing her to show up on New Year's Day to pay her delinquent $2 rent for her meter. Then, as now, bureaucracy took no holidays.

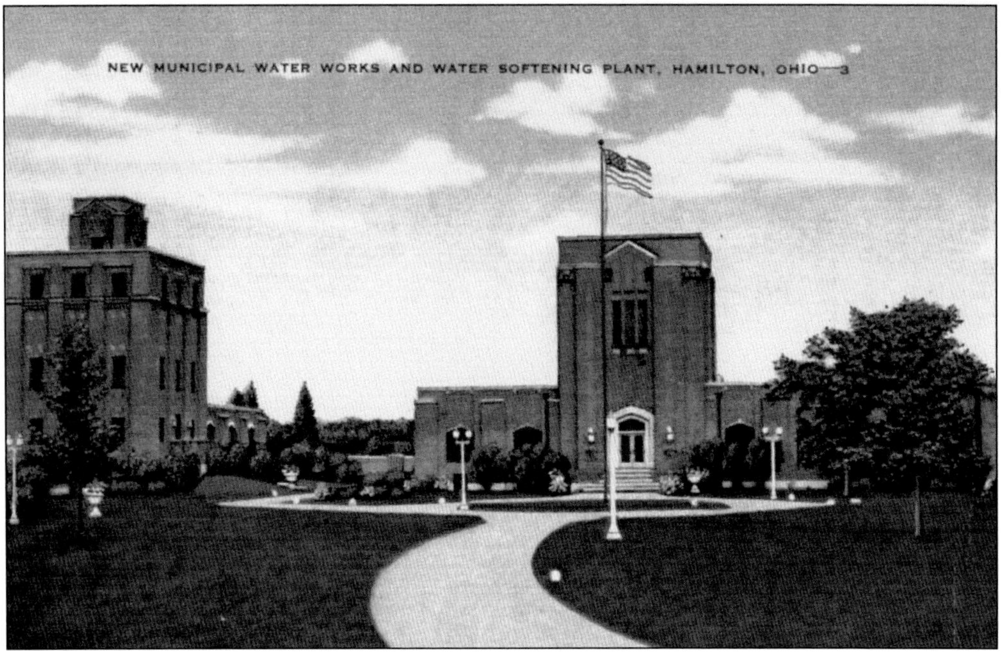

The new, modern Hamilton Water Works and Softening Plant is shown on this postcard. The plant was a Public Works Administration project that began in 1934 after years of study and development by city officials. The caption on the back notes the "abundant supply of good, pure water" taken from underground wells. "Miles of mains distribute the water to all sections of the city," according to the card.

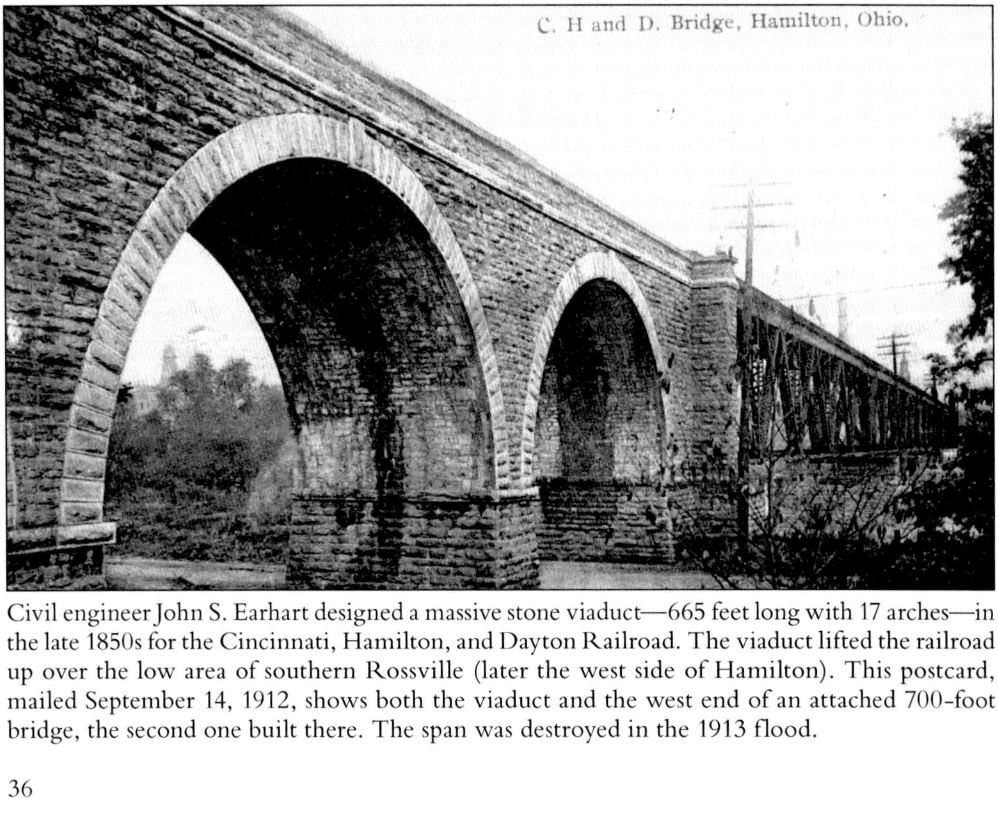

Civil engineer John S. Earhart designed a massive stone viaduct—665 feet long with 17 arches—in the late 1850s for the Cincinnati, Hamilton, and Dayton Railroad. The viaduct lifted the railroad up over the low area of southern Rossville (later the west side of Hamilton). This postcard, mailed September 14, 1912, shows both the viaduct and the west end of an attached 700-foot bridge, the second one built there. The span was destroyed in the 1913 flood.

Three

Churches

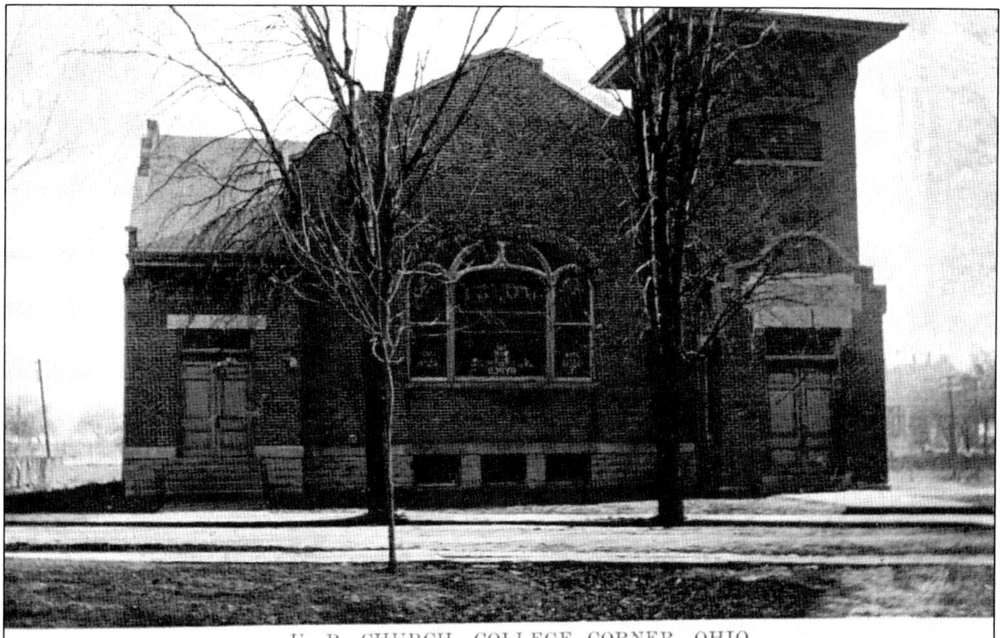

U. P. CHURCH, COLLEGE CORNER, OHIO.

The United Presbyterian Church in College Corner was organized in 1845. Dr. John Scott, the father-in-law of Pres. Benjamin Harrison, proved a major force in the congregation. Scott had been a Miami University professor in the 1830s and served as director of the Oxford Female Institute in the 1840s. The church's early preachers were Miami professors from Oxford. In the 1880s, a new church was built on the Indiana side of the town, called West College Corner.

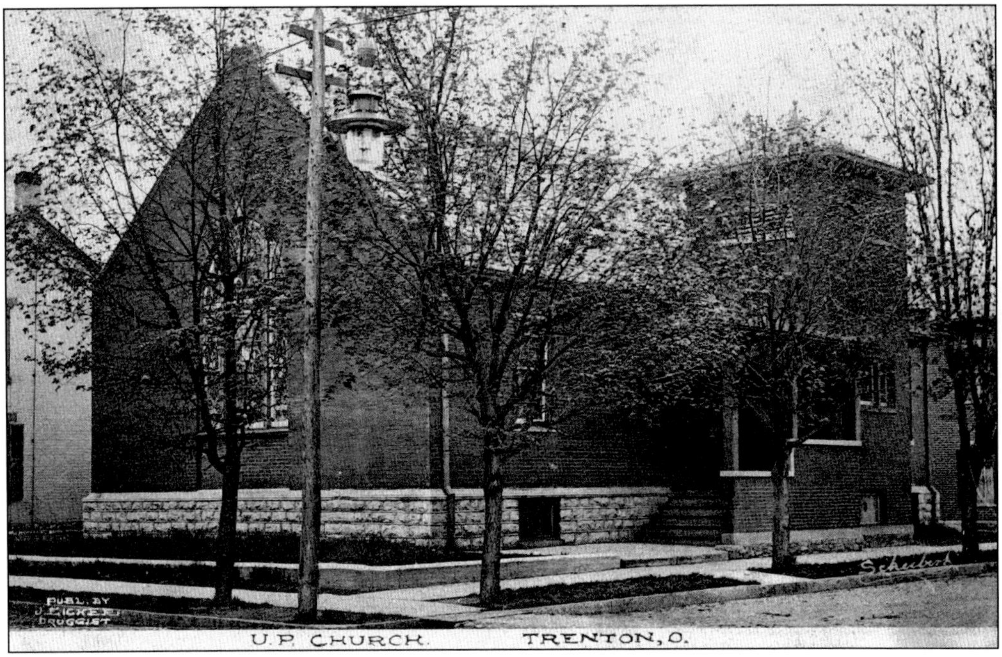

This card of the United Presbyterian Church in Trenton is postmarked August 21, 1908. At that time, the church was called the finest in the village. It was built in 1904 and dedicated by a Rev. Dr. Moorhead on January 29, 1905.

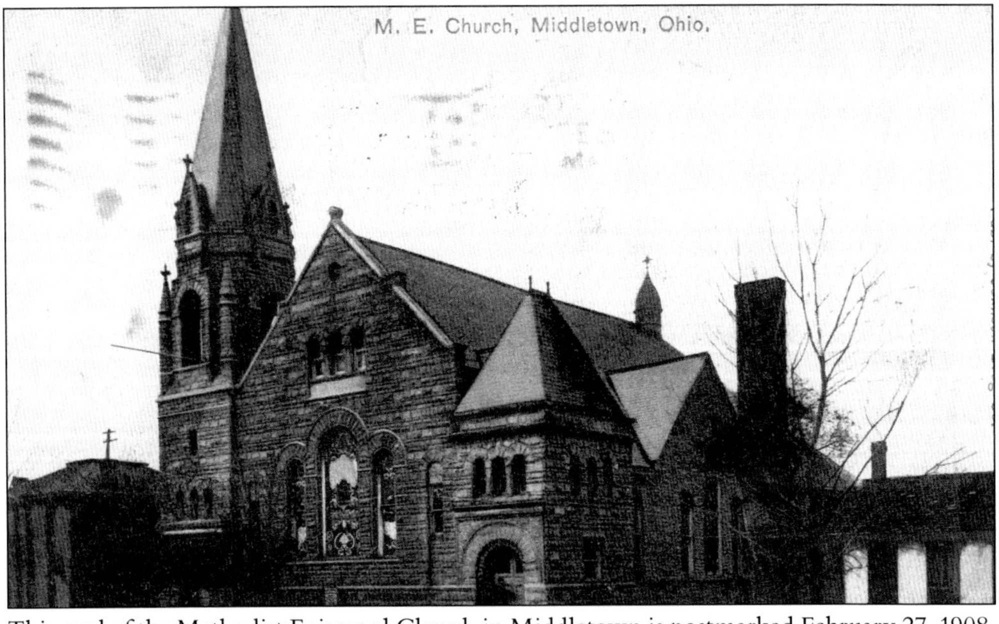

This card of the Methodist Episcopal Church in Middletown is postmarked February 27, 1908. The cornerstone for the second Broadway Methodist Episcopal Church was laid on May 31, 1890, and the building was dedicated by Bishop J. W. Joyce in front of 1,200 people on May 1, 1891. The church was built of native blue limestone; the front was made of Berea sandstone. Construction costs hit $50,000, which the congregation had paid off by 1905.

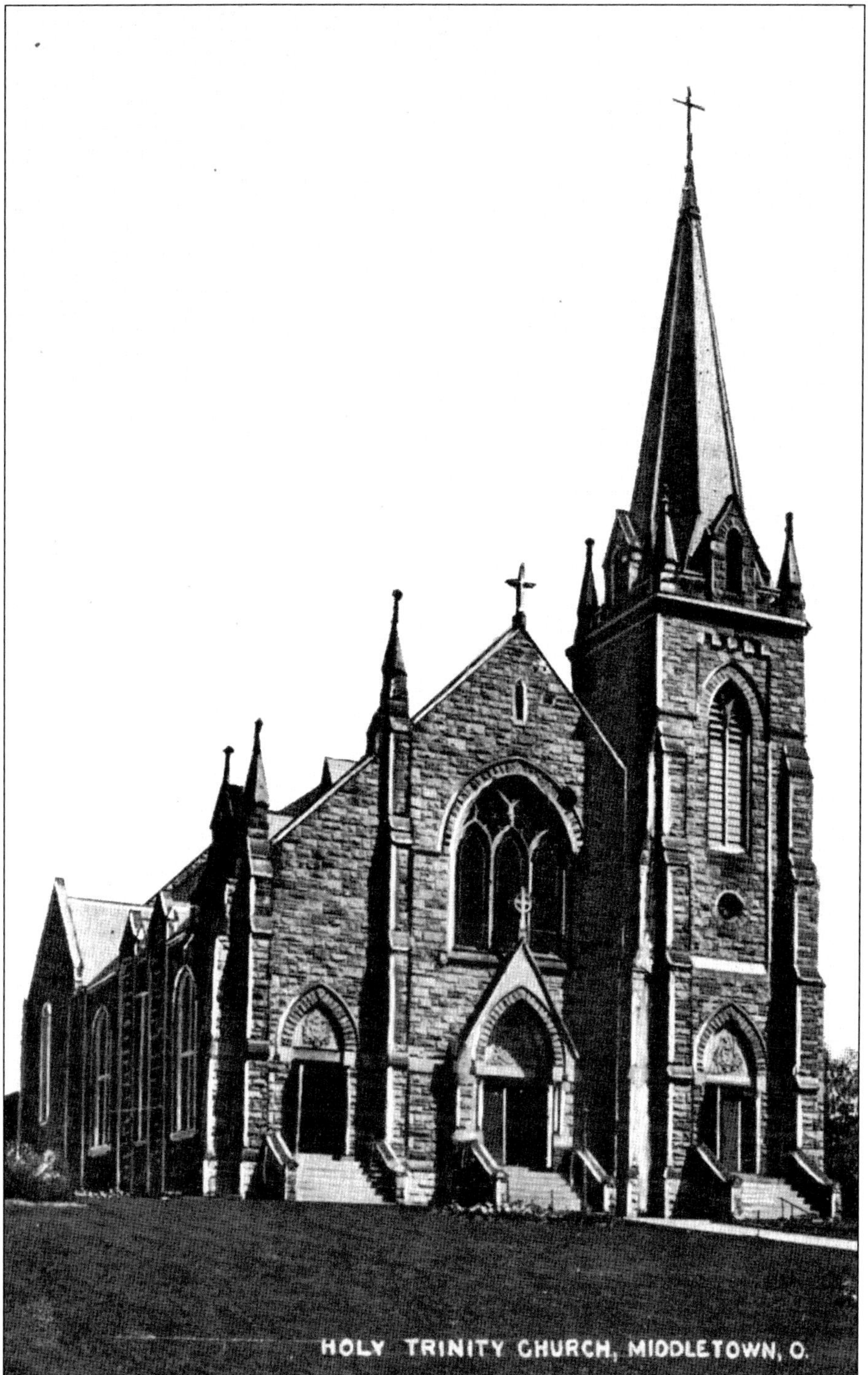

Holy Trinity Church, located on Clark Street in Middletown, was dedicated on September 3, 1899, as the New Holy Trinity. An earlier church on the site had been built in 1853 and a two-story parochial school added in 1891.

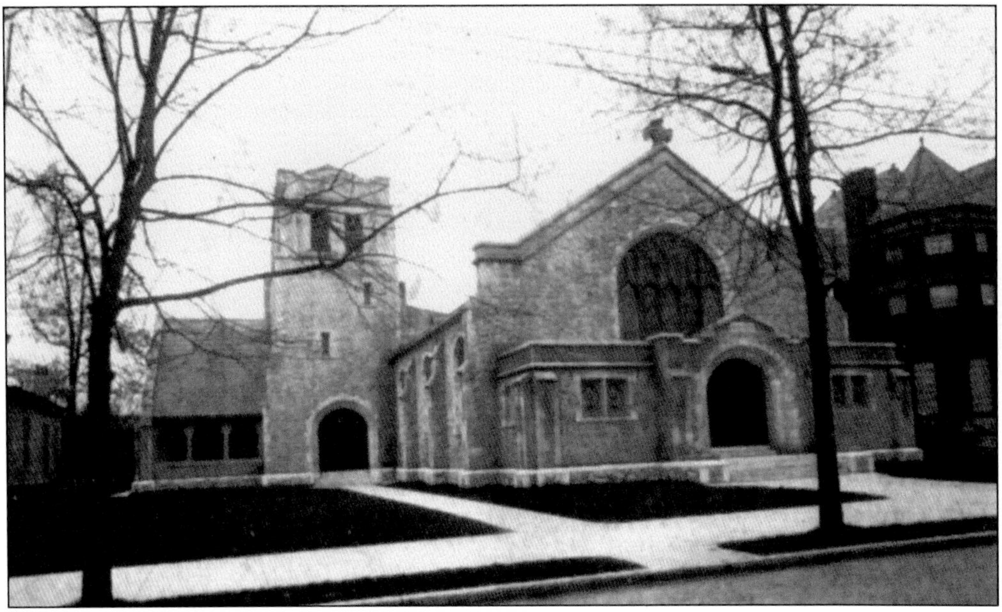

This card of the First Baptist Church, situated at 415 South Main Street in Middletown, was mailed without comment to Bessie Kearfott in West Liberty on October 2, 1909. The congregation formed in 1808 as the Salem Baptist Church, and members changed the name 20 years later. In 1889, the pastor was Rev. Edward A. Ince, who wrote a book about the church that year. In 1916, the congregation was led by Rev. D. F. Rittenhouse.

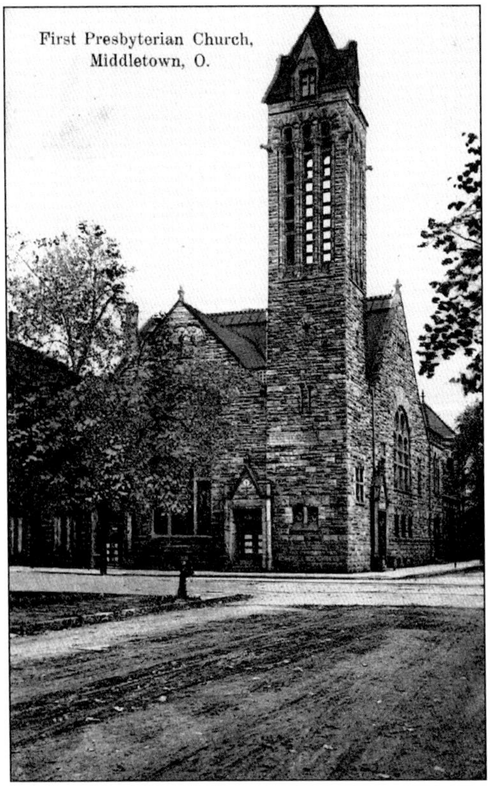

The congregation of the First Presbyterian Church of Middletown was founded in 1819, and a church was built in 1832 on lower Broadway. In 1854, the congregation moved to the northeast corner of Fourth and Main Streets, where it built a large brick church at $15,000. In 1892, the church was razed and a stone church constructed for $50,000. The congregation had a reputation of being wealthy and conservative. In this undated postcard, published about 1915, the structure looks European in design.

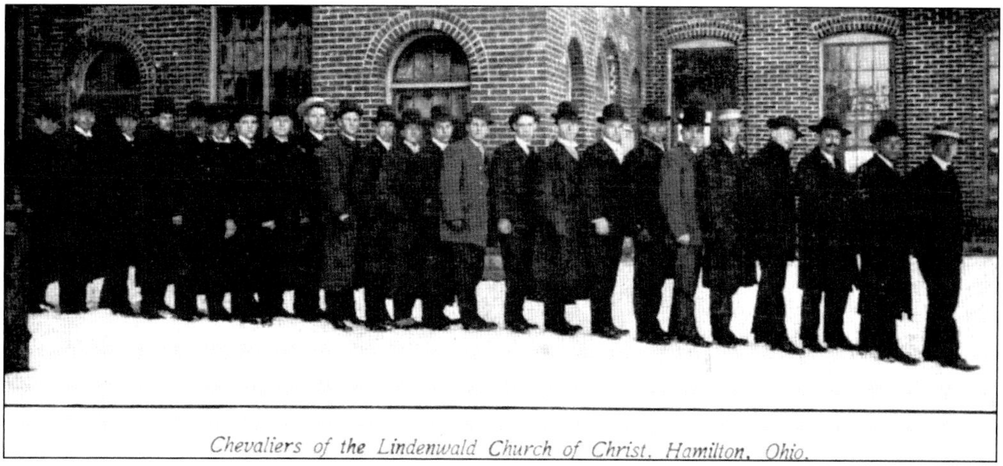

In this undated card, the Lindenwald Church of Christ men's choral group poses in front of the church at Forest and Benninghofen Avenues in Hamilton's southernmost neighborhood. Rev. William T. Mullins served as pastor in 1922. Judging by the clothing, this photograph was probably taken late in the second decade of the 20th century or in the early 1920s.

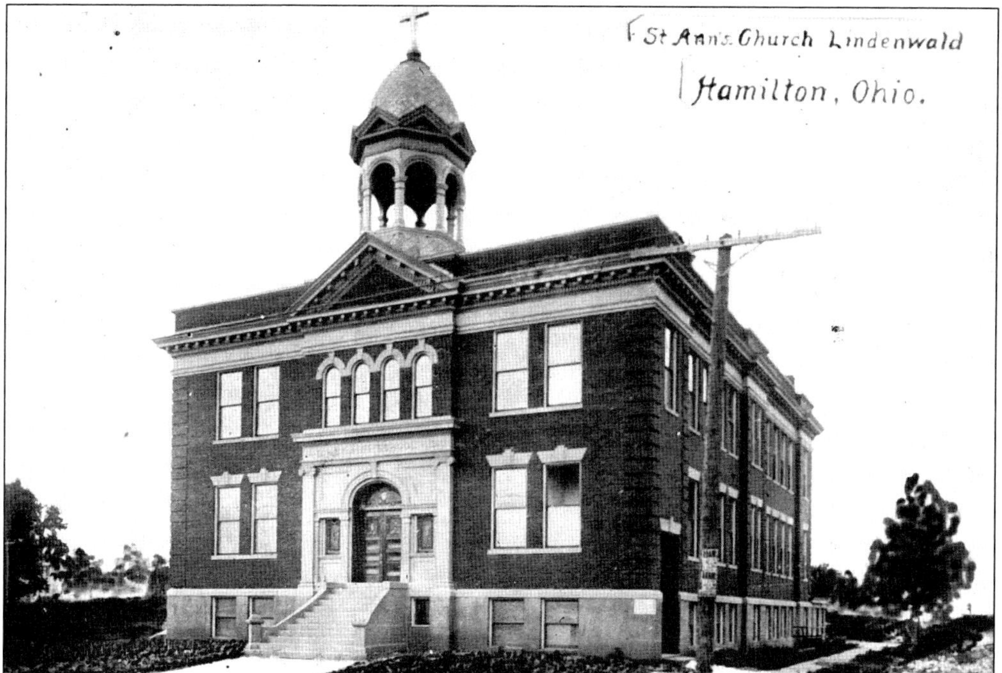

St. Ann's Catholic Church was built in 1911 on Pleasant and Clinton Avenues to serve the growing Lindenwald community of south Hamilton. Rev. Herman N. Santen was pastor during that period. The building pictured is still in use, and St. Ann's bells ring every day.

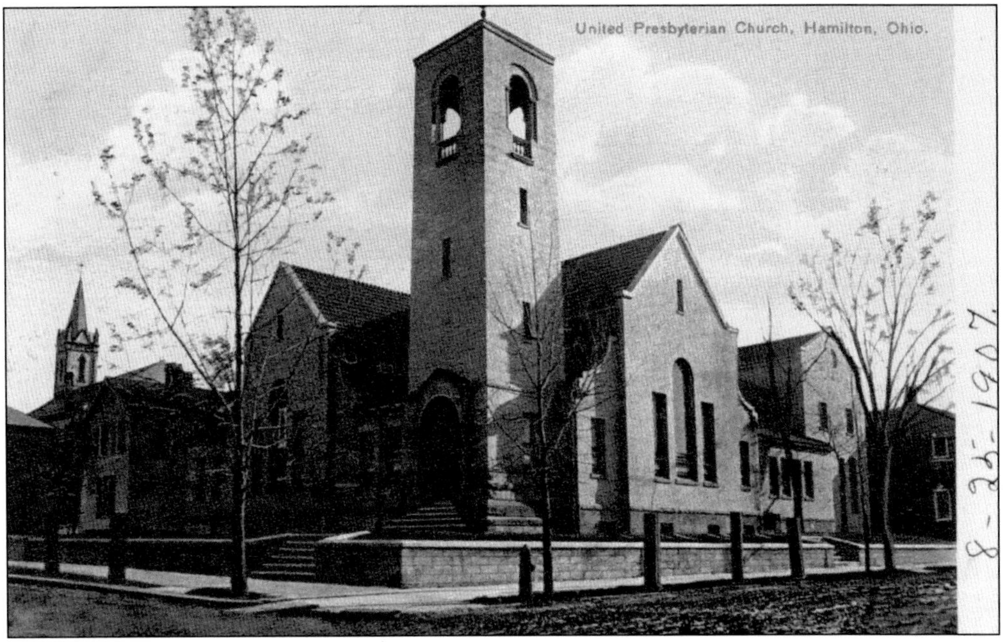

This card of the United Presbyterian Church on North Front Street in Hamilton is dated August 25, 1907. Rev. Francis Monfort led the first congregation to build a church on this location in the early 1800s. Another Presbyterian church was built on Water Street in 1818 but was demolished in 1831 when the Great Miami River Basin was established.

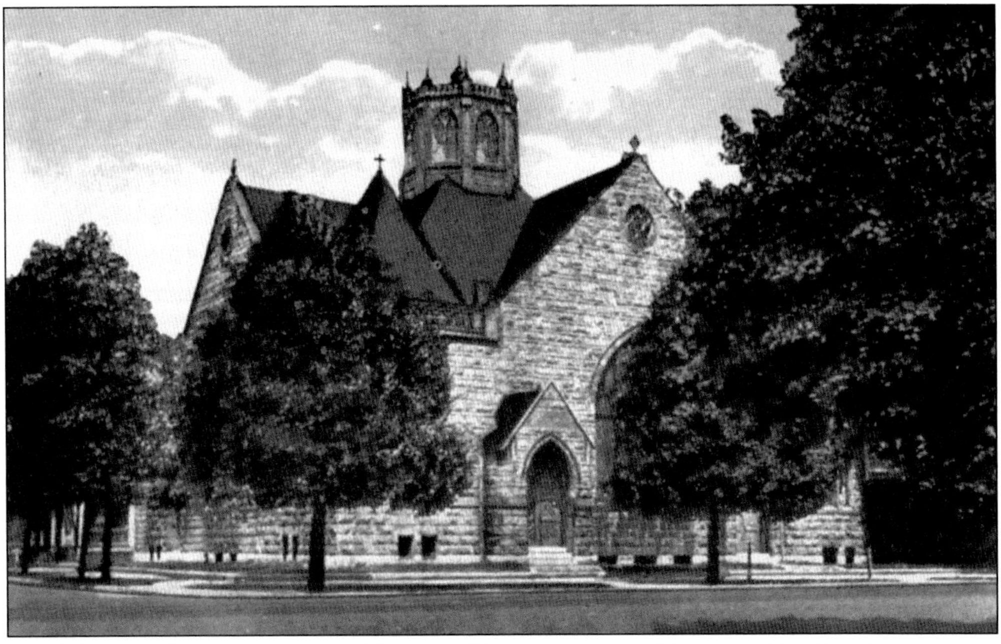

In 1895, some 100 members seceded from the First Presbyterian Church in Hamilton because they thought its practices were too liberal. They opened their own house of worship, the Westminster Presbyterian Church, whose first preacher was Rev. J. S. Edenburn. For the first year, the congregation held services in the courthouse. Later in 1895, a church was built on the northeast corner of High and Seventh Streets. By 1903, the church had grown to 400 members.

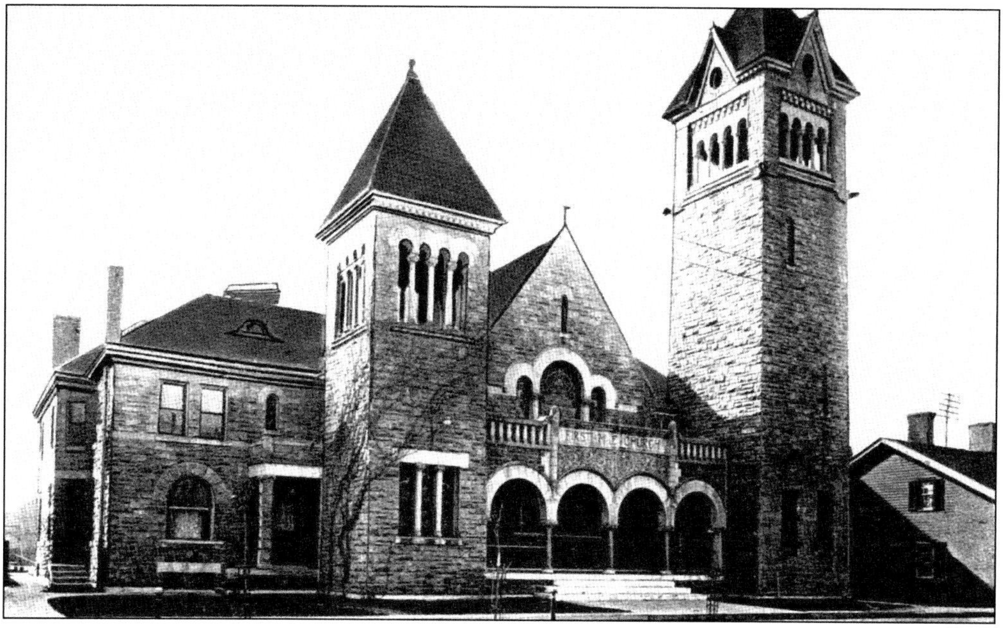

The Methodist Episcopal congregation of Hamilton dates back to 1819, when it was organized by Rev. Samuel West. In 1893, members built a brick church that could seat 400 people on Ludlow Avenue between Second and Third Streets. Rev. Greenburg R. Jones served as the minister. This card of the remodeled church is dated June 9, 1909.

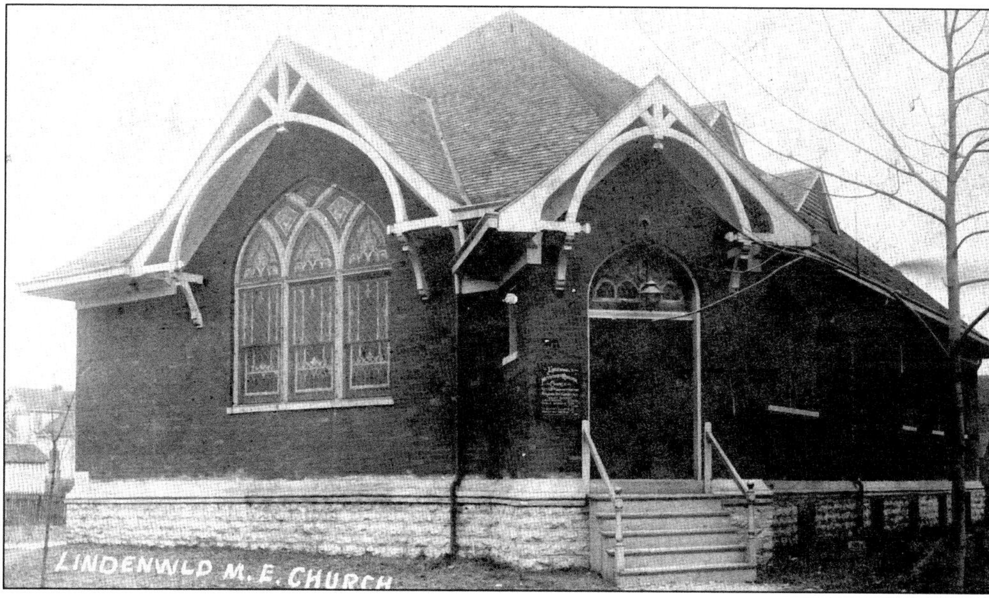

The Lindenwald Methodist Episcopal Church, an outgrowth of a mission of the main Hamilton church, opened in 1903 on Fairview Avenue and by 1905 was going strong. The minister was Rev. S. A. Stephans. Coauthor Randy McNutt attended this church as a child in the early 1950s. In 1955, the congregation built a new, larger church on Pleasant Avenue in southern Lindenwald. It held its first formal service on Palm Sunday that year. The congregation, now known as United Methodist, still occupies the Pleasant Avenue church. The old building has been used by different denominations over the last half century.

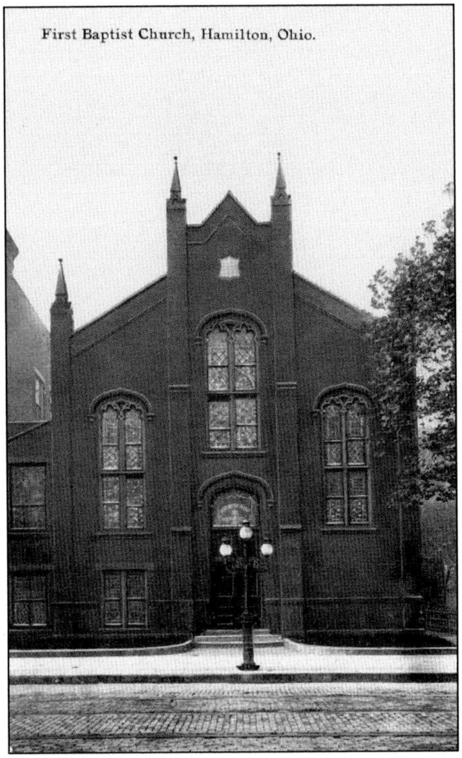

In this exterior real-photo postcard, published around 1912, the First Baptist Church in urban Hamilton looks inviting. Notice the globe streetlamp in front of the main entrance and the traction car tracks embedded in the brick street. The building appears Gothic in design.

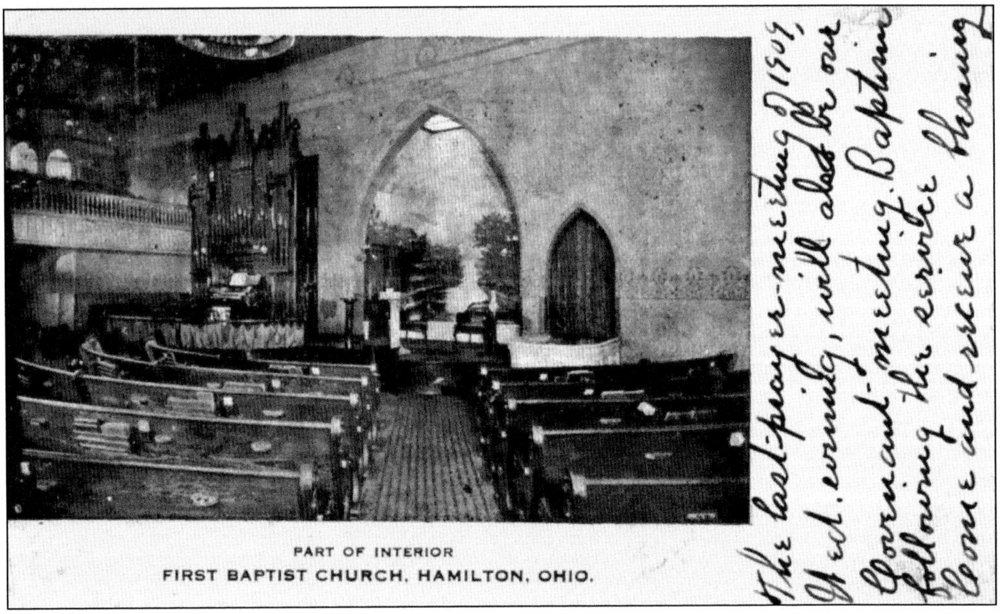

The interior of the First Baptist Church of Hamilton is shown here. The card, apparently one of many sent to both existing and prospective members, was mailed to Mrs. Andrew Boyer of 1150 Central Avenue in Hamilton on December 28, 1909. Note the massive pipe organ on the left side and the interesting arch in the center. The unidentified sender wrote, "The last prayer meeting of 1909, Wed. evening, will also be our covenant meeting. Baptism following the service. Come and receive a blessing."

Four

Education

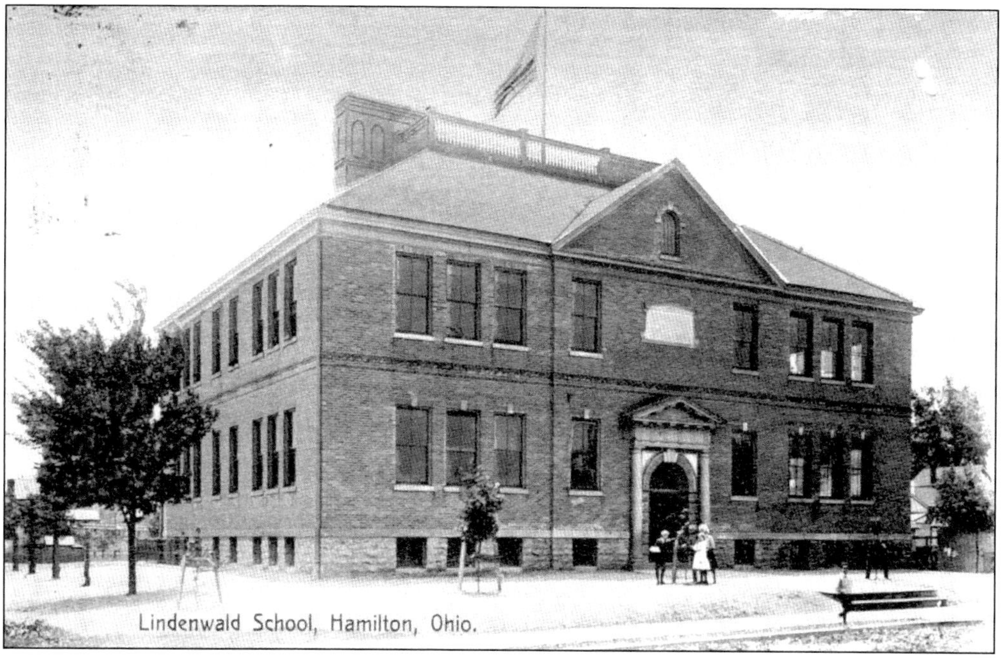

Lindenwald School served a growing neighborhood in southern Hamilton in 1910. With factories, churches, and shops just blocks away and a family-run grocery store on every corner, Lindenwald residents did not have to go far for whatever they wanted.

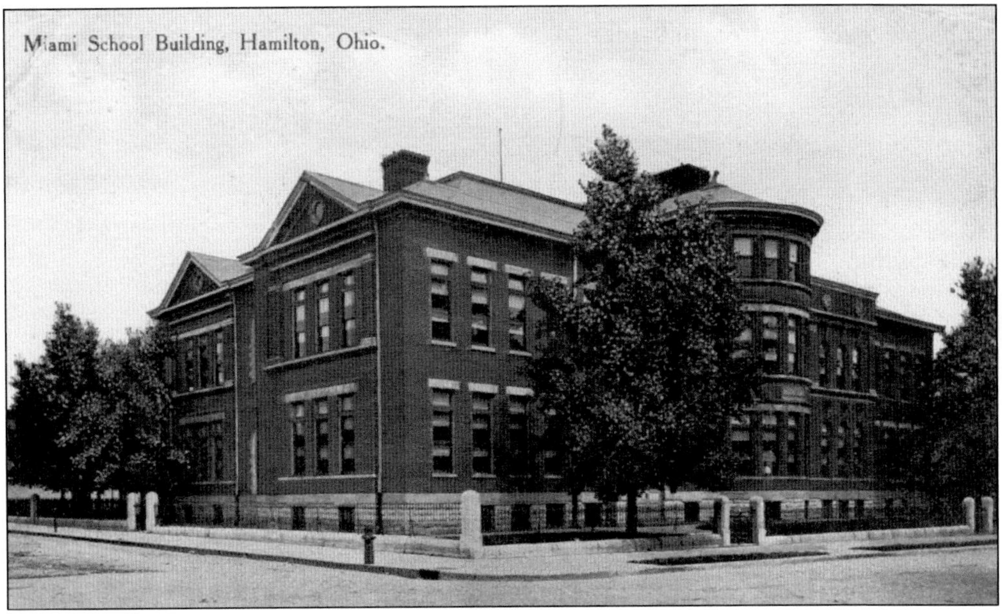

The Miami School building, located at C Street and Ross Avenue in Hamilton, catered to students of the west side's Rossville community. The card is postmarked May 23, 1912. Today the building is occupied by the Butler County Senior Citizens' group.

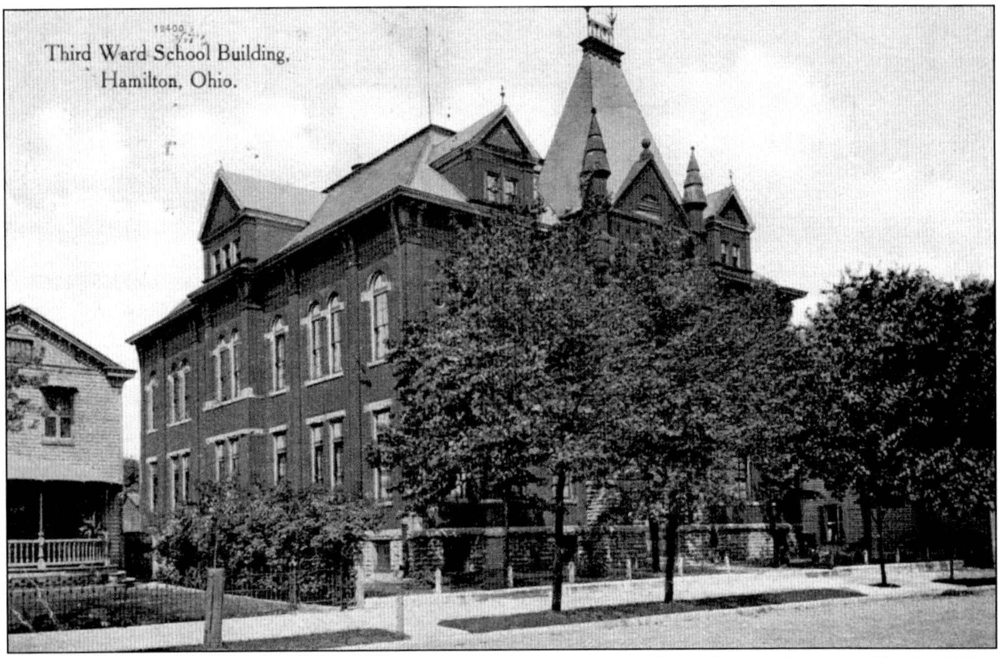

Hamilton's Third Ward School was located on Dayton Street when this card was mailed in 1912. The school, built in the Victorian Romanesque style in 1889, featured symmetrical facades and a truncated hip roof with a large gable and dormers. The building was used as a school until 1948, when the Hamilton Board of Education moved its offices there. Although the board has now transferred up the street, the old school is still used for city school purposes.

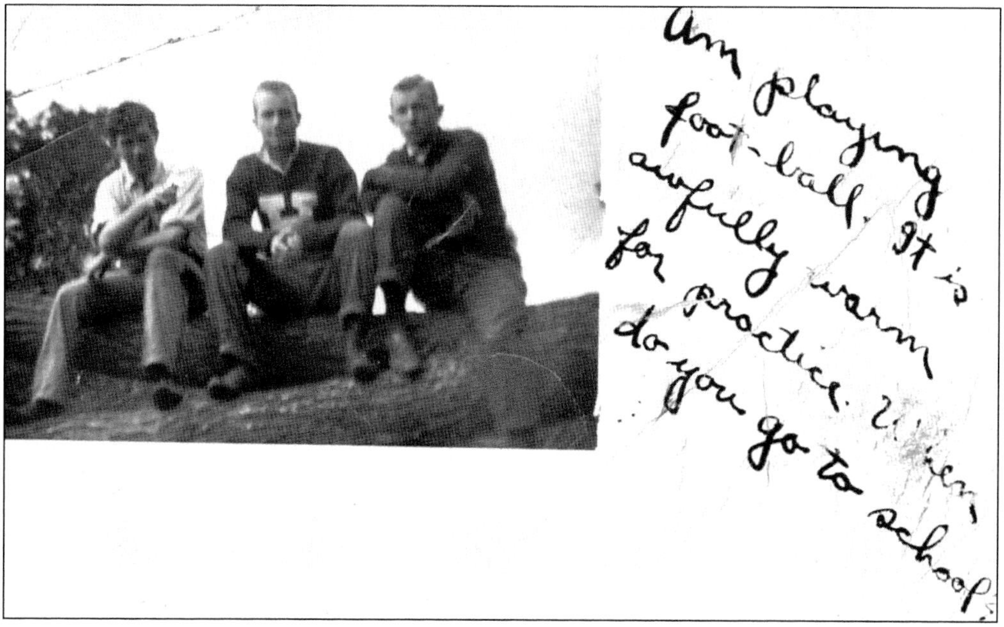

Early September 1912 was particularly warm for football practice, according to this card mailed by Bill, a Hamilton High School player, to his friend Charles "Brownie" Brown Jr. in Vicksburg, Michigan. "Four bats received," Bill added. "Much obliged." The Hamilton students on the card are unidentified.

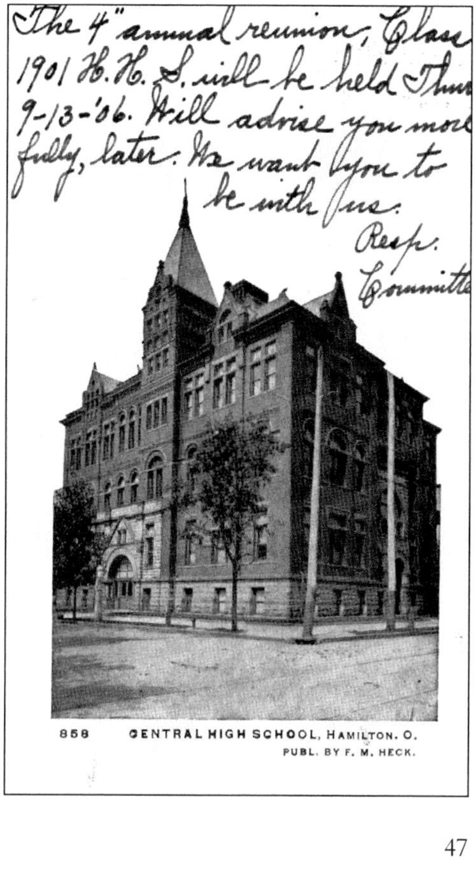

This postcard was mailed to Nina and Grace Flickinger of Seven Mile, Ohio, on August 13, 1906, to invite them to the Hamilton High School class of 1901 reunion. Hamilton High was located at the corner of Second Street and Ludlow Avenue.

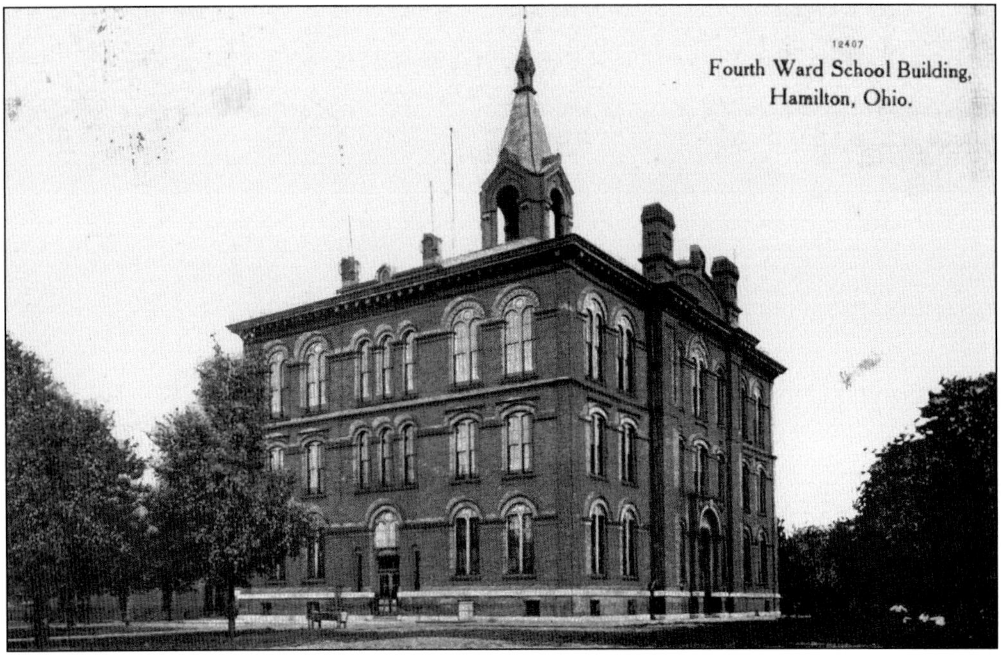

The impressive Fourth Ward School was located on Hamilton's Eighth Street, between Rigdon Avenue and Chestnut Street. The card is postmarked 1909.

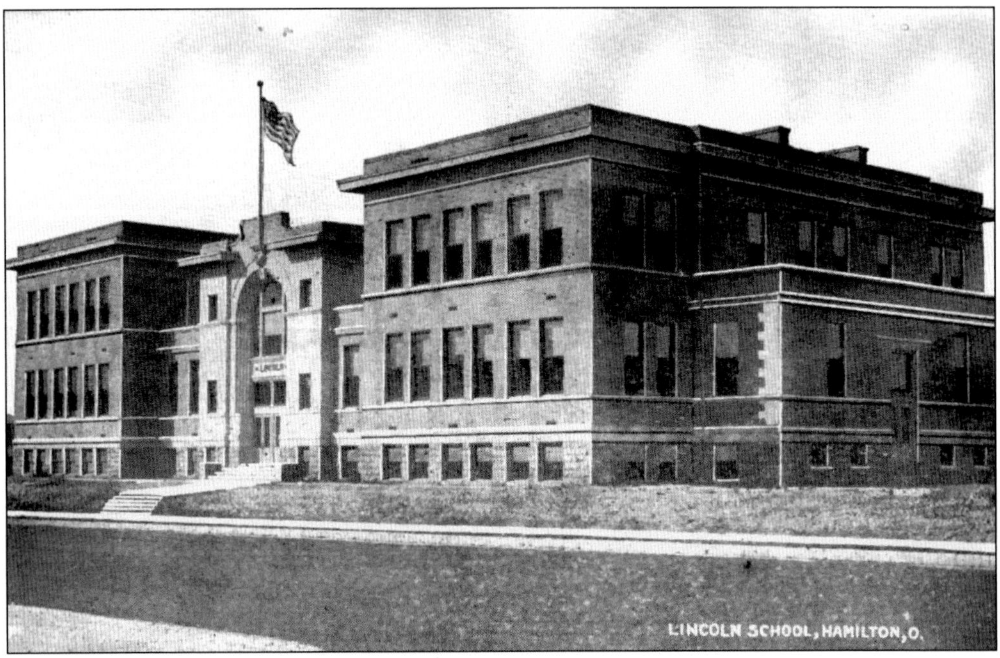

Lincoln School, at 401 North E Street on Hamilton's west side, was one of a number of city schools opening in the first 30 years of the 20th century. Lincoln, one of the older schools in the group, was named for Pres. Abraham Lincoln.

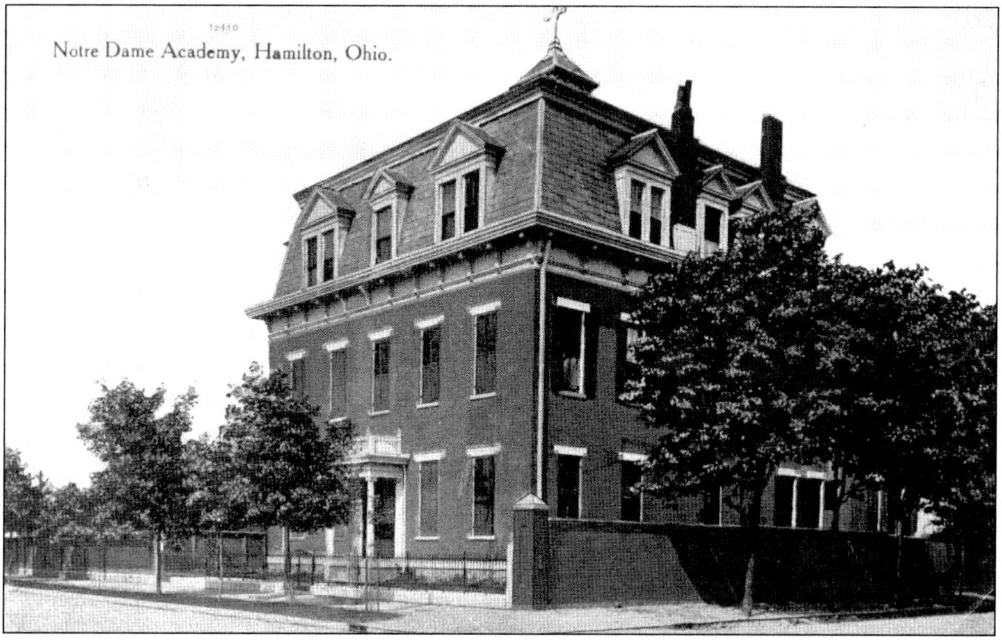

The Roman Catholic Church first provided parochial education in Hamilton in 1908. The Sisters of Notre Dame operated St. Veronica Catholic School at the corner of Shuler and Beckett Avenues. Notre Dame Academy, depicted on this 1909 card, stood on the northeast corner of Second Street and Hancock Avenue.

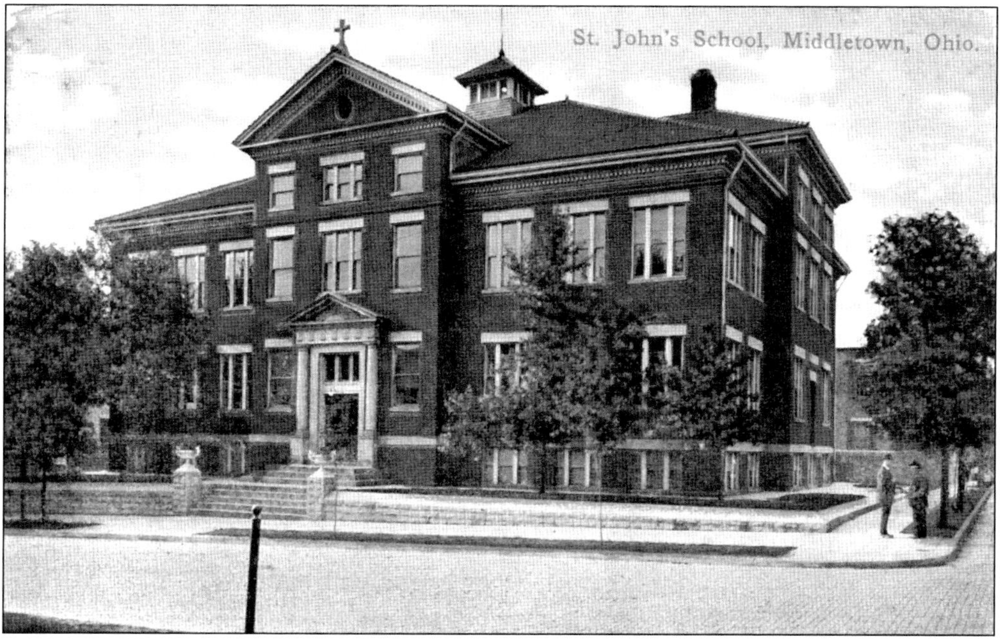

Construction began in 1908 on the new St. John's Parochial School on First Avenue in Middletown. The school was first established in 1872. Christina Zeier Nunlist, who attended the old two-room school from 1900 to 1907, remembered parish priest Father Gerdes playing baseball with the boys during lunch and cutting up an apple in class to teach fractions. This card was mailed as a Thanksgiving greeting in 1913.

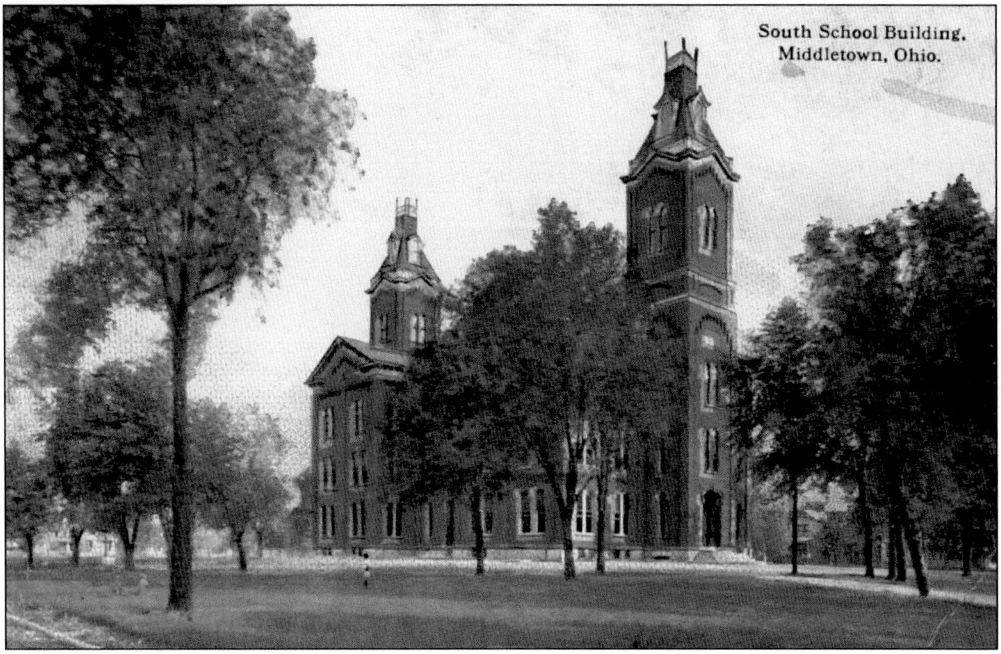

South School was built in 1872 on South Main Street, Middletown, to accommodate a growing student body. The three-story brick structure stood on the site of the former Arthur Lefferson estate. The nucleus of Middletown High School began in Room 12 on the third floor of this building. Four students graduated in the class of 1871.

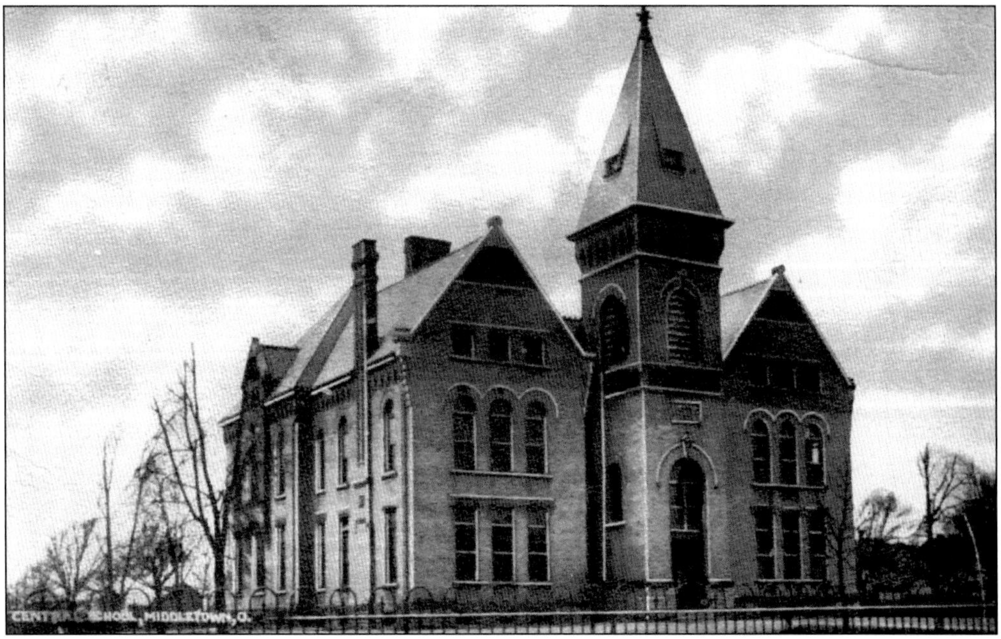

Central School in Middletown began holding classes in 1888 in eight "splendid, well-equipped and well-lighted rooms," according to a contemporary history. The card is postmarked April 28, 1910.

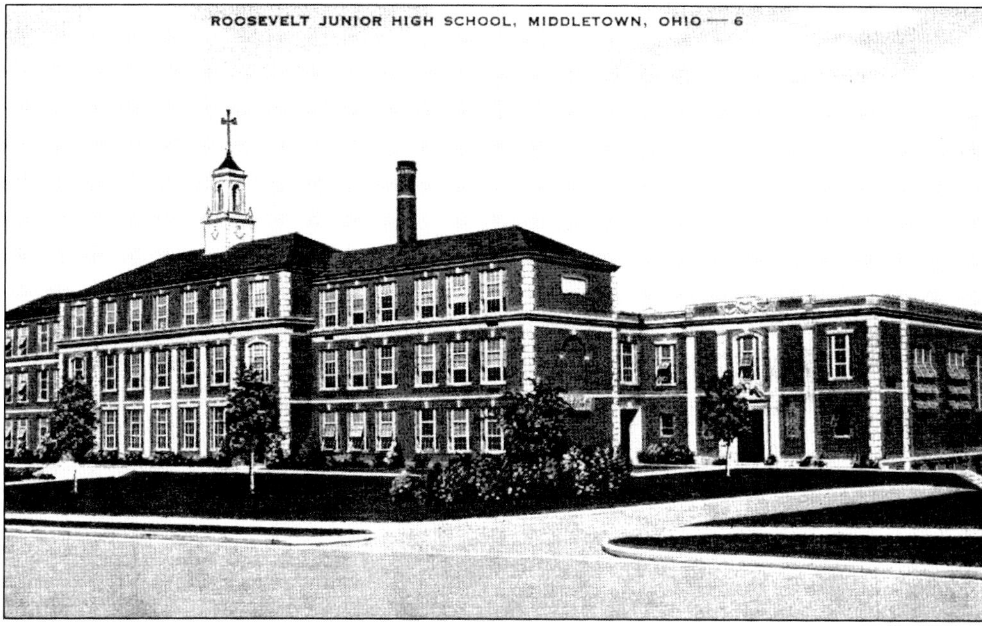

Roosevelt Junior High School opened in 1930 on East Central Avenue in Middletown. McKinley, the city's other public junior high, started the same year on Verity Parkway.

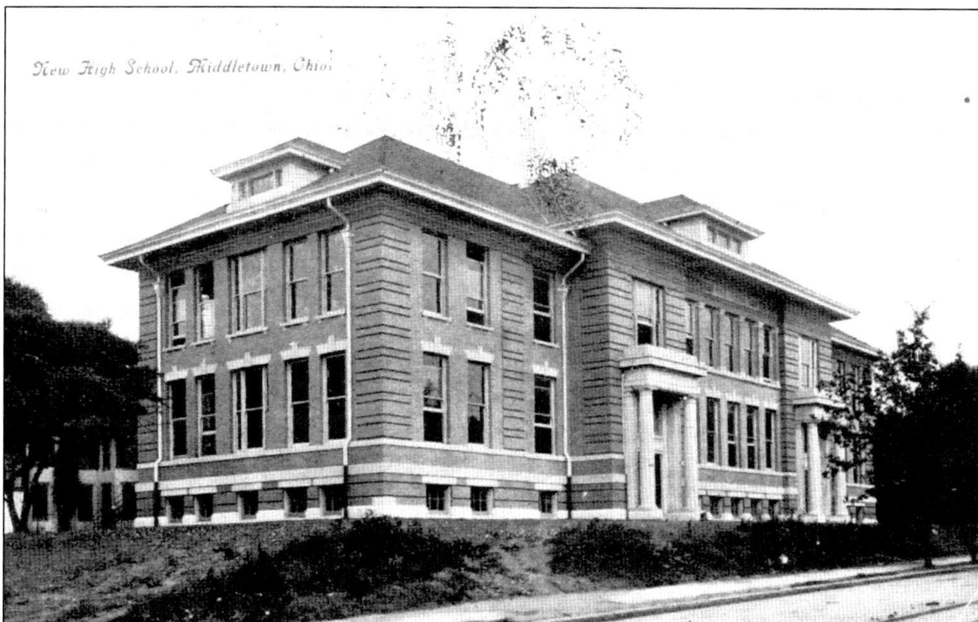

Middletown's new public high school was ready for students during the 1908–1909 school year. Located on Central Avenue, the building is shown in 1916. A surge in the student population necessitated the construction of a new high school on Girard Avenue in 1923. The Central Avenue School was then converted into an eighth-grade building.

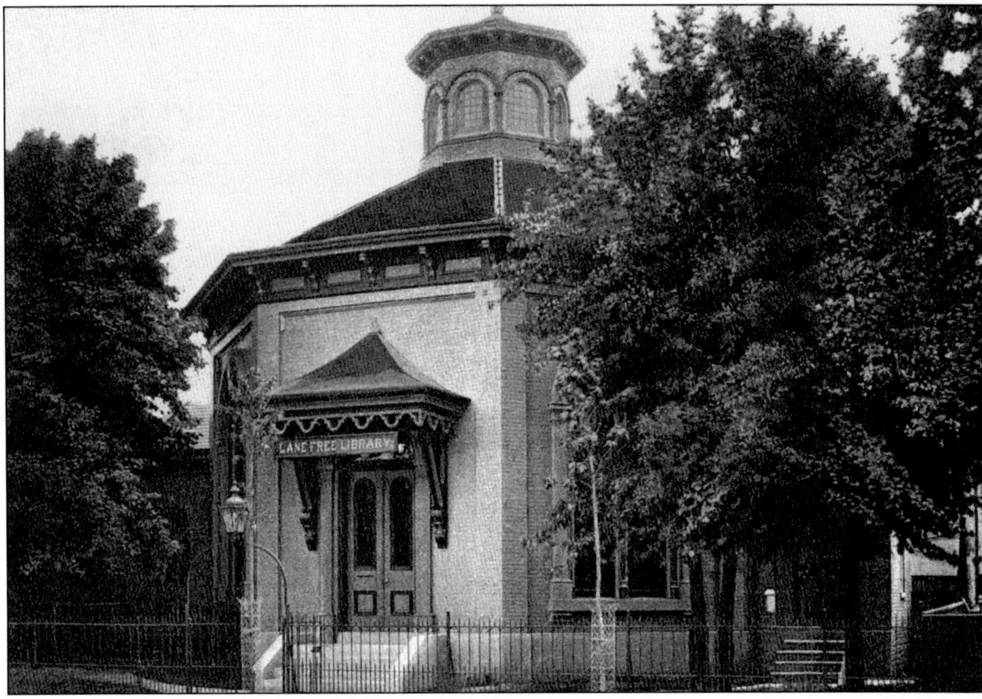

Industrialist Clark Lane built and designed the Lane Free Library at Third and Buckeye Streets in Hamilton to serve Butler County residents. Voters formally accepted Lane's gift in 1868. By 1908, the library had 9,000 volumes. Florence S. Schenck served as librarian and Hattie James as assistant librarian. Lane Public Library still operates out of Clark Lane's original building, although it has been expanded and remodeled over the years. The main library also oversees a large library in Fairfield.

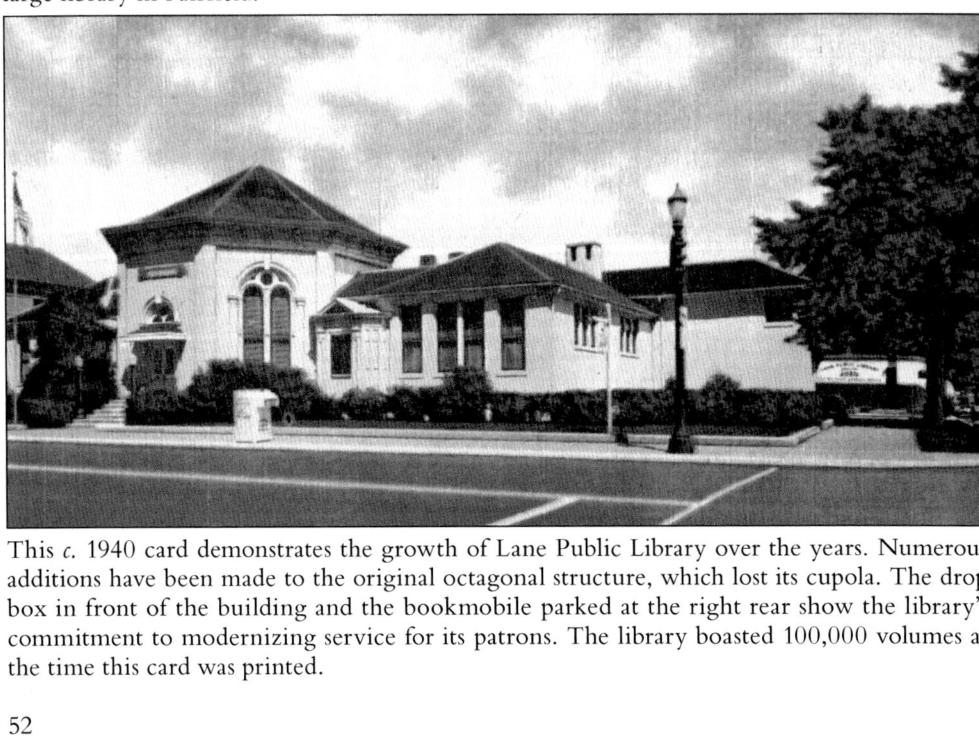

This *c.* 1940 card demonstrates the growth of Lane Public Library over the years. Numerous additions have been made to the original octagonal structure, which lost its cupola. The drop box in front of the building and the bookmobile parked at the right rear show the library's commitment to modernizing service for its patrons. The library boasted 100,000 volumes at the time this card was printed.

Five

College Days

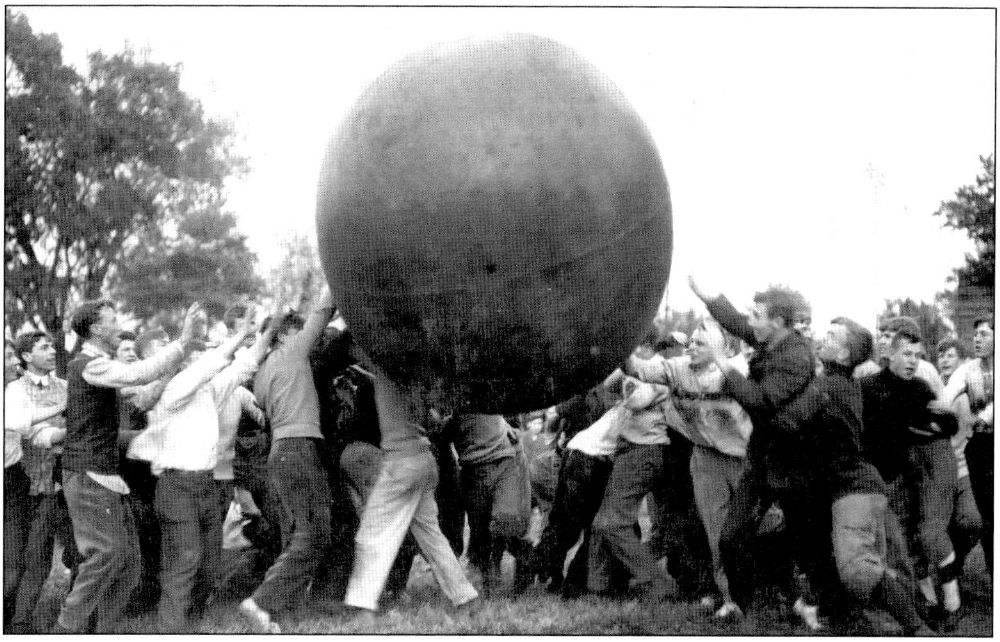

On a mild October day in 1909, two groups of Miami University students met for a big game in Oxford. The ball, nine feet in diameter, was rented from the University of Michigan for the intramural event. New balls of this sort cost between $250 and $600, according to one participant. There are no real winners in this type of game, but everyone looks as though he is having fun.

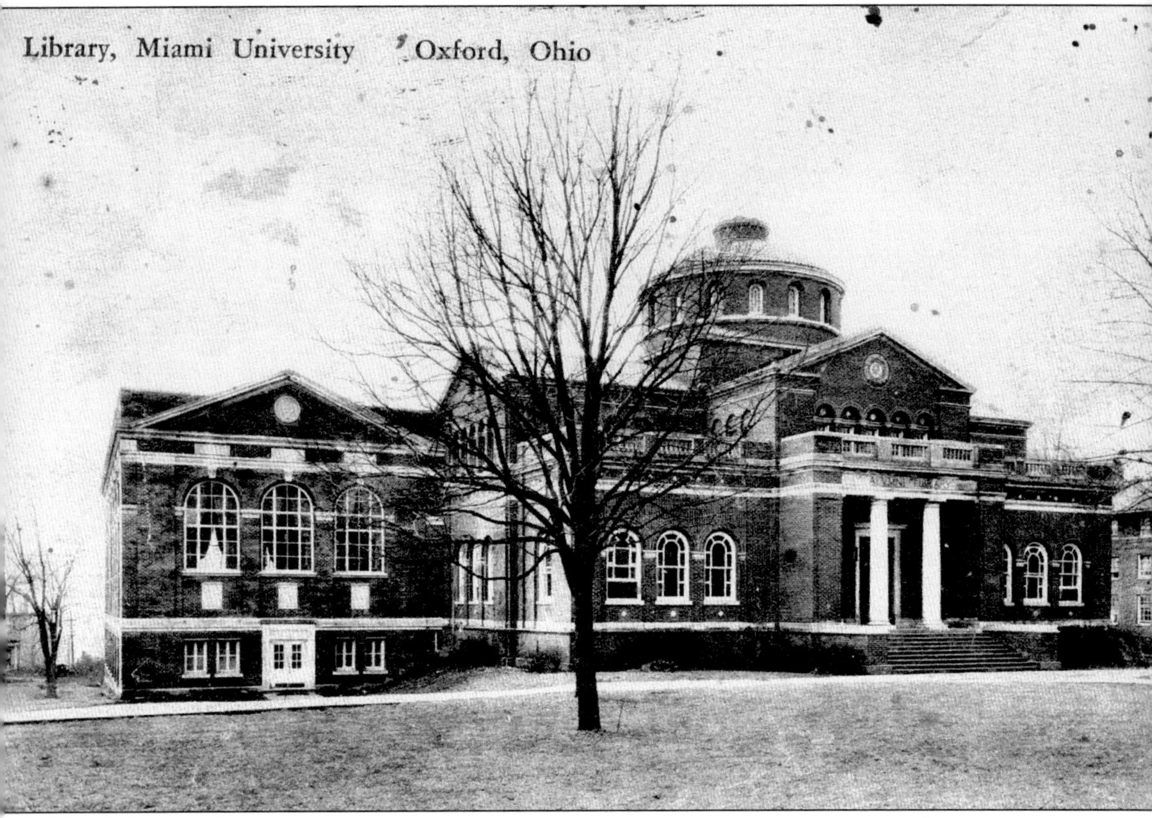

Alumni Library was an intellectual and social center for Oxford residents, full-time Miami University students, and visitors who arrived for conferences and seminars. Joseph Dues of Saint Henry, Ohio, arrived in Oxford in late August 1934 for "one more week of good and hard studying." He mailed this postcard to his young son Joseph Jr. to let him know he had arrived safely. Opening in 1909, the library was funded through the Andrew Carnegie Foundation and matching money donated by Miami alumni. The east wing, shown on this card, was built in 1924; a west wing was added in 1955. The building was called Alumni Hall after King Library was constructed.

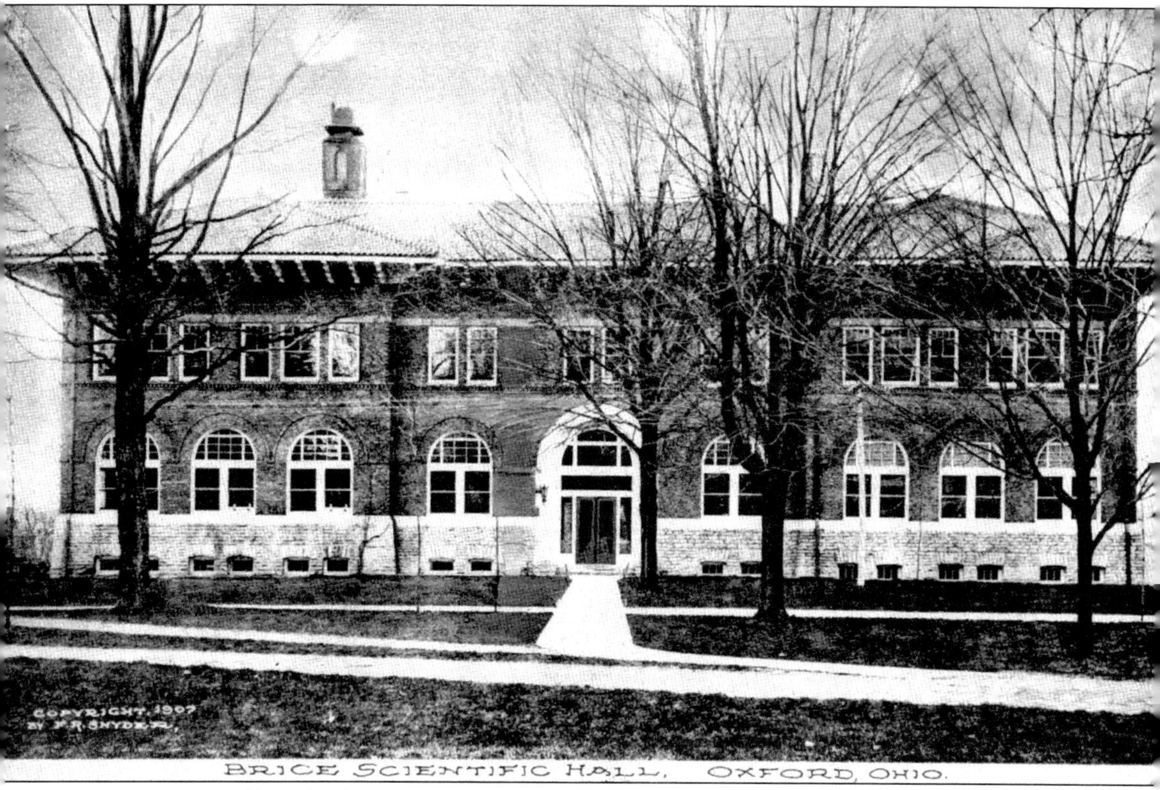

Brice Scientific Hall was built in 1892 and named for Calvin Brice, a Miami alumnus who became a U.S. senator. Student Grace Bardon sent this card to her friend Olive Young in Delaware, Ohio, about 1910. Grace was one of an increasing number of women attending colleges and universities as the 20th century began. She had just attended a student reception and a basketball game and was enjoying collegiate life.

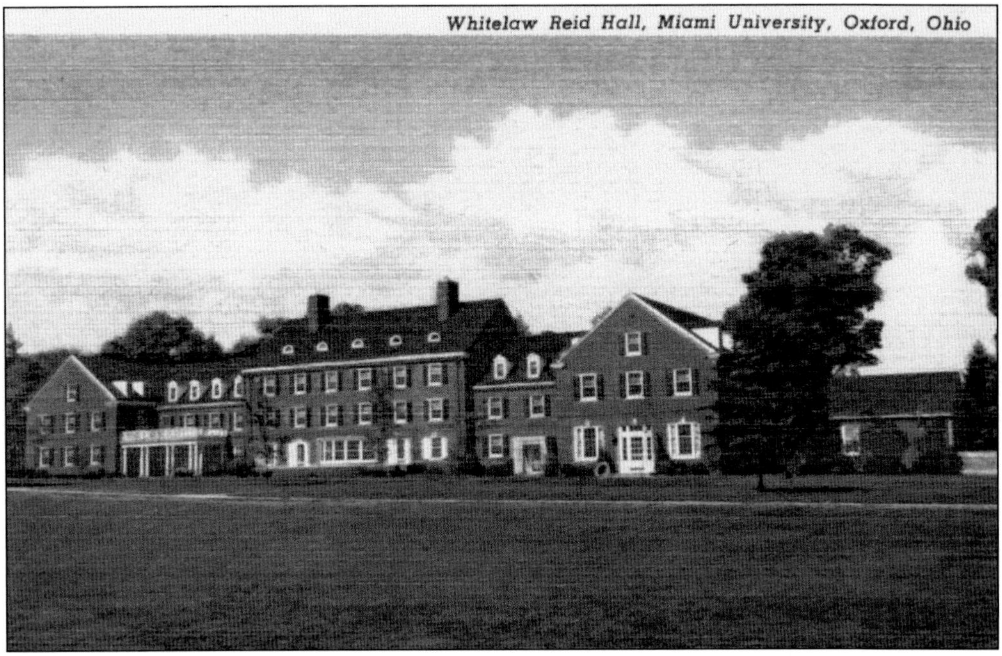

Whitelaw Reid Hall, a men's residence at Miami University, was constructed in 1948 and named for a member of the class of 1856. A journalist and diplomat, Reid was born in Xenia, Ohio, in 1837. He covered the Civil War for the *Cincinnati Gazette* and later wrote a history of Ohio during the war years. Reid was the unsuccessful Republican nominee for vice president in 1892.

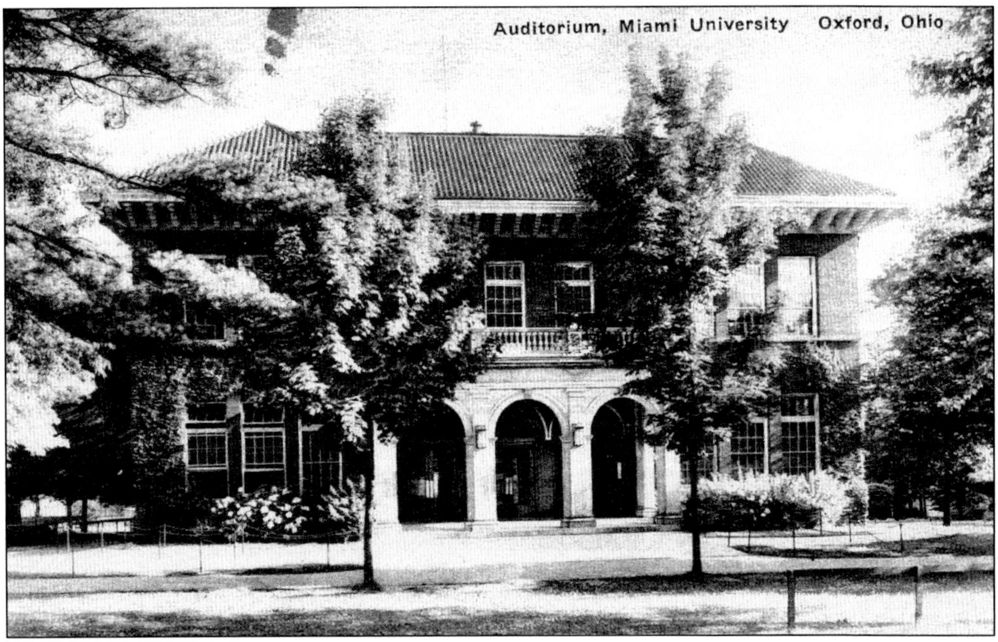

Miami University's auditorium, built in 1908, also served as its administration building when this card was mailed on August 8, 1930. The university president and deans had offices there. The auditorium could seat 700 people.

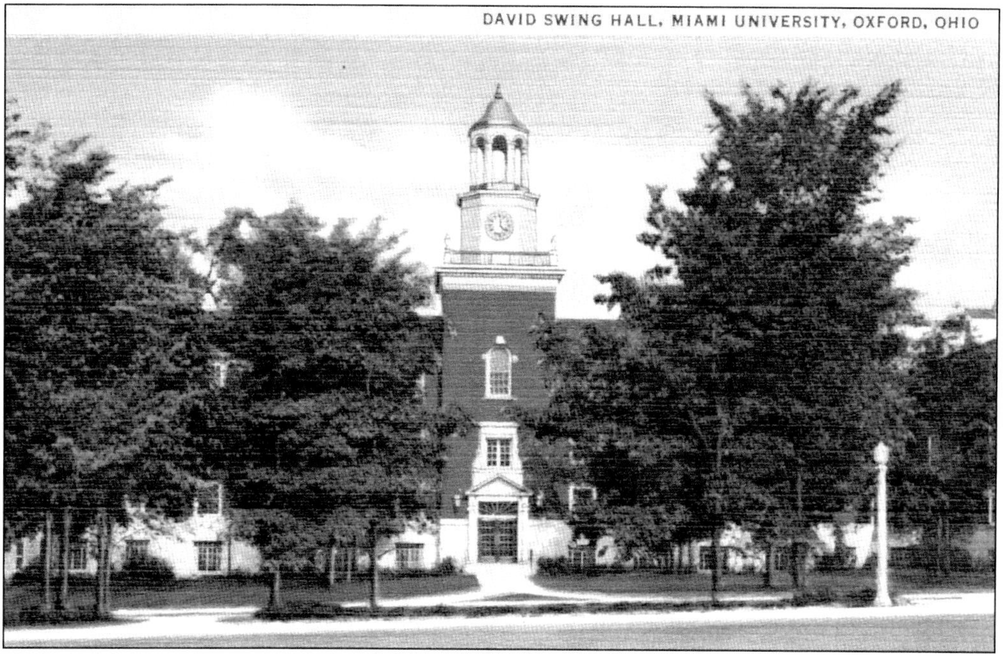

David Swing was principal of Miami's preparatory department from 1853 to 1866. After moving to Chicago to pastor a Presbyterian church, he became a nationally known preacher. The Miami building named for him was used as a men's dormitory.

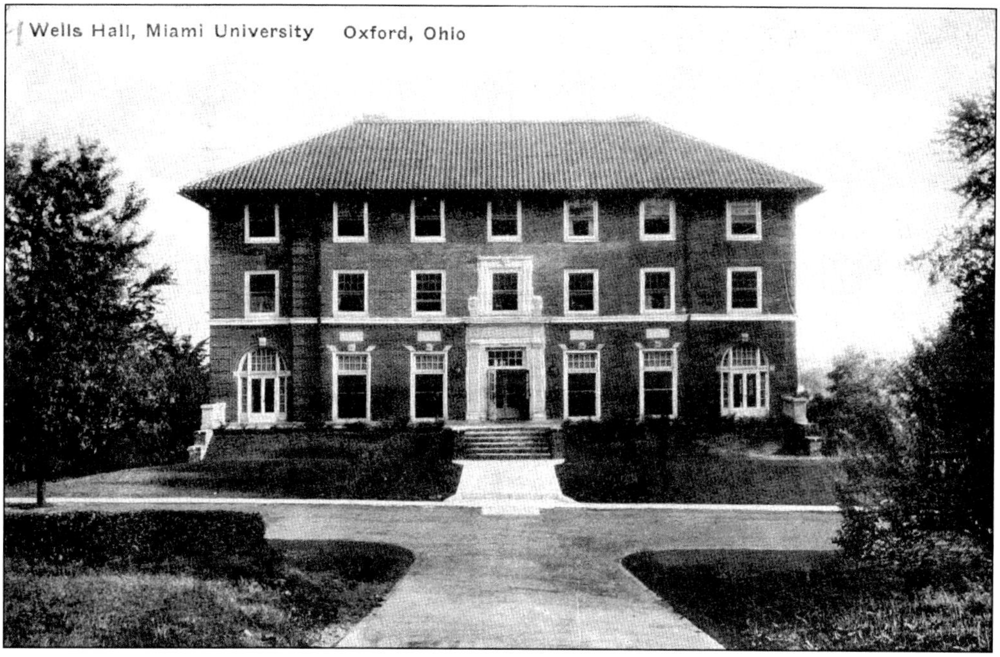

"Pretty place here, although Pickaway Co. is better," wrote Bill, who was apparently from the mentioned county and whose last name is unknown. This postcard, mailed June 22, 1926, shows Wells Hall, a women's dormitory built in 1923 on Spring Street. The hall was named for financial donor William B. Wells, who had served as director of the St. Louis World's Fair and Exposition.

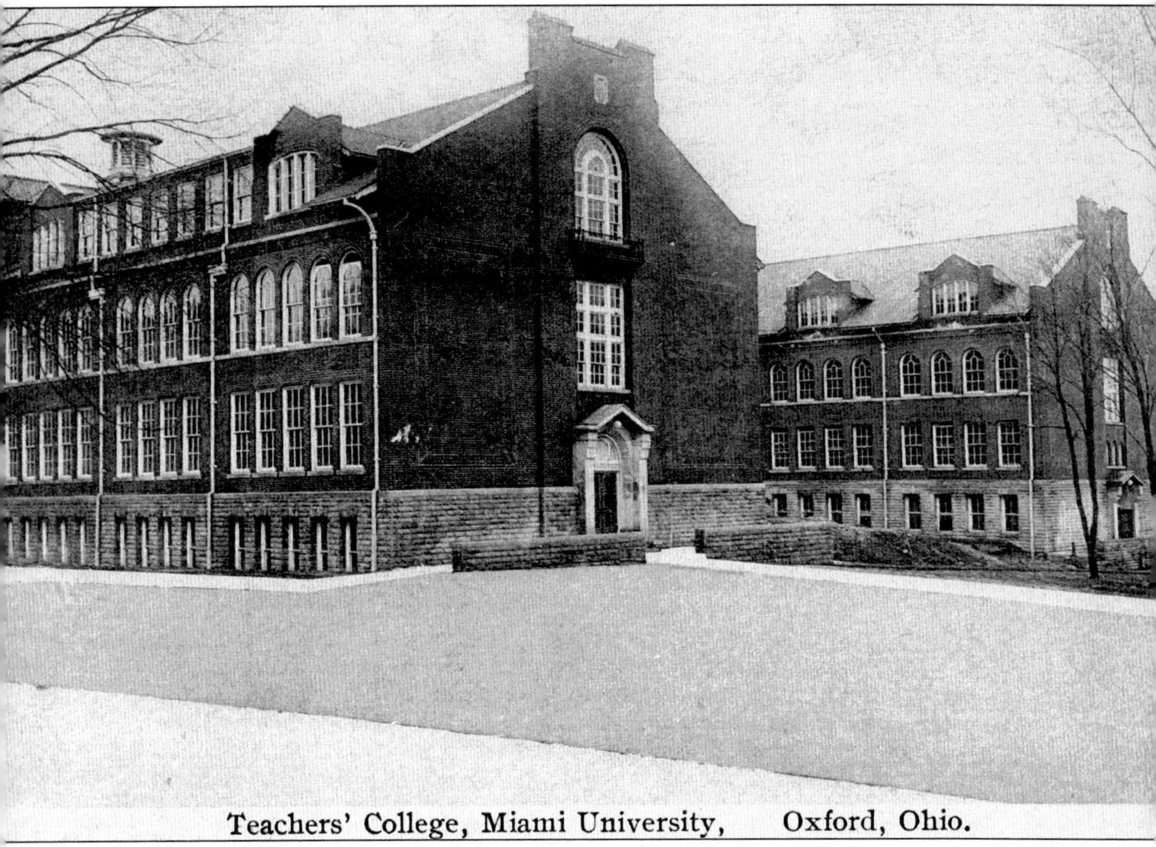

Lois Banta was taking summer classes at Miami University on July 10, 1917, when she sent this card to Amanda Gates in Lewisburg, Ohio. Many teachers came to McGuffey Hall, referred to here as Teachers' College, in the summer to learn new theories and techniques to help in their own classrooms. Later McGuffey was filled with teachers on summer recess who were working on advanced degrees. By the middle of the 20th century, Miami's teacher education program was well known nationally. Miami will forever be associated with the building's namesake, William Holmes McGuffey, who taught there from 1826 to 1836 while developing his famous McGuffey Readers series of instructional books. The hall was built in stages from 1910 through 1925.

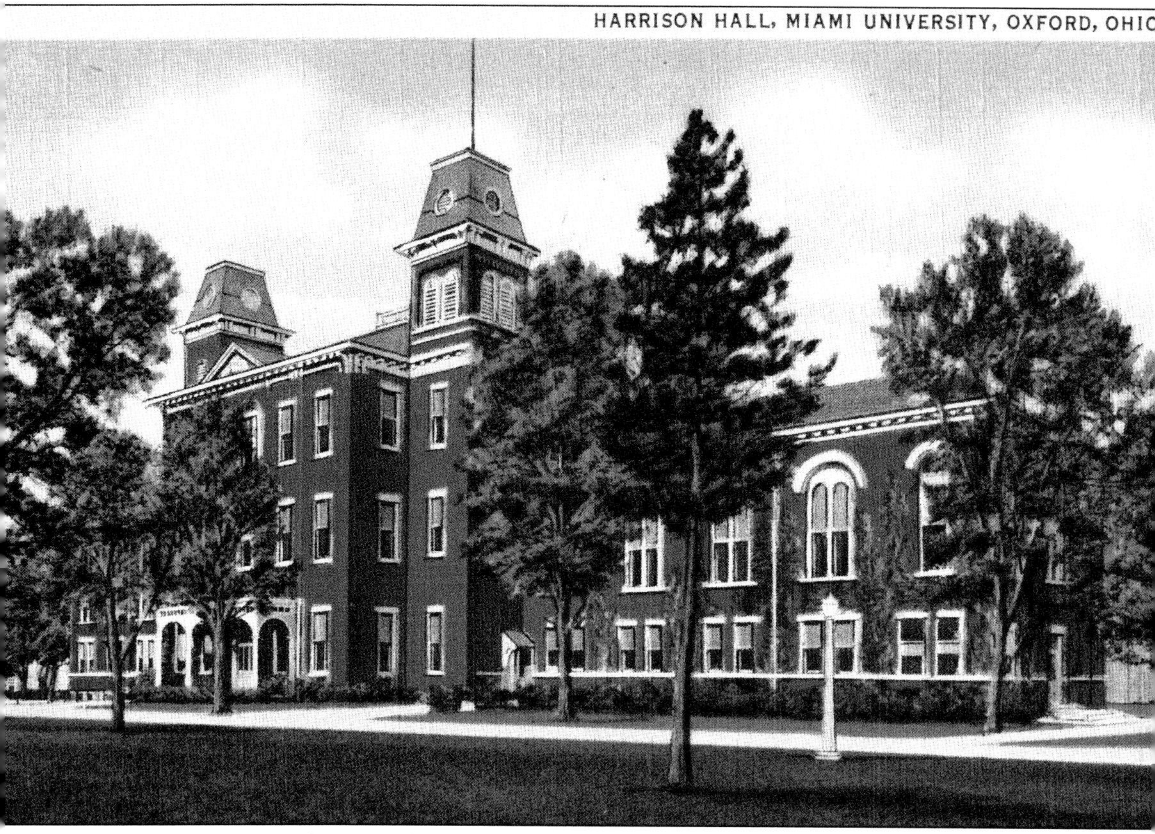

Harrison Hall, named for one of Miami's most famous graduates, started life as Old Main after the Civil War. Classrooms, a chapel, a library, and meeting rooms filled the red-painted structure. The hall was renamed Harrison about the time this postcard was printed in the 1930s. Pres. Benjamin Harrison, an 1852 Miami graduate, is the namesake. First Lady Caroline Scott Harrison, who became the first president general of the National Society of the Daughters of the American Revolution (DAR), was also honored by a DAR memorial on campus. The Harrison-Miami connection dates back to 1832, when Caroline was born in Oxford and her father, Dr. John Witherspoon Scott, taught at the university. Dr. Scott was dismissed by Miami in 1845 for his abolitionist views. When he returned to Oxford to head the Oxford Female Institute in 1849, Caroline's beau, Benjamin Harrison, enrolled at Miami. Caroline completed her education at the institute in 1853, and the couple married at the Scotts' Oxford home that same year. The Harrisons returned there the following year for the birth of their first child.

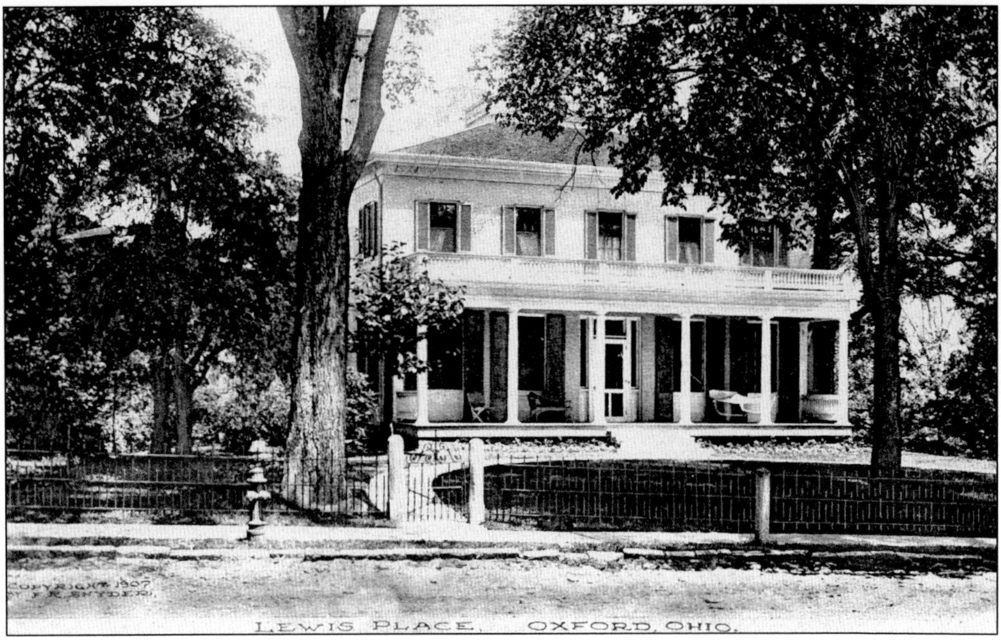

Jane and Romeo Lewis built this gracious home at 310 East High Street in Oxford in the 1830s. Miami University first rented, then in 1929 purchased, the home to be the residence of the university president. This view is postmarked 1909.

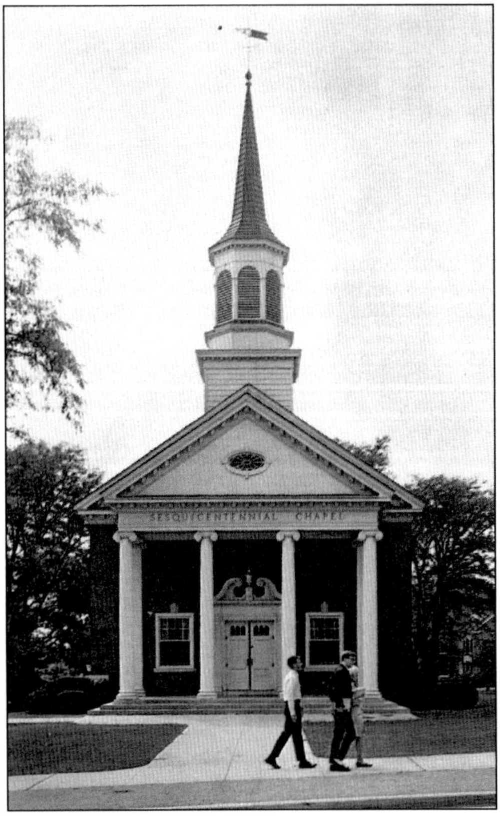

The Sesquicentennial Alumni Chapel provides a place for private meditation and for services sponsored by campus groups of all faiths. The chapel was dedicated in 1959 as a commemorative gift of Miami alumni and friends during the university's 150th anniversary festivities.

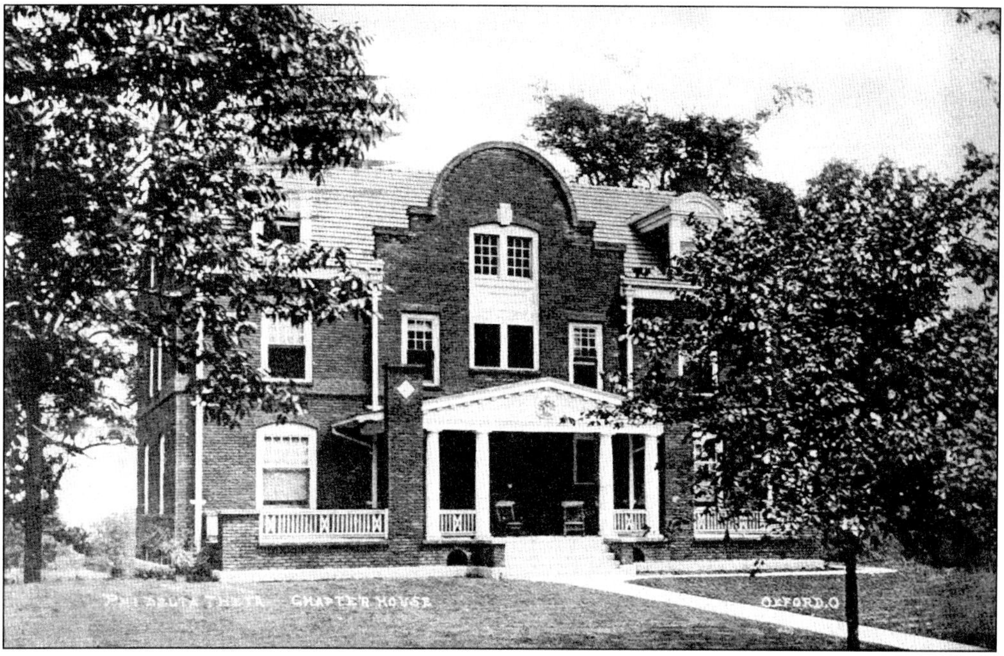

Phi Delta Theta Fraternity was created in Oxford in 1848. The fraternity built this chapter house in 1908 on the north side of High Street on land owned by Miami University. The building was later razed when the university needed the property. The fraternity's national headquarters and foundation offices are still located in Oxford on South Campus Avenue. This card is postmarked 1915.

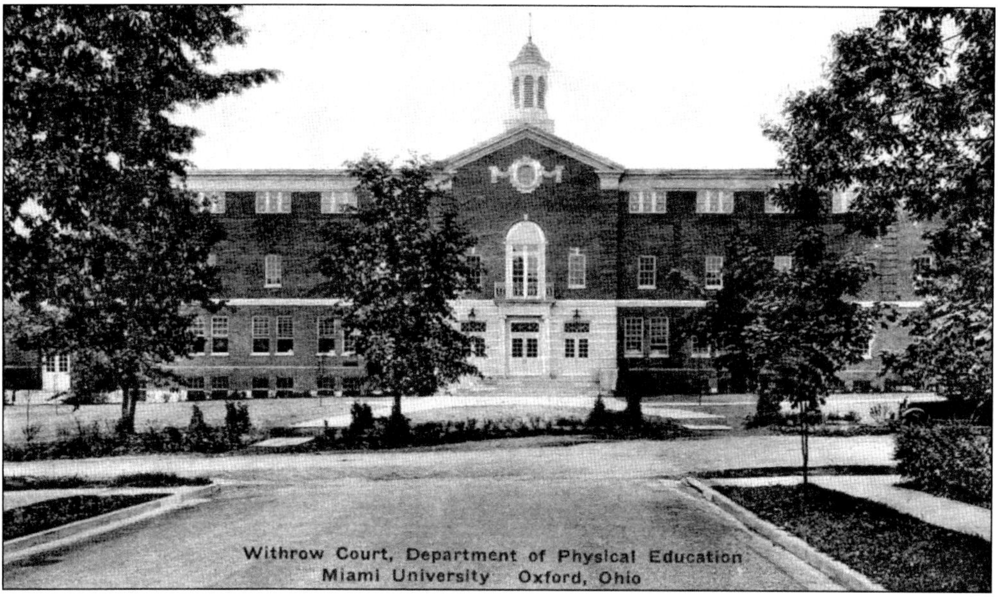

Withrow Court was just four years old when this card was mailed in 1935. The building accommodated gym classes, student assemblies, formal dances, intercollegiate basketball games, and commencement exercises. Withrow was named for Dr. John W. Withrow, class of 1875, who became a physician educator at Cincinnati's Ohio Medical College and a trustee of Miami University.

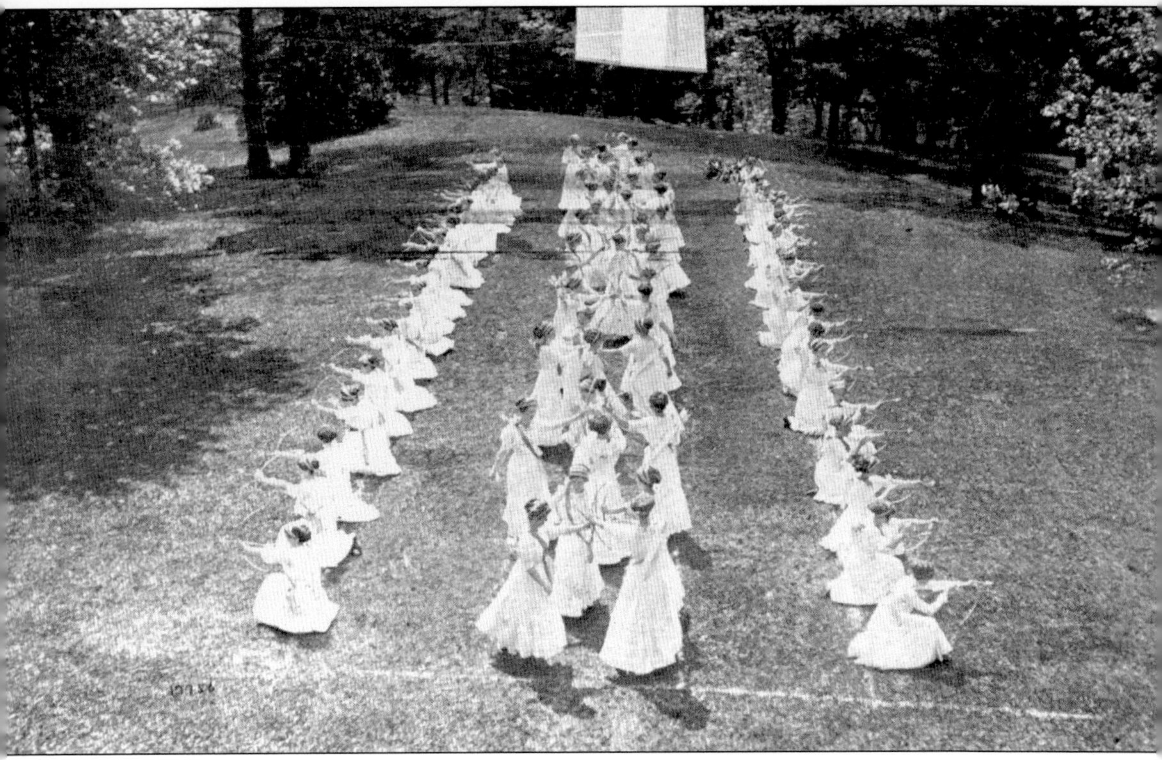

Looking like 20th century Dianas, the freshmen of Western College participate in a drill exercise on Tree Day. The spring event was modeled after one at Mount Holyoke Seminary in Massachusetts, the school that had served as a blueprint for Western. Students typically planted a new tree, raised class flags, and sang school songs as part of the festivities. Tree Day observances began around 1890 and continued through World War II. In those early days, Miami University was just the first of several institutions for higher learning in Oxford. The Western Female Seminary was chartered in 1853 to train teachers and missionaries. With a broadened curriculum, the name changed to the Western College for Women in 1904. This postcard was mailed to a prospective student in June 1913 to announce the availability of the new college catalog.

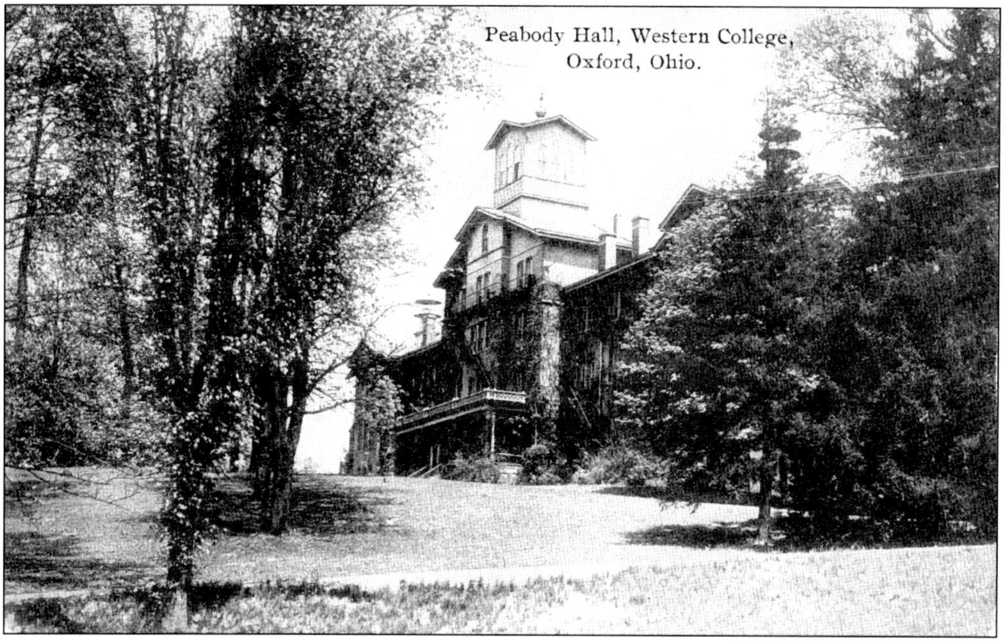

Peabody Hall, Western's original building, was named for Helen Peabody, the Mount Holyoke graduate who became Western's first principal in 1855. Fires in 1860 and 1871 seriously damaged the structure, but it was rebuilt both times and named for Helen Peabody in 1905. Miami acquired Western in 1974.

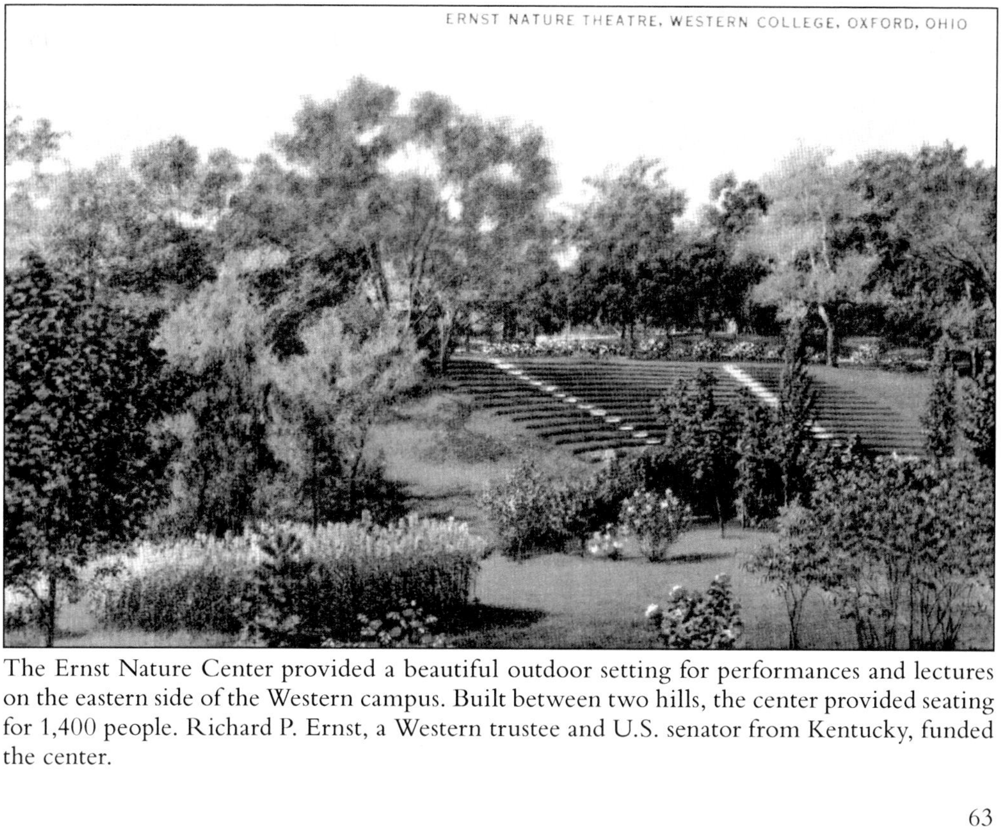

The Ernst Nature Center provided a beautiful outdoor setting for performances and lectures on the eastern side of the Western campus. Built between two hills, the center provided seating for 1,400 people. Richard P. Ernst, a Western trustee and U.S. senator from Kentucky, funded the center.

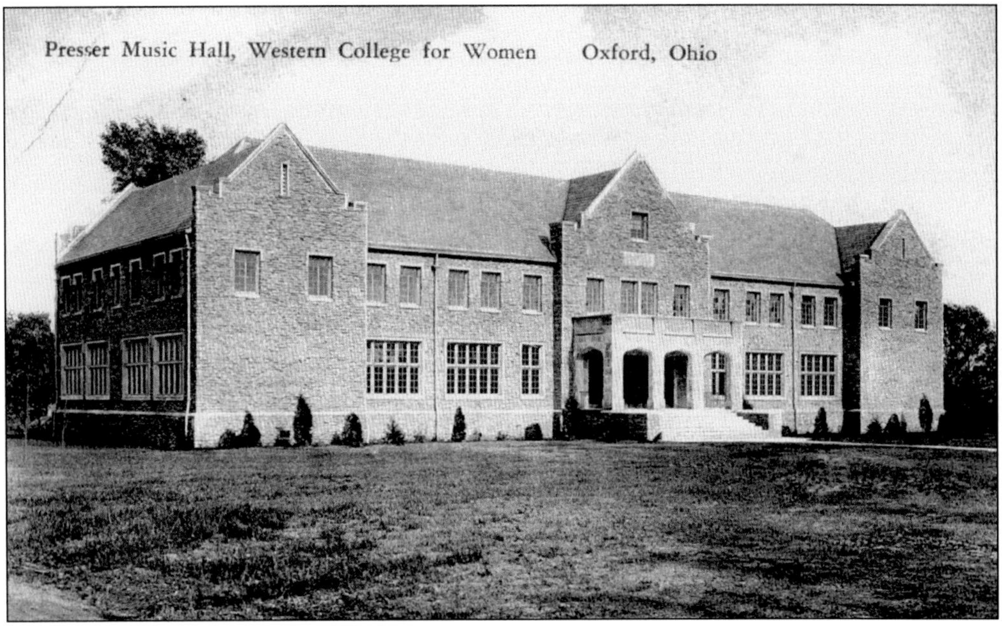

Musician Theodore Presser's foundation paid for half of the construction costs of Western's music building, used for instruction and performance. Presser founded the *Etude*, a monthly music magazine in 1883. Although Presser never taught at Miami University, he taught at three other Ohio universities. The hall was completed in 1931.

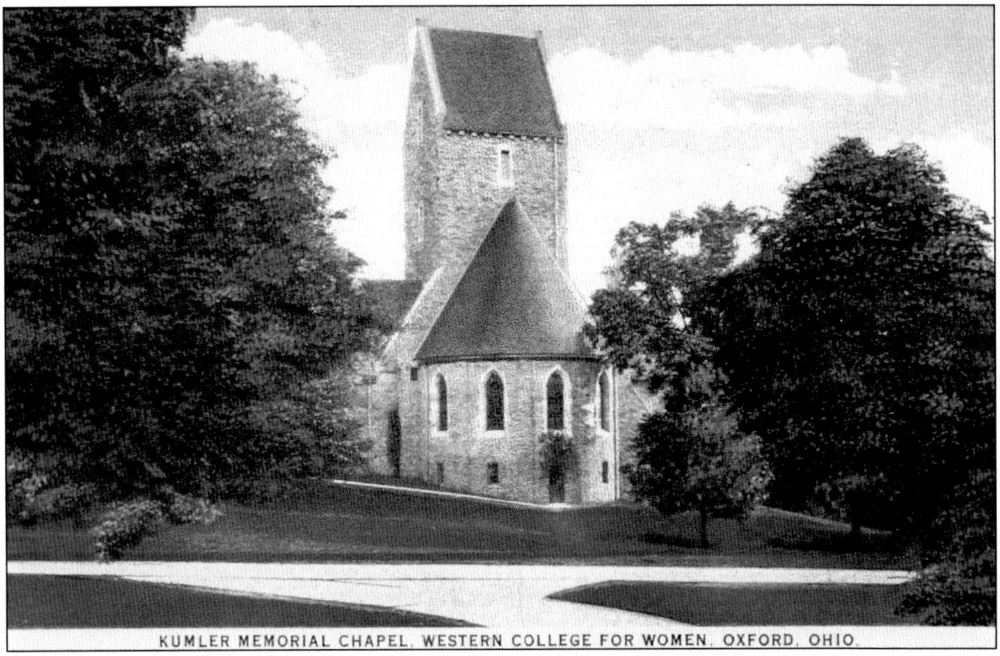

"Hope your school is as satisfactory as mine! This is where I go to church every morning at 8 a.m.," wrote the correspondent of this *c.* 1930 card. Kumler Memorial Chapel contains several beautiful stained-glass windows, including one that was exhibited at the 1893 World's Columbian Exposition. Anna Kumler Wright and Ella Kumler McKelvy donated funds for the chapel in honor of their father and grandfather.

Six

LEISURE

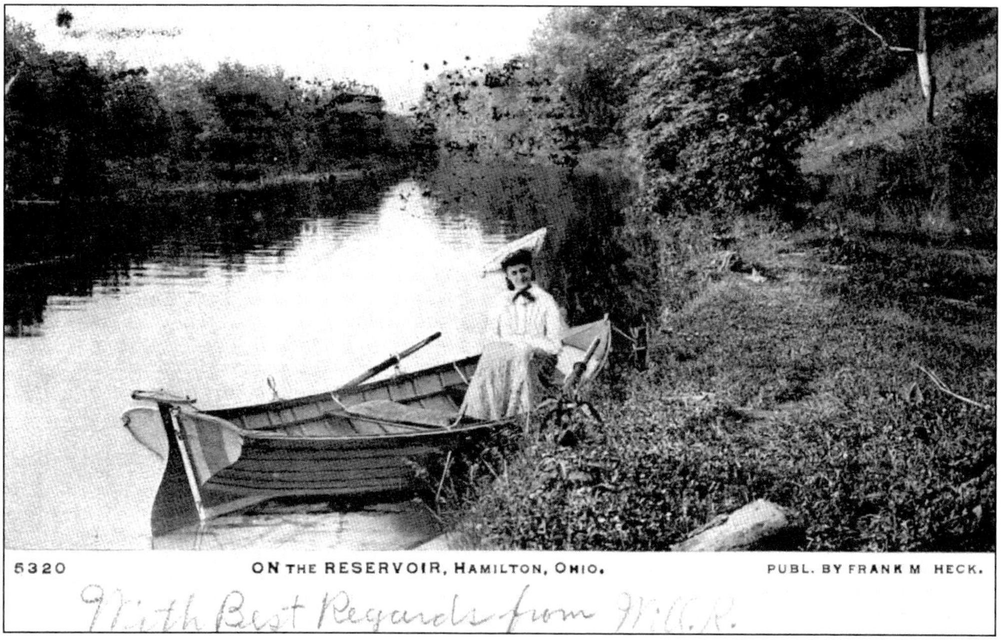

Long after the Miami and Erie Canal ceased to be used by towboats, the waterway and its locks provided Butler County residents with picturesque spots for canoeing, swimming, and relaxing. Dignitaries from Ohio and New York attended the canal groundbreaking at Middletown in 1825. The canal stimulated industrial growth in Butler County for decades until the railroads made canal transportation obsolete. By the time this card was mailed in 1906, the canal's use was more recreational. The canal officially closed in 1929.

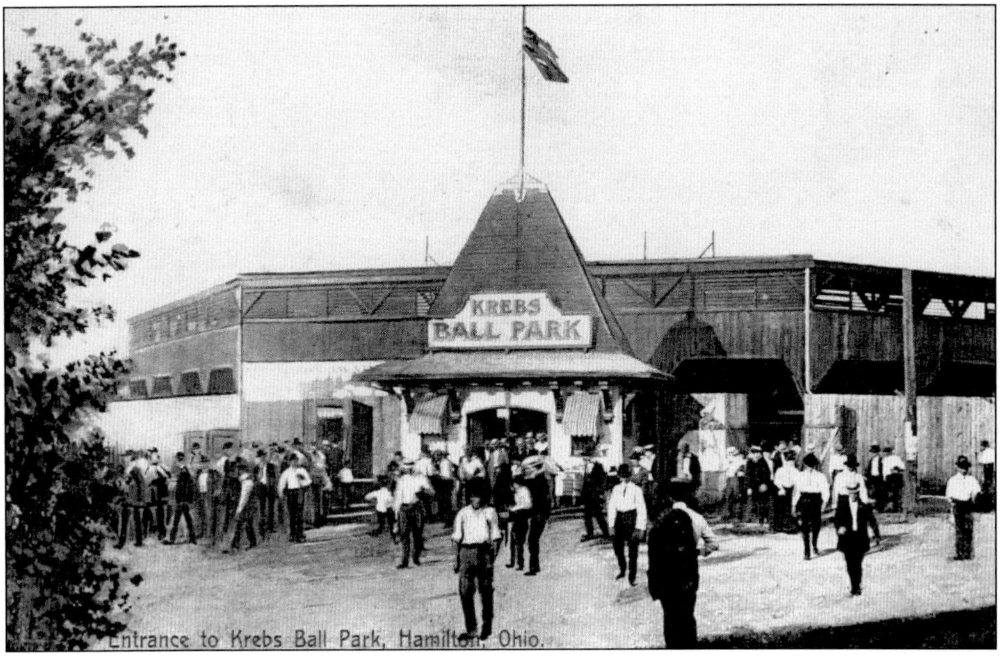

Americans' passion for baseball made Krebs Ball Park a popular Hamilton destination in the early 1900s. Local residents were devoted to their major-league team, the Cincinnati Reds, but they also loved to watch their hometown teams play at Krebs, a city park located at the northeast corner of High Street and Lockwood Avenue. This artist-enhanced card shows real patrons exiting the stadium to the right. Drawn figures appear on the left.

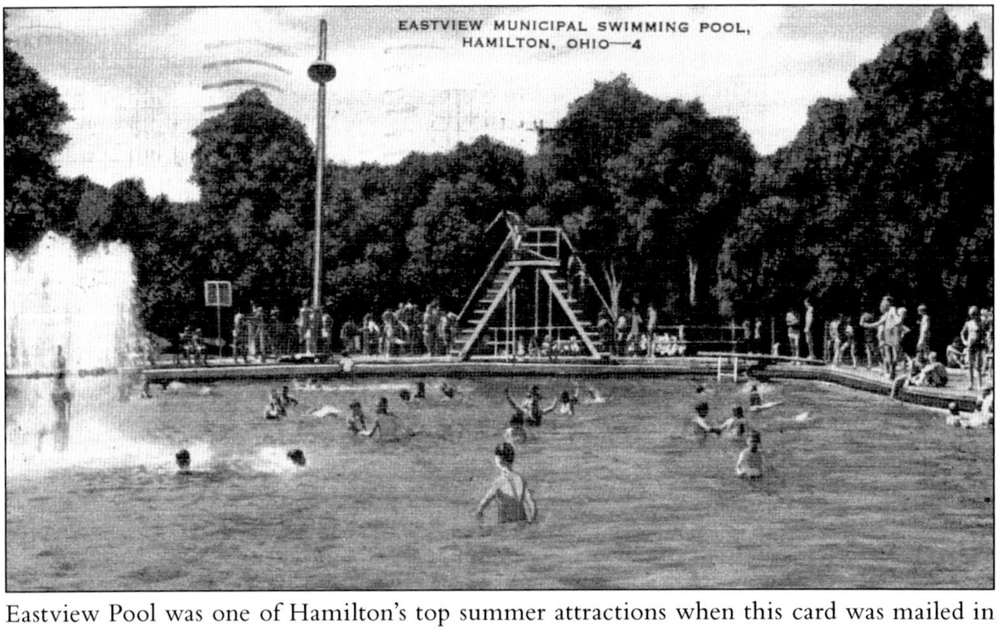

Eastview Pool was one of Hamilton's top summer attractions when this card was mailed in 1957. Hamilton boasted 45 municipal parks at the time, including wading pools, playgrounds, tennis courts, ball diamonds, and "one of the most beautiful golf courses in Ohio," as this card states. Ellis M. Potter's gift of 100 acres for a golf course and park is still appreciated by residents today.

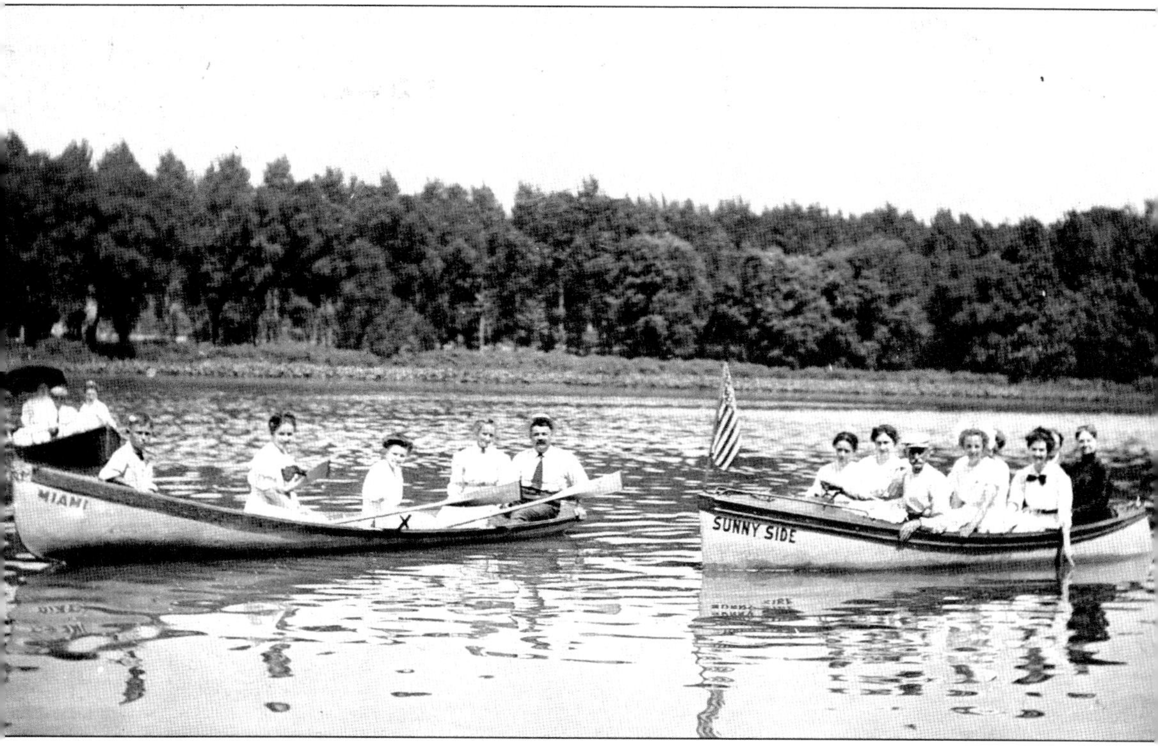

Butler County residents have always enjoyed the water, with some notable exceptions during floods. But the skies were fair and the water calm on the day when this photograph was taken. The view, possibly of the Great Miami River, was sent to a friend in Cincinnati on September 10, 1910, from Middletown, just after the correspondent—identified only as May—returned home from vacation. May marked her position with an *X* in the boat on the left. The Paris family is aboard the *Sunny Side*. The construction of a low-level dam in Hamilton in the 1980s led to more recreational use of the river by boaters, water-skiers, and Jet Ski users, as well as more habitation of wildlife.

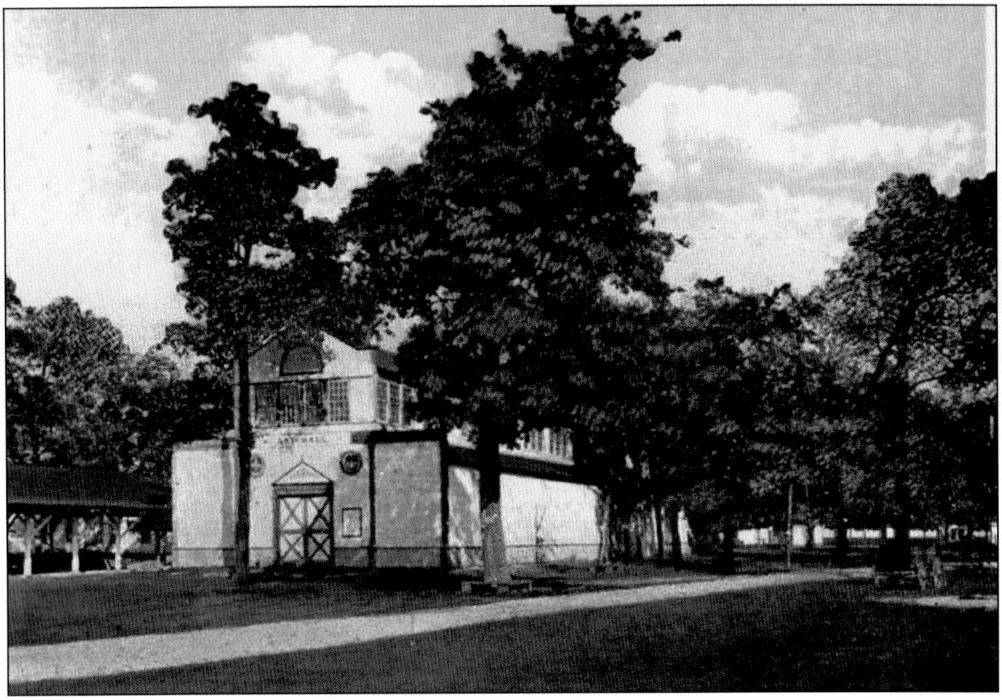

The Butler County Agricultural Society hosted the county's first fair on the streets of Hamilton on October 26 and 27, 1831. The current fairground, at State Route 4 and Fairgrove Avenue, was not established until the mid-1800s. The fair provides a showcase for farm families' livestock, produce, and crops, and a good time for everyone. Harness racing has always been a popular attraction.

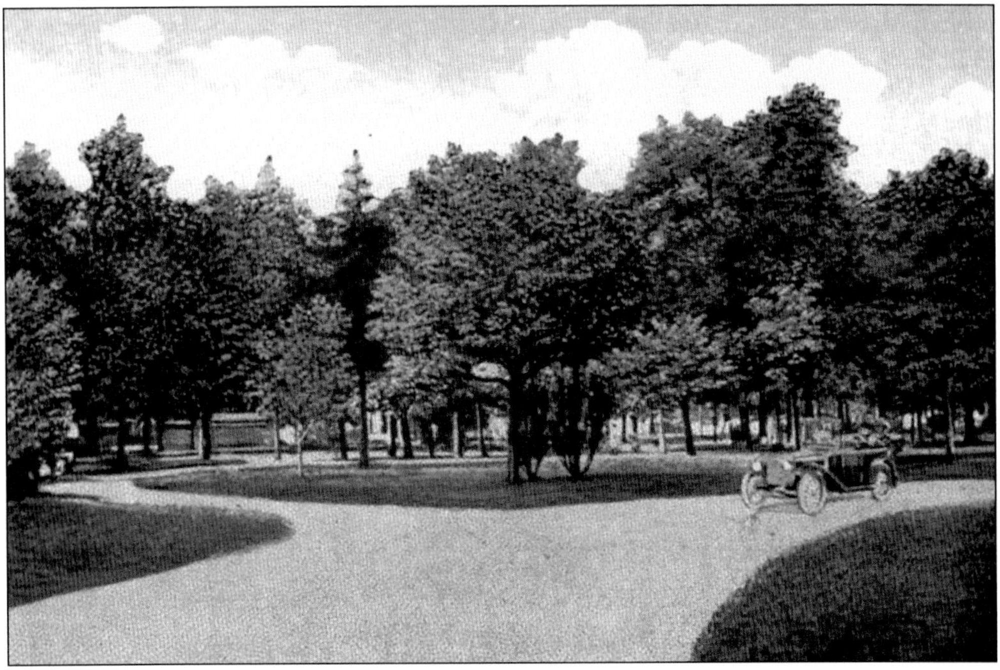

Hamilton's Fourth Ward Park provided a pleasant green space in a rapidly expanding industrial city in this *c.* 1910 postcard.

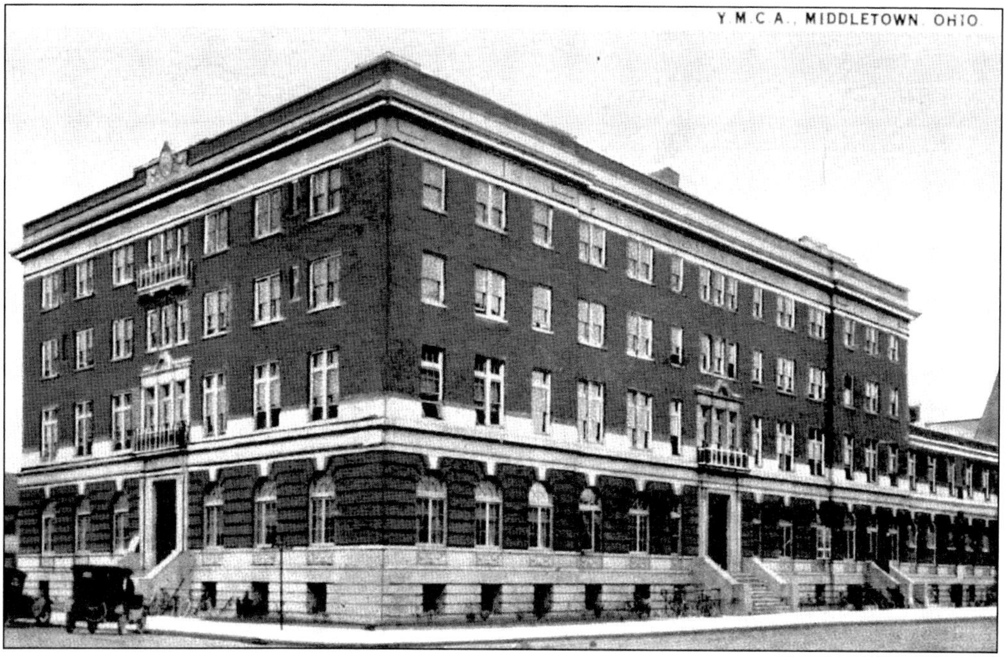

Development of mind, body, and spirit was the goal of the Middletown YMCA when it first organized in the city in 1867. Those goals carried over to the new YMCA, which opened its doors in October 1923 at Broadway and Manchester Avenue. The Greater Middletown Fund of the community's civic association financed the building, which offered classrooms, meeting space, dormitories, dining rooms, and offices.

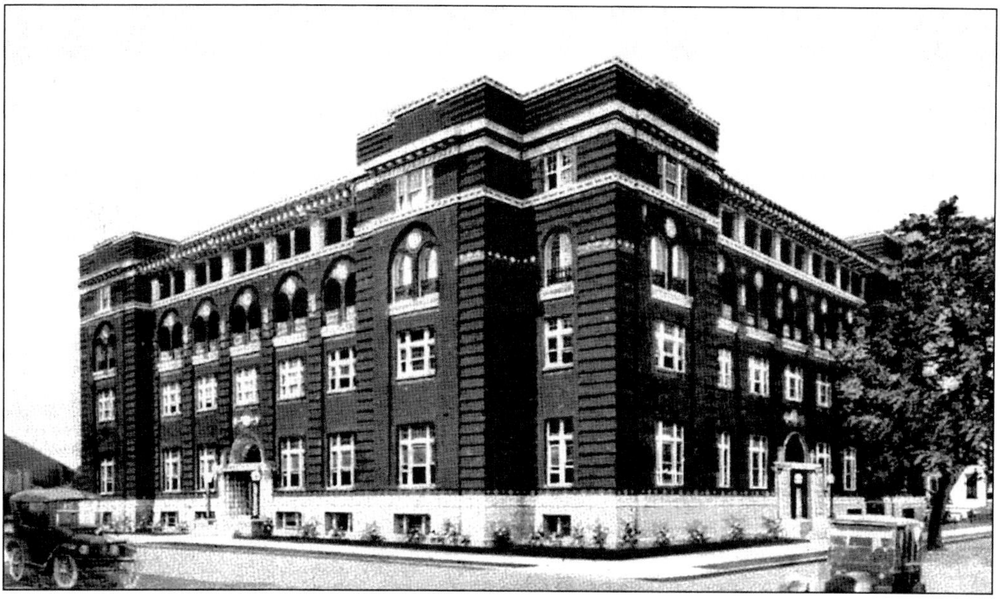

Josephus Daniels, secretary of the U.S. Navy for Pres. Woodrow Wilson, spoke at the dedication of Hamilton's new YMCA at Second and Market Streets on September 20, 1914. The local group was organized in Hamilton in 1889. Today YMCA facilities and/or programs exist in Fairfield city and township, West Chester, and Liberty Township. Thousands have attended Camp Campbell Gard in St. Clair Township.

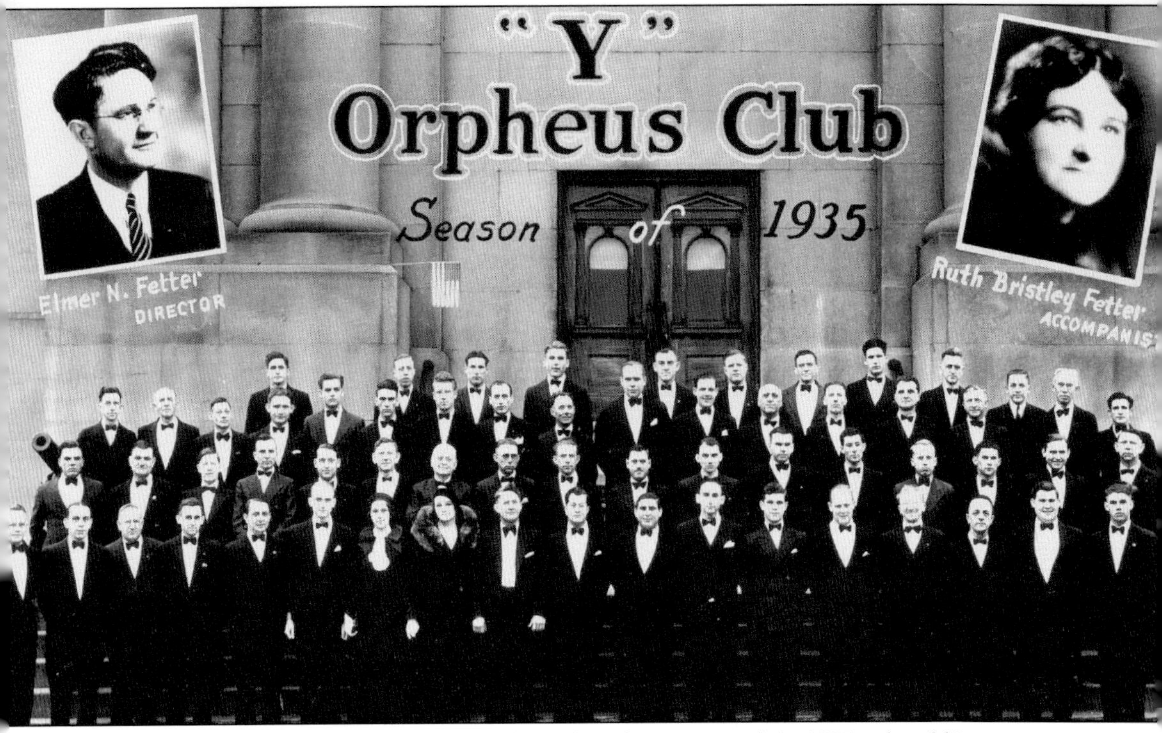

The YMCA's Orpheus Club mailed high-quality glossy postcards in 1935 to herald its new season. Elmer N. Fetter directed the choral group and Ruth Bristley Fetter accompanied. The group is posing on the front steps of the Butler County Soldiers, Sailors, and Pioneers Monument in Hamilton. In those days, downtown was a lively and prosperous place to visit and be entertained. The streets were filled with people buying everything from furniture to small gifts. Located only a block from busy High Street, the YMCA quickly became a focal point of physical, artistic, and intellectual stimulation. The Orpheus Club had plenty of opportunities to perform for city shows and at civic organizations that met in downtown centers and offices. The YMCA itself was so widely attended that dozens of clubs met in its rooms on weekday nights, and a reporter for the Hamilton bureau of the *Cincinnati Enquirer* was assigned to cover the entire organization. Editors knew that it was a good place to learn, play, and hear music.

Carved columns and architectural details enhance the facade of the Independent Order of Odd Fellows Temple in Hamilton in this 1907 postcard. The temple, located at 19 Third Street near Court Street, operated five different lodges, including the Butler County Encampment No. 7, formed in 1844. The Independent Order of Odd Fellows still functions in Hamilton, at 309 Court Street.

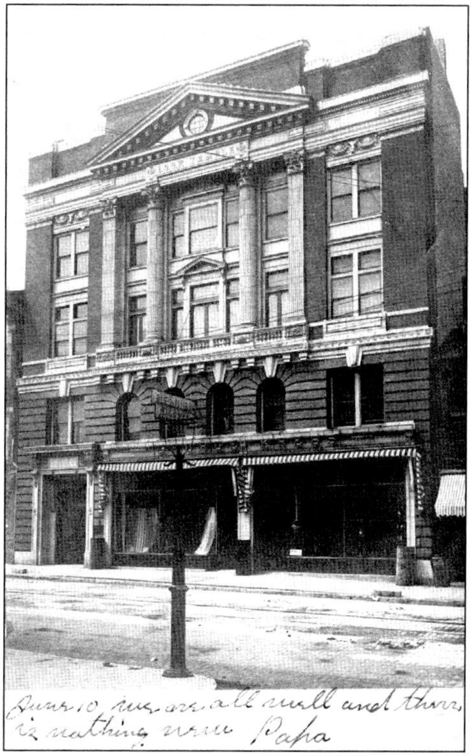

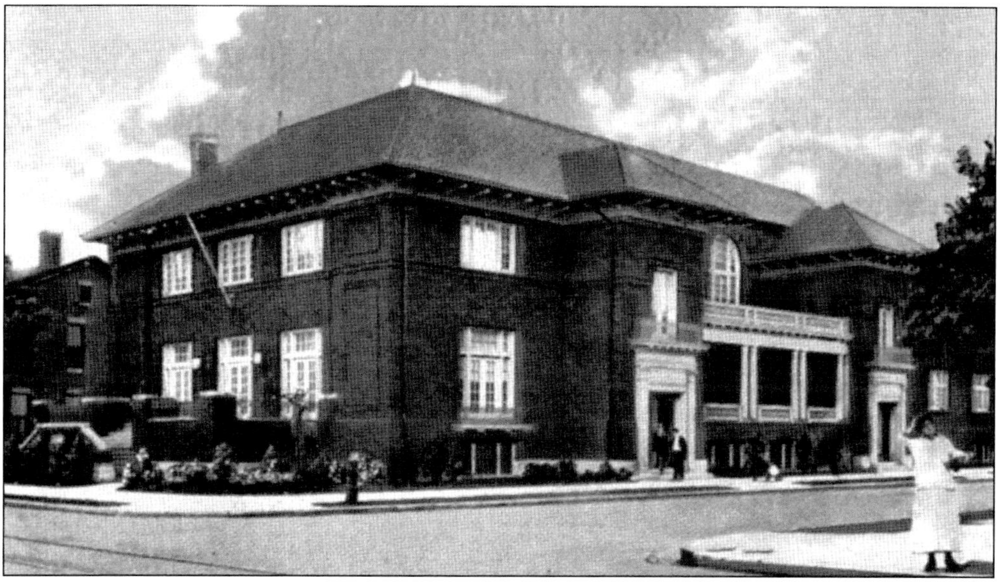

The Elks Club of Hamilton was one of a number of fraternal organizations operating in Butler County in the early 1900s. The national group was formed in New York in 1868 as the Benevolent and Protective Order of Elks. The mission was to further the principles of charity, justice, brotherly love, and fidelity, and to help promote welfare and happiness of members, to encourage patriotism, and to serve people with benevolent programs. This message was well received in Butler County. The group now runs a golf course and lodge on State Route 4, between Hamilton and Middletown.

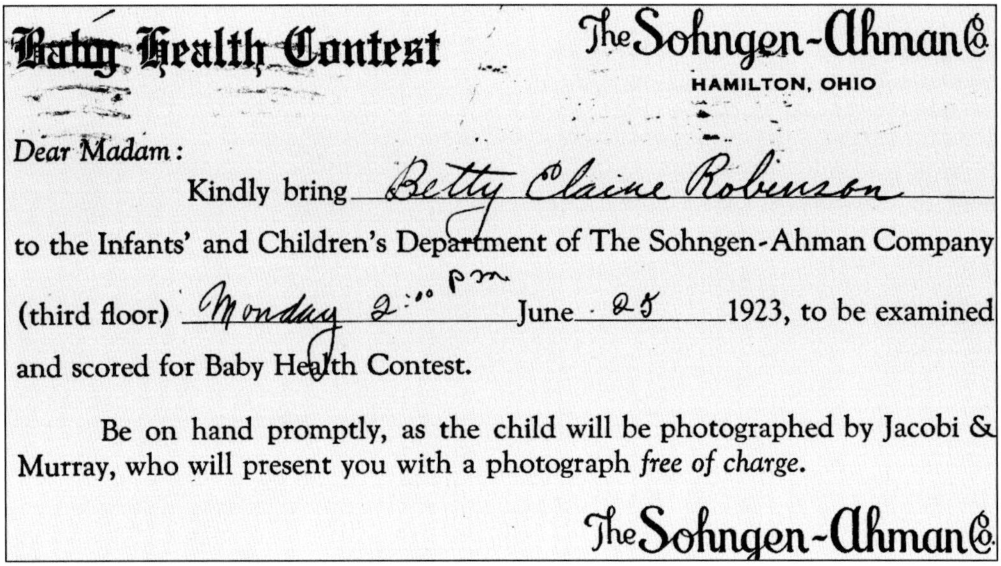

Baby Health Contest — The Sohngen-Ahman Co. — HAMILTON, OHIO

Dear Madam:

Kindly bring Betty Claine Robinson to the Infants' and Children's Department of The Sohngen-Ahman Company (third floor) Monday 2:00 pm June 25 1923, to be examined and scored for Baby Health Contest.

Be on hand promptly, as the child will be photographed by Jacobi & Murray, who will present you with a photograph *free of charge.*

The Sohngen-Ahman Co.

While providing an afternoon of entertainment for mothers and children in 1923, savvy merchants capitalized on the public's love of contests and the lure of a gift. The Sohngen-Ahman department store of Hamilton offered a free photographic portrait to each mother who entered her child in the Baby Health Contest.

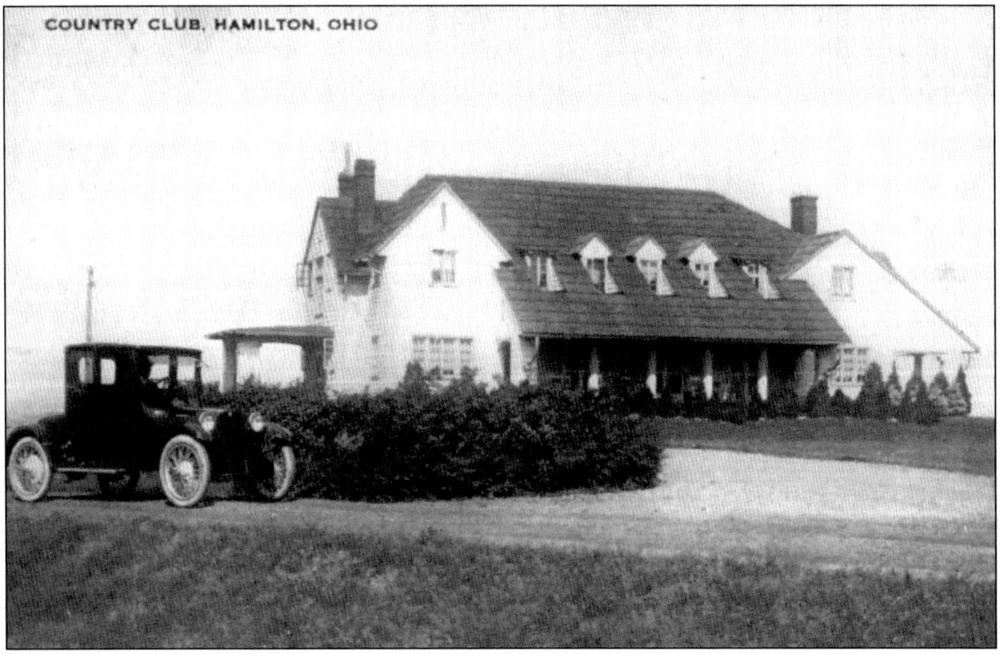

Prominent citizens from Hamilton and Middletown were among the members of the country club on Route 4. The caption on the back of the card mentions that the club is "particularly noted for its wonderful location overlooking the splendid Miami Valley, known since the days of its first settlement as the 'Garden Spot of Ohio.'"

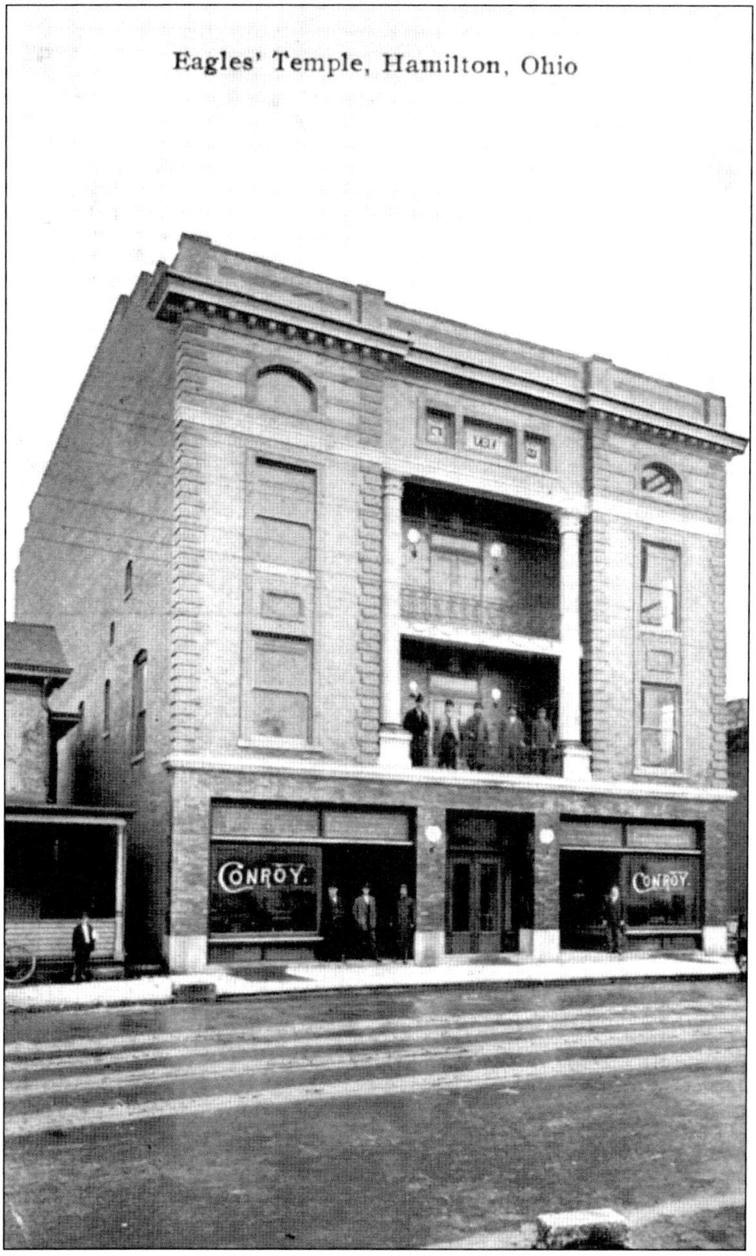

Several members of the Fraternal Orders of Eagles pose at their hall at Sycamore Street and Ludlow Avenue in Hamilton in this *c.* 1910 card. Conroy's Furniture is downstairs. Butler Aerie No. 407 met there twice monthly. In those times before television and radio and other forms of mass entertainment, fraternal organizations were important groups in the city and county. They provided people with friendship, entertainment, socializing, and even life insurance. The Eagles' mission is to unite people in the spirit of liberty, truth, and justice; to make life more desirable; and to promote peace, prosperity, gladness, and hope. Downtown Hamilton was filled with meeting halls for groups such as the International Order of Odd Fellows, the Monkey Mutual Aid Society, and the Eagles. Today Butler County still has its share of fraternal groups, but their popularity no longer matches that of the early 1900s.

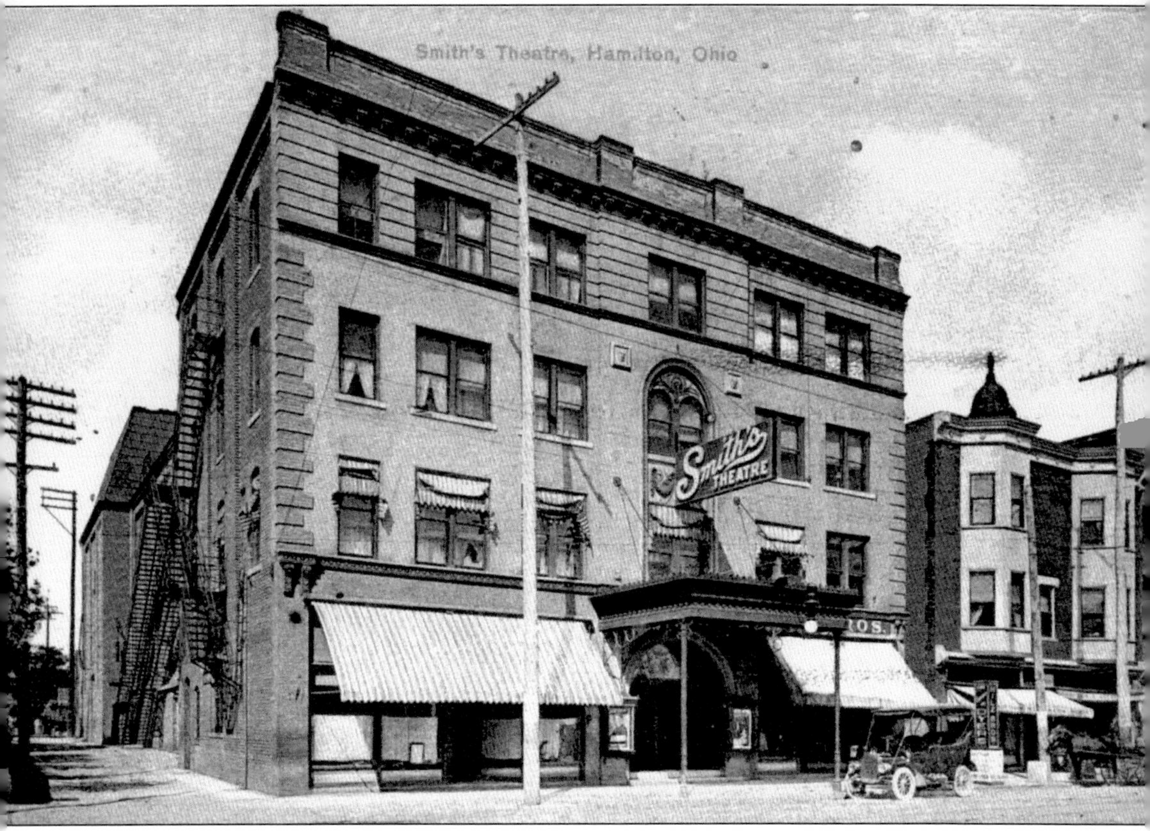

This postcard of Smith's Theatre, located on South Second Street between Ludlow Avenue and Court Street in Hamilton, is postmarked 1919. Tom A. Smith was manager. By then, Butler County had fallen under the spell of the motion picture. Hollywood reached into most every small town and burgh in America. Theaters popped up in all sorts of places, especially in the county's larger communities like Hamilton, Middletown, and Oxford. Hamilton boasted multiple theaters. The Smith's Theatre building hosted the Knights of the Pythias convention in 1911 and was one of Hamilton's more popular destinations. People were either stopping for entertainment or to stay in a number of overnight guest rooms that were rented upstairs.

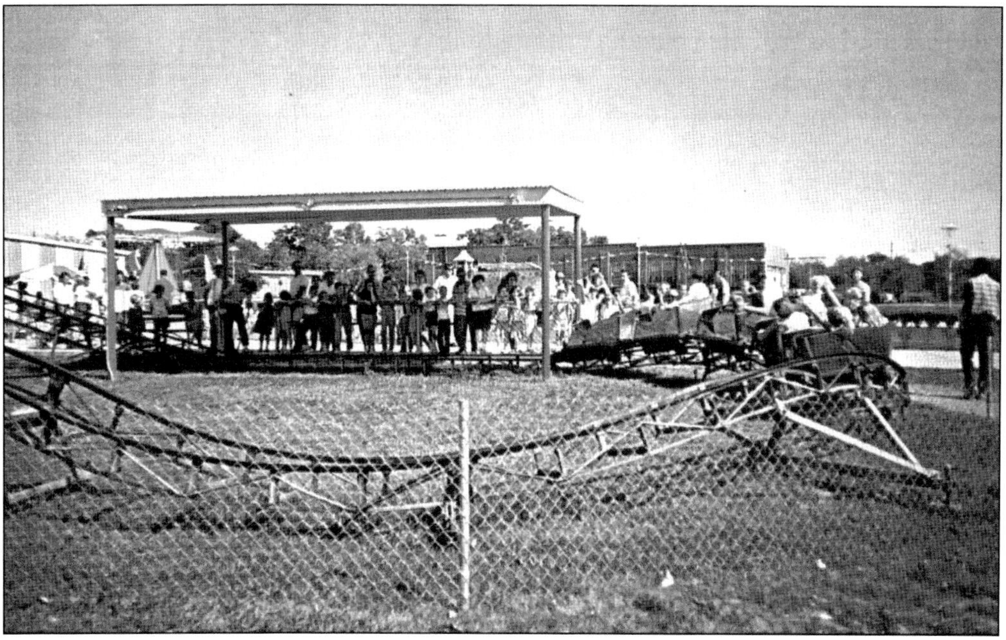

The kiddie roller coaster was one of the most popular carnival rides at Fantasy Farm Amusement Park on State Route 4 south of Middletown. Storybook Land, farm buildings and equipment, a picnic orchard, and a petting zoo of farm animals provided fun for families with young children. Edgar Streifthau opened the park in 1960 after selling LeSourdsville Lake Amusement Park, which he had founded next door.

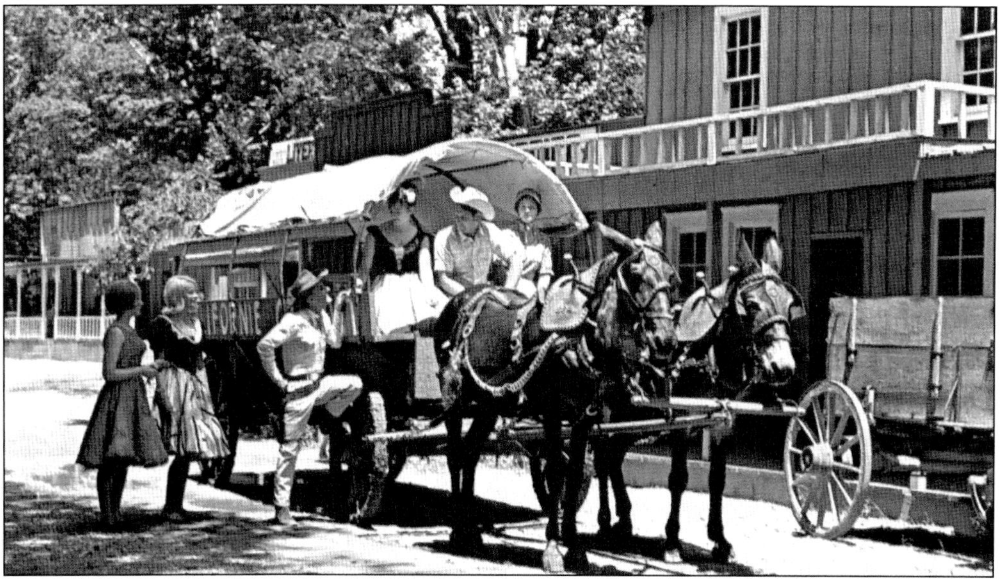

Edgar Streifthau and Bill Rothfuss started LeSourdsville Lake Amusement Park in 1922 as a safe, clean place for families to swim and picnic. The man-made lake was once used as an ice-making facility. Generations of young people took their first roller coaster ride or played their first game of Fascination at LeSourdsville. On the other side of the lake, the town of Tombstone provided a Hollywood version of the Old West. In 2006, the owner of the park announced that LeSourdsville Lake will never reopen.

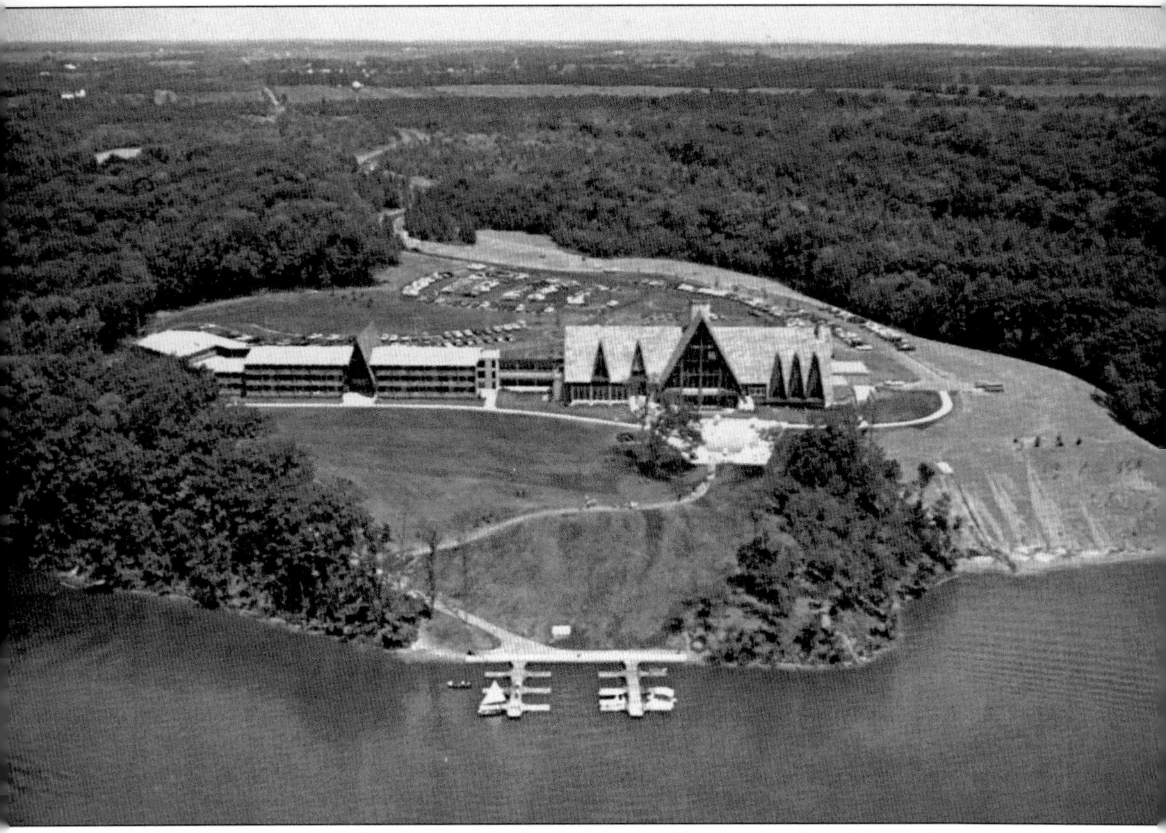

Most of Hueston Woods State Park is located in Preble County, but Butler County residents have always considered it their own. The 3,600-acre park, just north of Oxford and filled with old-growth forests, draws visitors from all over the region. Deer, fox, eagles, hawks, rabbits, and countless other creatures roam the land. A nature center and an animal rehabilitation facility give visitors a close-up view of their wild neighbors. The imposing lodge provides lodging, dining, indoor swimming, and a variety of games just steps from the man-made Acton Lake. Boating, fishing, hiking, horseback riding, and camping are some of the activities that guests can participate in.

Seven

At Home

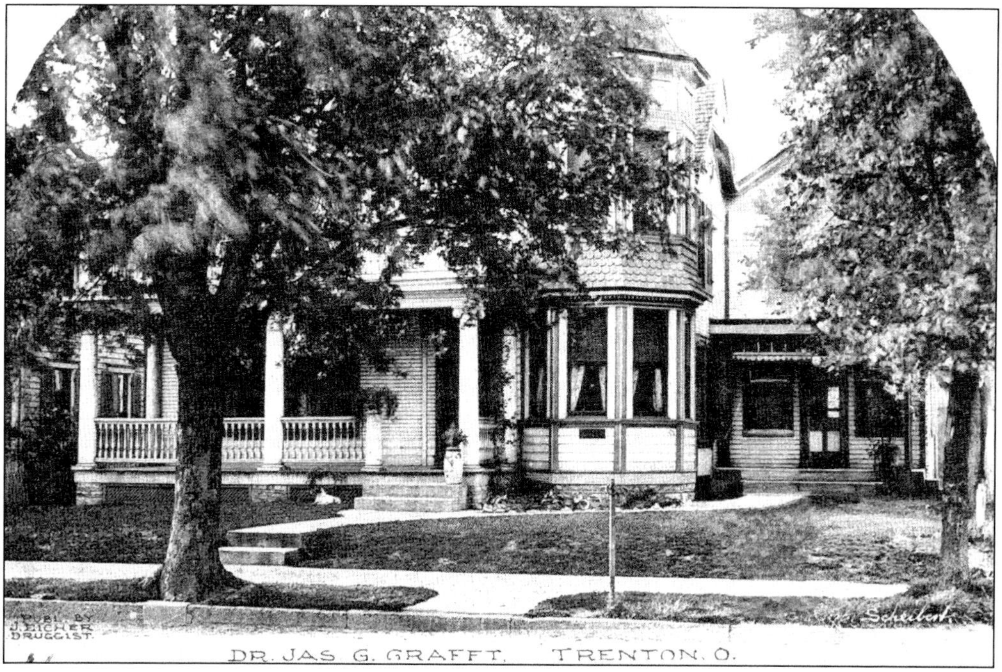

In the early 1900s, physicians commonly set up their practices in their residences, and Dr. James G. Grafft conducted his medical practice at his residence in Trenton. Grafft, who was born in Wayne Township in 1867, received his medical training from the Miami Medical College in Cincinnati in 1893 and then established his practice in Trenton. He and his wife, Eliza Grafft (née Williamson), raised three children—Helen, Jennie, and Walter—in this home.

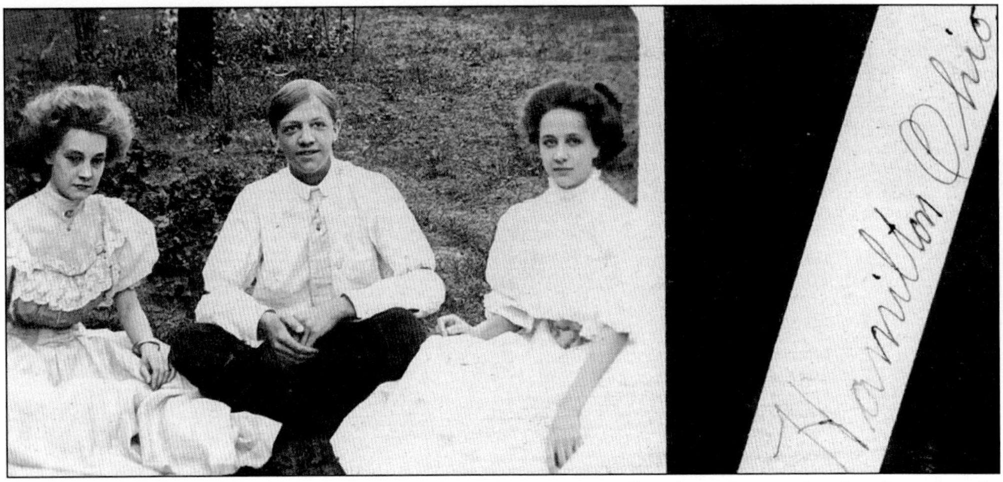

More people started using real-photo postcards as personalized stationery in the first decade of the 20th century. These elegantly attired young people posed for a personal card that was addressed to Mrs. William Klenk, 416 North Third Street, Hamilton.

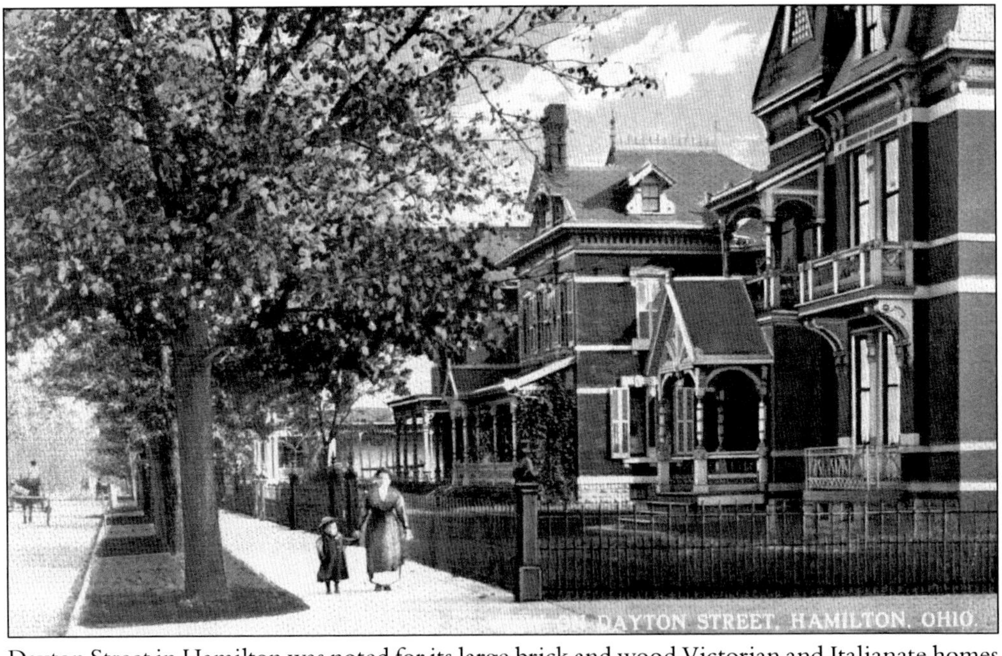

Dayton Street in Hamilton was noted for its large brick and wood Victorian and Italianate homes and tree-lined median when this card was mailed in the summer of 1914. The correspondent wrote to her mother in Indianapolis about visiting Butler County communities, including Millville and Ross (then called Venice).

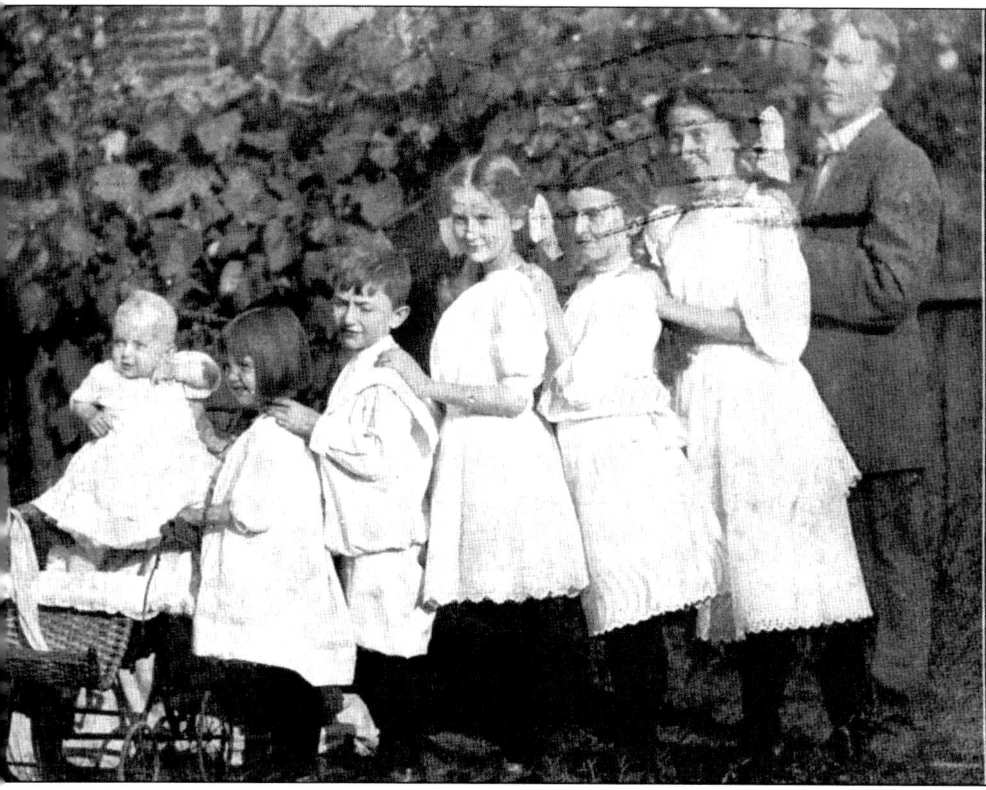

"WE ARE SEVEN"

Mrs. Allwardt of Hamilton was apparently content to stop with seven children when she had this real-photo postcard printed in 1908. She sent it as a New Year's greeting in 1909 to Ida Gayman of Canal Winchester, Ohio. The children, seen here from left to right, are Paul, Clara, Theophilus, Bertha, Elsie, Vida, and Carl. At the time she sent the card, personal portrait postcards were at their height of popularity. People mailed them as holiday greetings; to announce a birth, wedding, or other momentous occasion; or to just to show off their home or farm. The trend continued for a few more years.

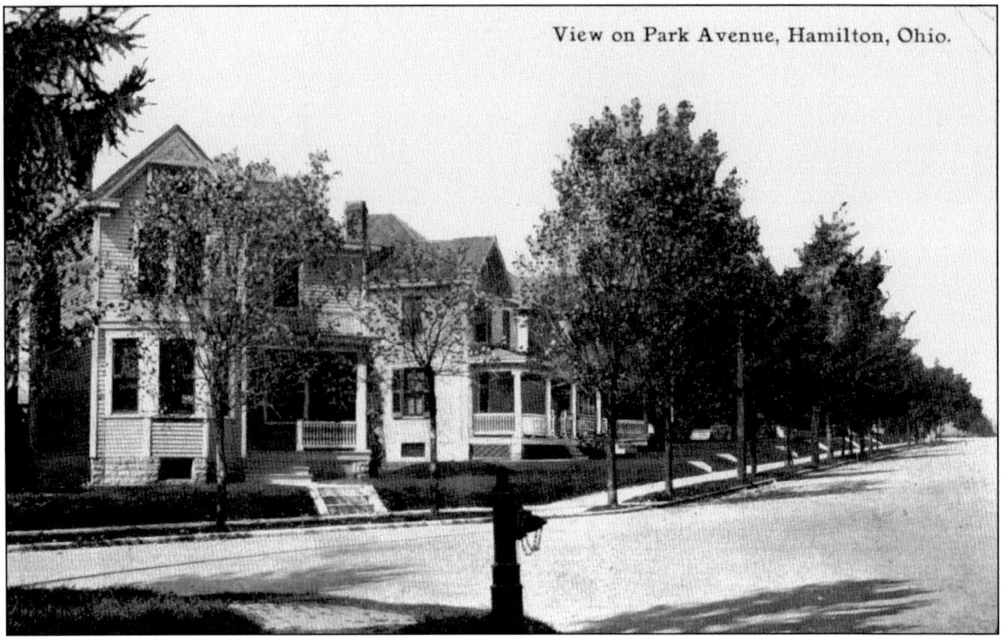

Hamilton's Park Avenue was home to middle-class families when this card was mailed in 1911. Wide front porches and numerous windows on the frame homes pulled in summer breezes from the tree-lined avenue.

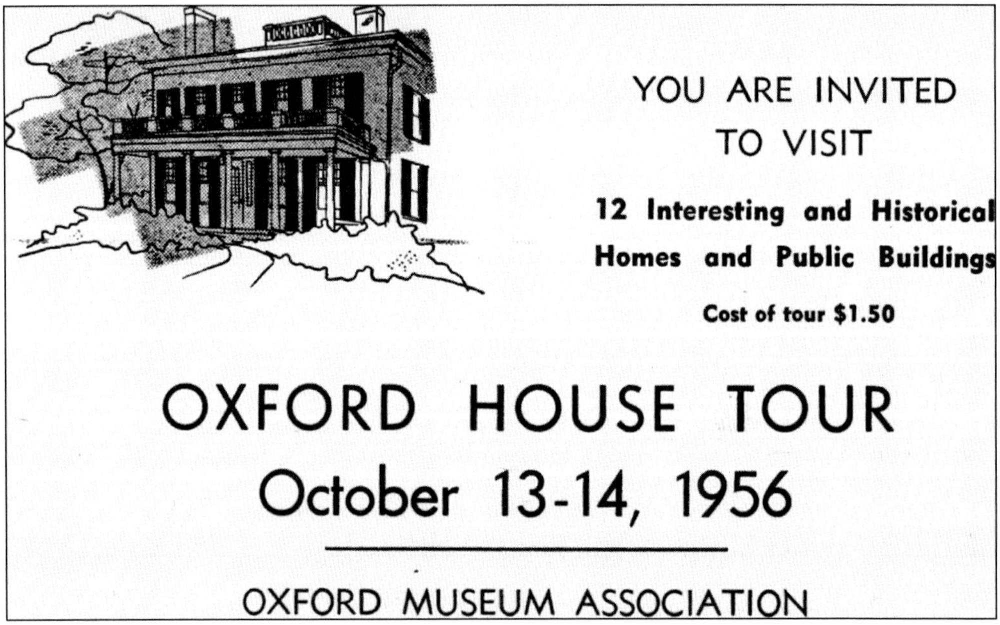

Strolling down Oxford's brick streets on an autumn afternoon recalls the New England villages that many "western" settlers came from in the first quarter of the 19th century. Oxford's House Tour of 1956 featured tours of buildings in the Victorian, Federal, Italianate, and Queen Anne styles. The Oxford Museum Association charged $1.50 to tour 12 buildings.

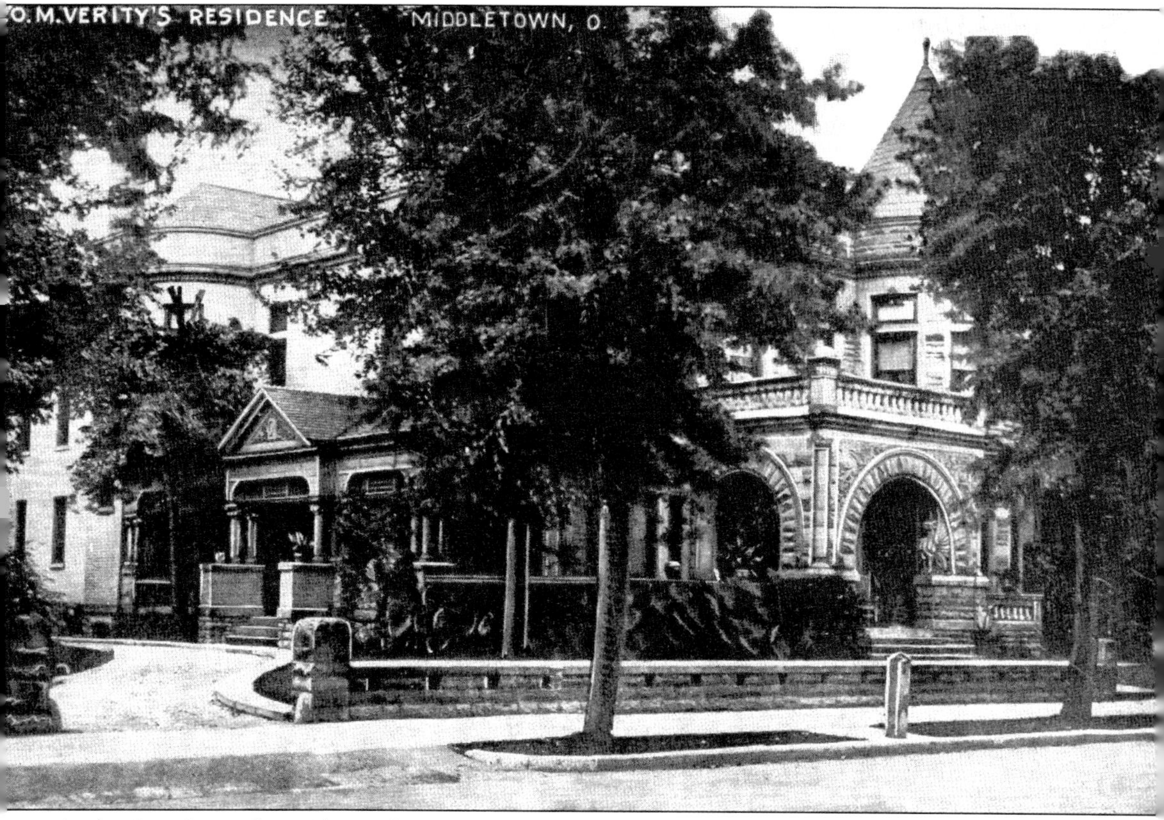

As the founder and president of Armco Steel, George M. Verity lived in one of the grandest homes in Middletown. The son of a Methodist minister, Verity grew up in a middle-class home. After graduating from Nelson's Business College in Cincinnati, he worked at the American Steel Roofing Company for 10 years, rising to the position of manager. When he decided to start his own company in 1900, he moved to Middletown. He bought this house on South Main Street from the estate of banker Charles F. Gunckel and remodeled it extensively. During the 1913 flood, the Verity family had to move to the second story of the home to escape high waters. Like many townspeople of the period, the Veritys kept their own milk cows in a barn on their property. Maude Hinkle Bake Schenck, whose brother-in-law worked for the Veritys, remembered bringing the cows into the mansion and tying them to the fireplace mantel so they would not float away. Waters rose several inches on the table legs in the kitchen, but the cows presumably survived.

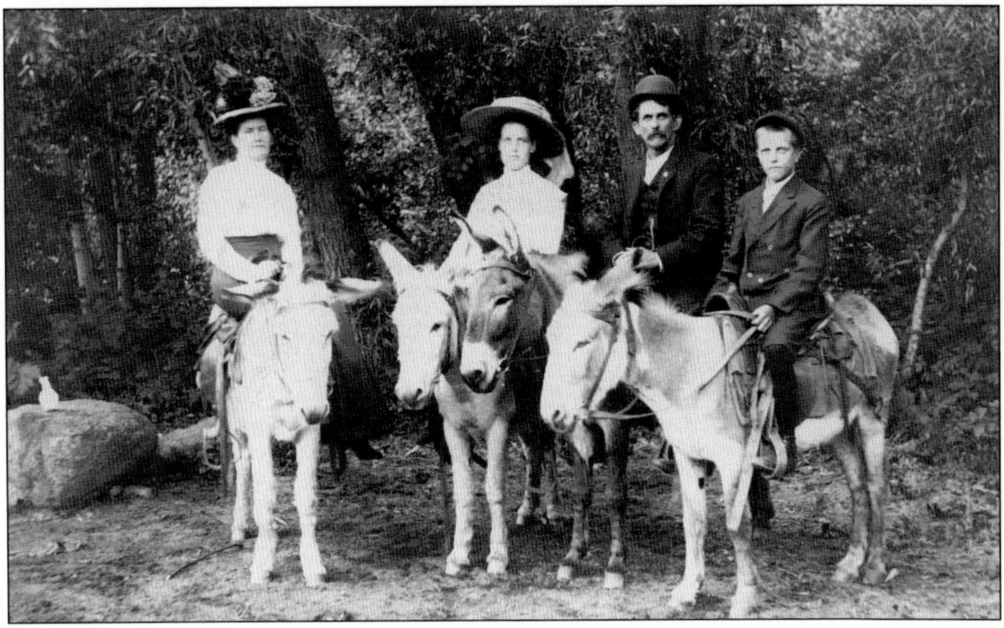

Personal real-photo postcards allowed residents a glimpse of what the rest of the country looked like in pretelevision days. Mrs. Horace Johnston of Lindenwald received this *c.* 1910 card from area relatives who were visiting Colorado Springs and Denver. Vacations then were still relatively rare, special occasions. Notice how nicely the group members are dressed. The only identifications given are, from left to right, Aunt Lizze, Jennie, and Uncle Ike Brannon.

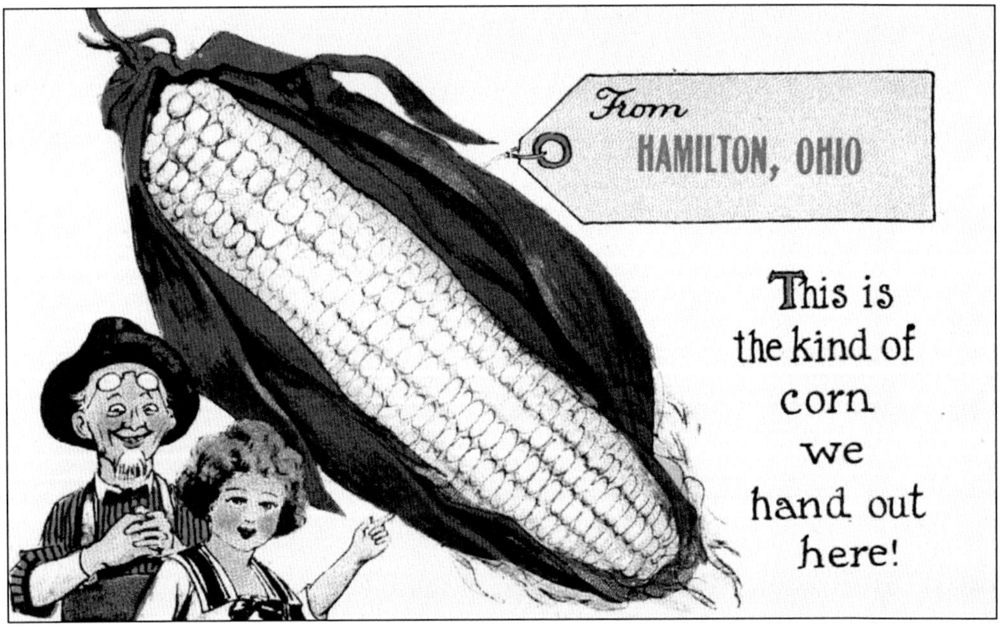

Novelty cards were especially popular from 1900 to the beginning of World War I. Makers of such cards typically inserted the name of the local community onto a generic scene. More specialized novelty cards featured a local landmark with an image added by an artist. Exaggerations like a two-ton turnip or 12-foot-tall heifer are examples of what would often be found on these hybrid cards.

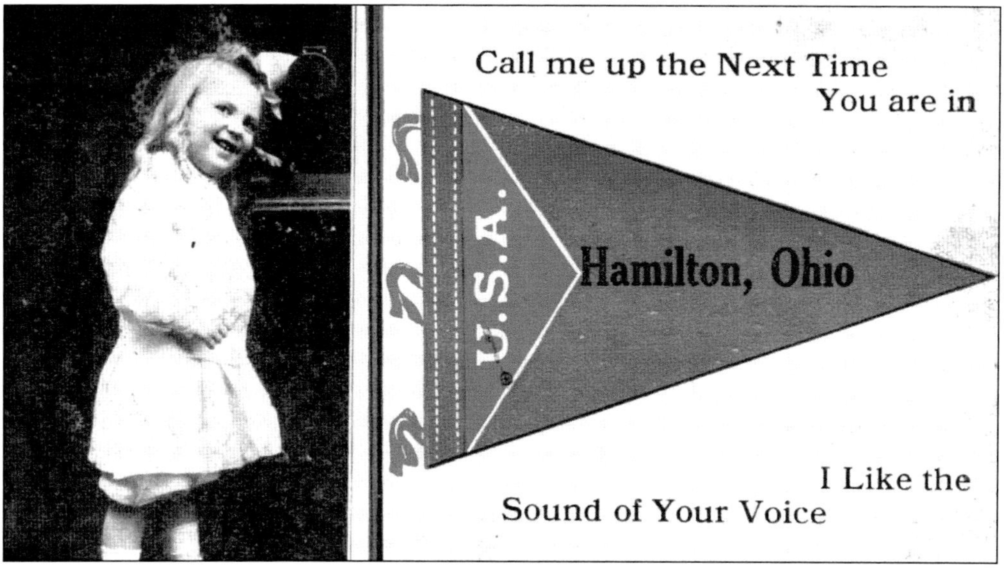

In a time before e-mail and instant messaging, postcards helped with many budding romances. Arthur Bolton of Connerville, Indiana, received this card, mailed from Hamilton in 1915. The message on the back reads, "From a Friend. *Guess.*" One can only hope that he did.

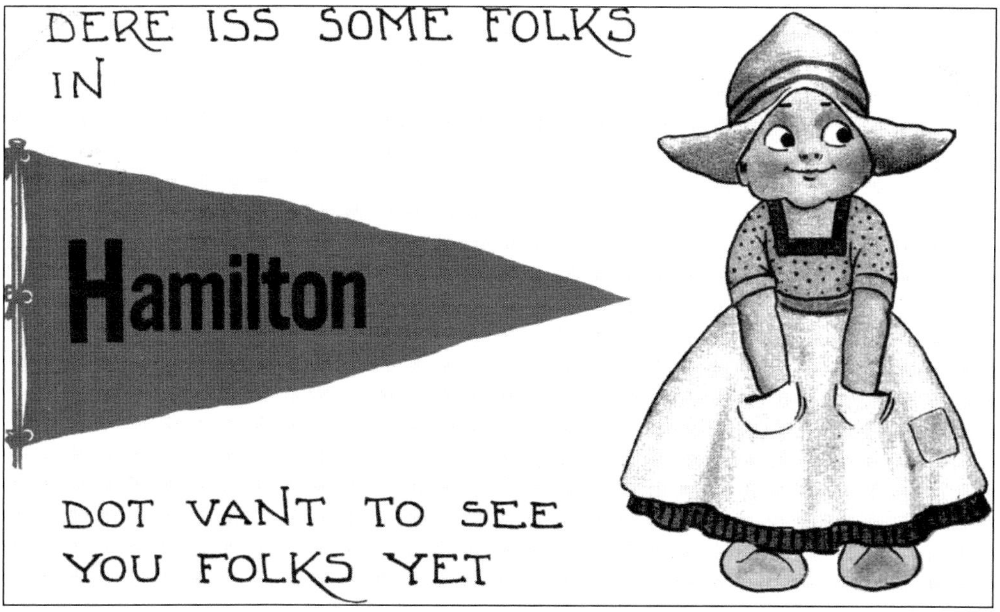

This "Dutch" card plays off Butler County's large German population. German immigrants from Hamilton fought in the Civil War and later helped found important businesses and industries. When this card was mailed in 1913, a large percentage of county residents were of German descent. An active German-American Society offered many cultural, educational, and recreational events to the public.

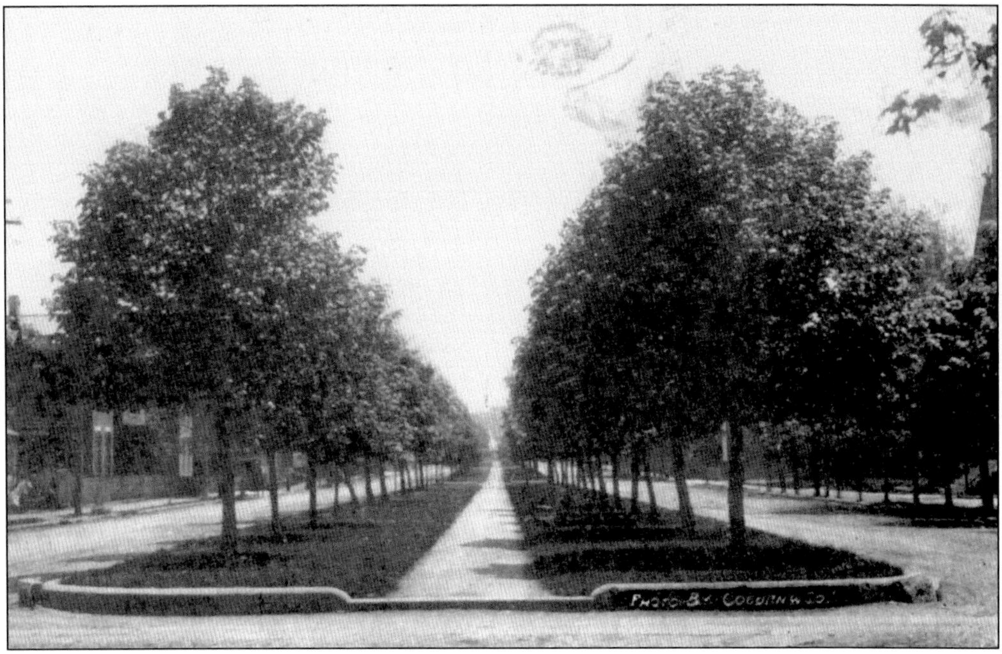

Rows of sturdy brick houses lined this alley of trees on Hamilton's Campbell Avenue, depicted here on a *c.* 1910 card. Trees in a large industrial city such as Hamilton provided more than an aesthetic function; they offered shade and cooling breezes, and an antidote to the industrial smokestacks and fumes from an increasing number of gasoline-operated vehicles. By 1910, many scientists and physicians were preaching the health benefits of trees.

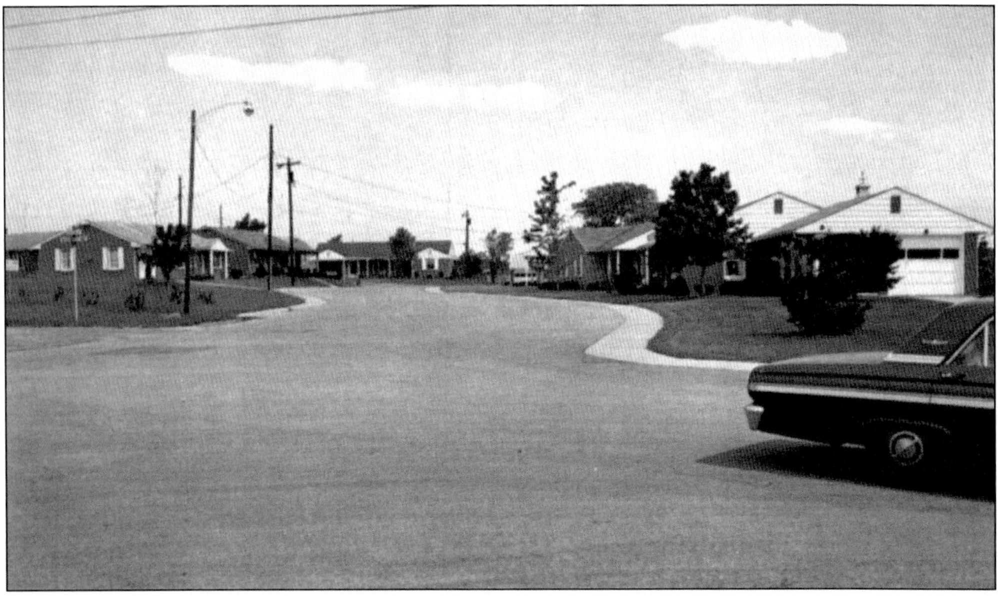

By the late 1950s, some people were living longer but had no extended family close by to help care for them. Retirement communities like the Mount Pleasant Presbyterian Home in Monroe were developed to provide "gracious and independent living with care and security." This card shows the fourth phase of the Monroe community, which was operated on a nonprofit basis by the Ohio Synod of the United Presbyterian Church.

Eight

Downtown and Beyond

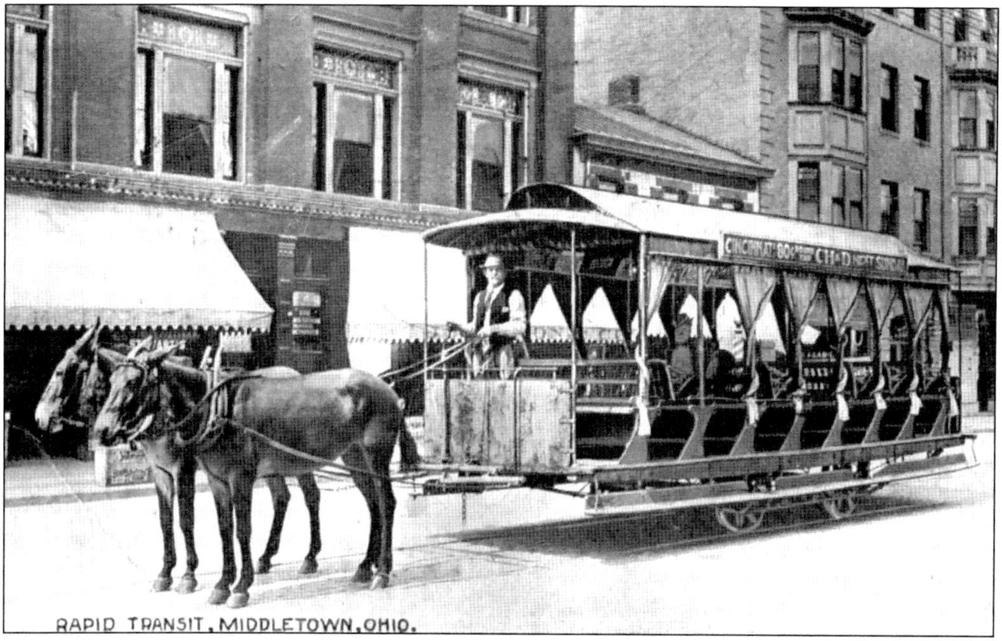

"This is the car we took from the depot in town. Ain't it a dandy?" asked the sender of this 1911 card. Fine teams of mules pulled the traction cars in Middletown from 1880 to 1914, when electricity began powering the trolleys. The line started at the Charles Street depot and traveled down Central Avenue to the west side of the city. Middletown resident Margaret Barber recalled that a quarter bought her two trips on the "mule cart" with a nickel left over for a large cone at Elite Ice Cream.

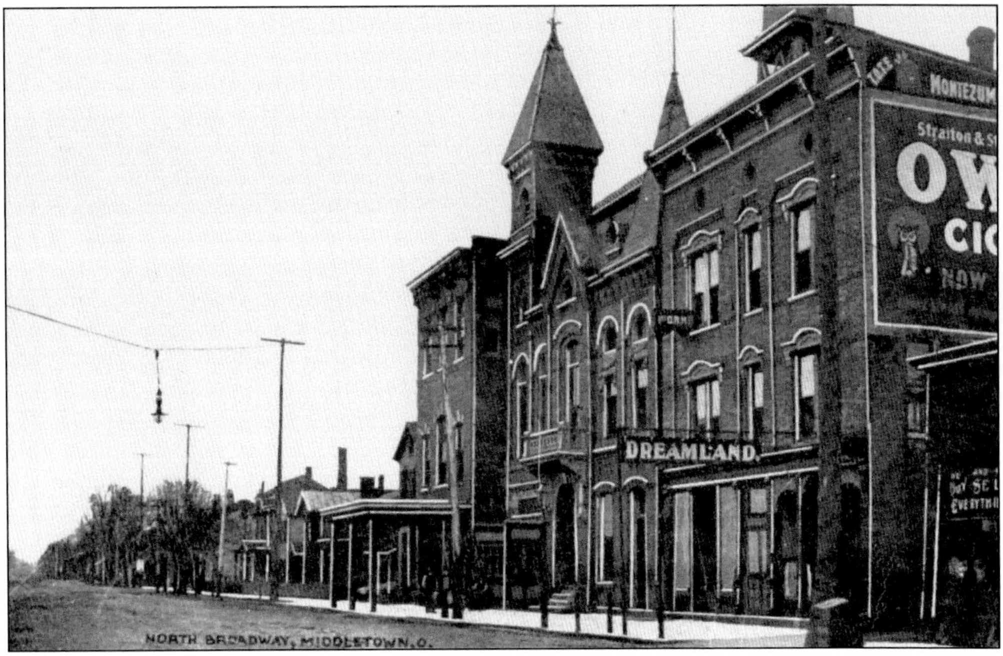

North Broadway in Middletown appears on a 1909 card. A large signs reads "Dreamland," while an advertisement on the side of the building promotes Owl cigars and Montezuma. Broadway was the home of varied enterprises, including W. N. McCoy, "funeral director and embalmer," at 405 South Broadway and the police headquarters at 219 South Broadway.

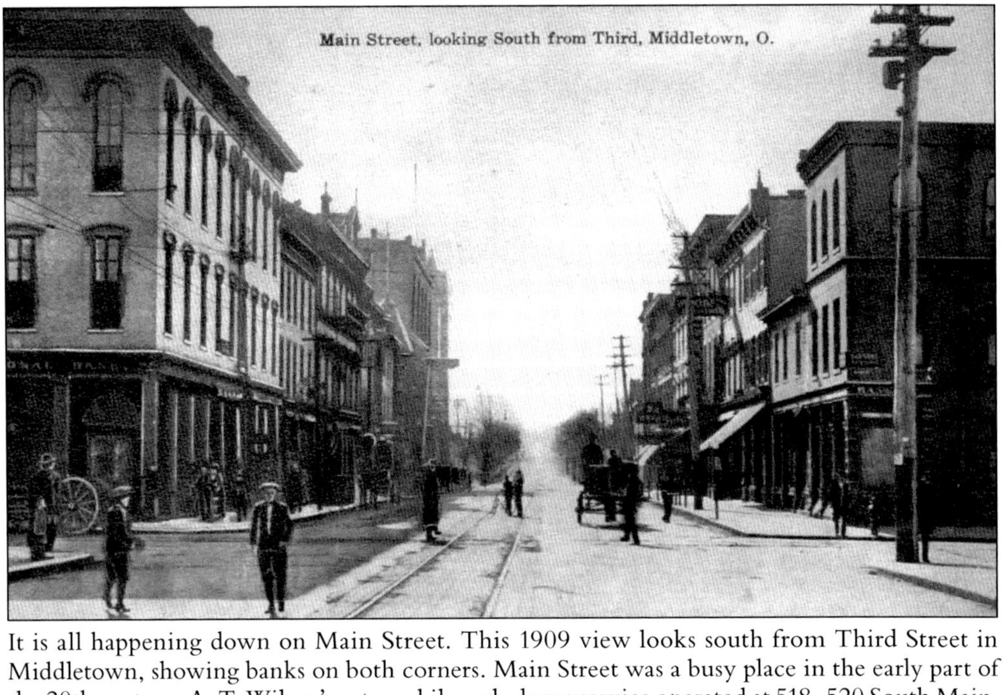

It is all happening down on Main Street. This 1909 view looks south from Third Street in Middletown, showing banks on both corners. Main Street was a busy place in the early part of the 20th century. A. T. Wilson's automobile ambulance service operated at 518–520 South Main, F. Cappel Furniture Company at 310 South Main, and the Middletown Real Estate and Brokerage Company at 232½ South Main.

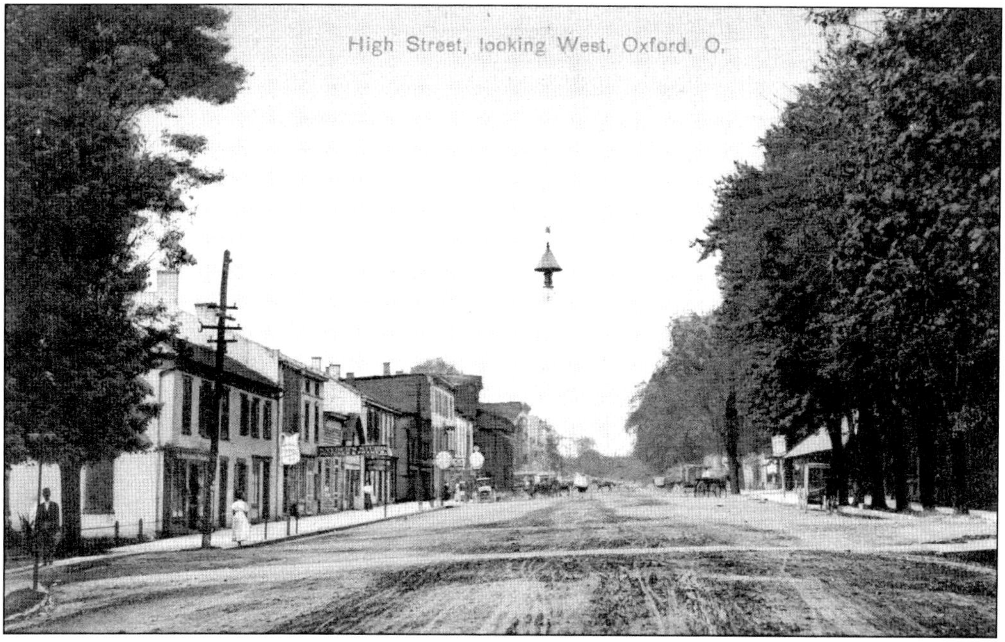

Frank R. Snyder, a well-known Oxford photographer and businessman, took this photograph of Oxford's High Street in 1909. His studio is visible on the left. Snyder's business expanded over the years to include selling art and photography supplies, gifts, cards, and Miami University items. Snyder's remained in business until April 2006. To the end, it continued to sell film and camera supplies.

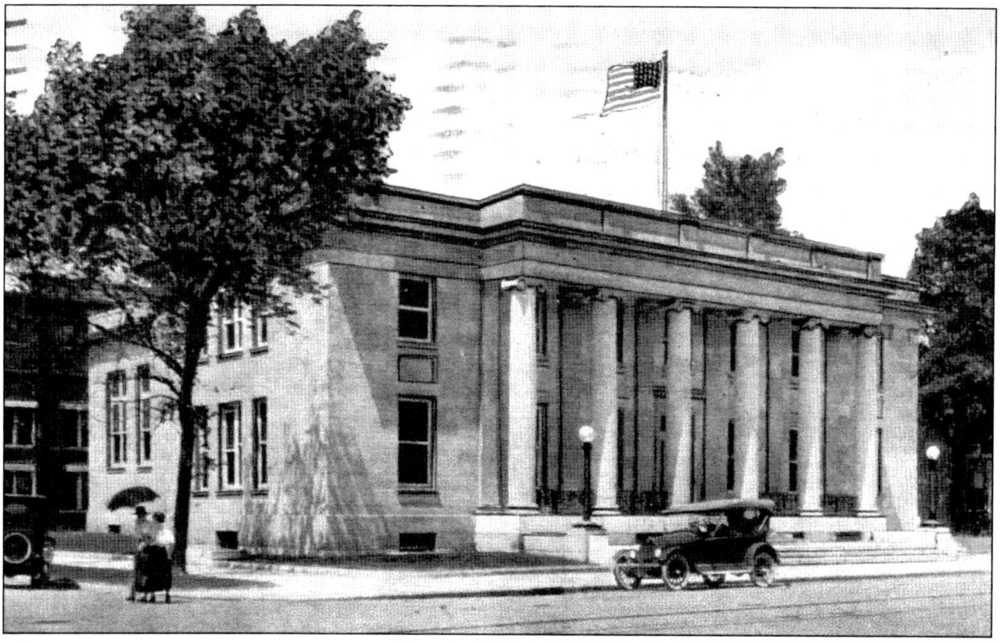

This card, postmarked 1928, shows the Middletown Post Office at the corner of Main Street and Manchester Avenue. Frank B. Pauly served as postmaster in the mid-1920s, with Richard C. Dawling as assistant postmaster. Postcards were mailed for 1¢; first-class mail traveled for 2¢ per ounce.

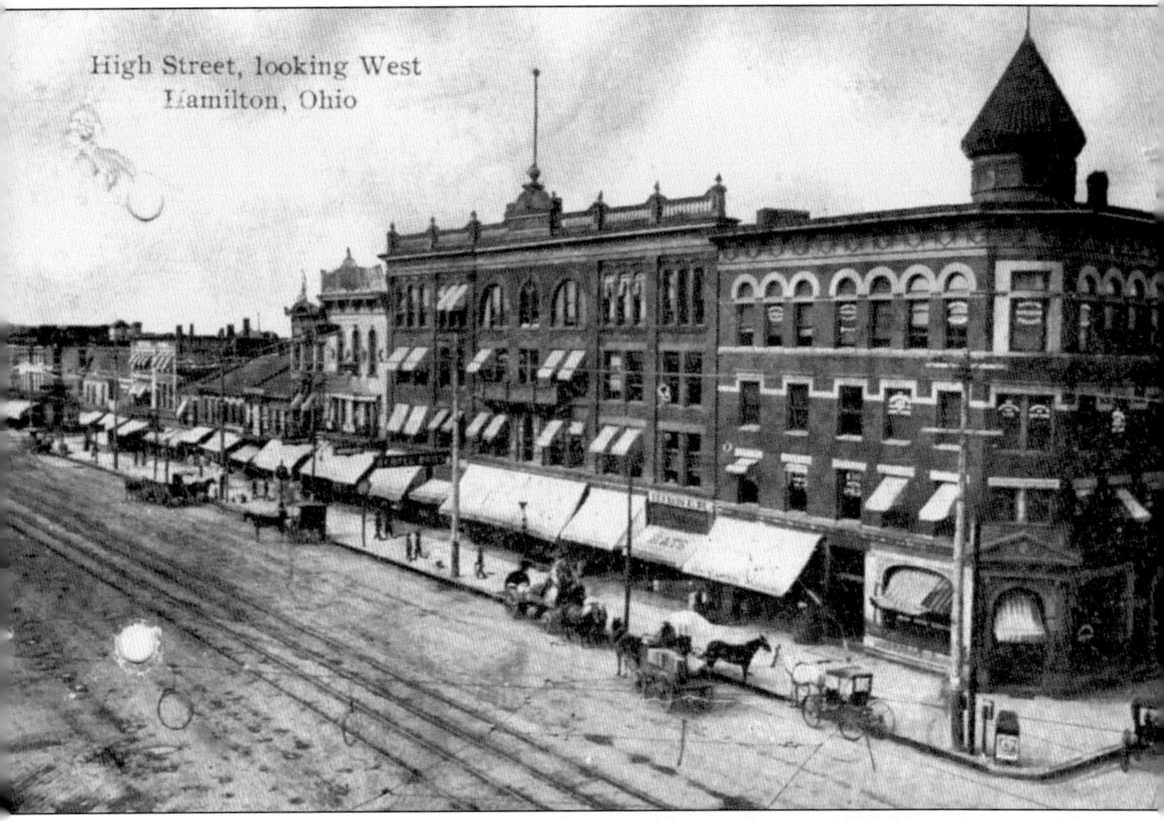

Whether shoppers arrived by traction car or horse and buggy, they could find just about anything they needed on Hamilton's High Street in 1911. A sign for Bentel Brothers is among the visible business advertisements.

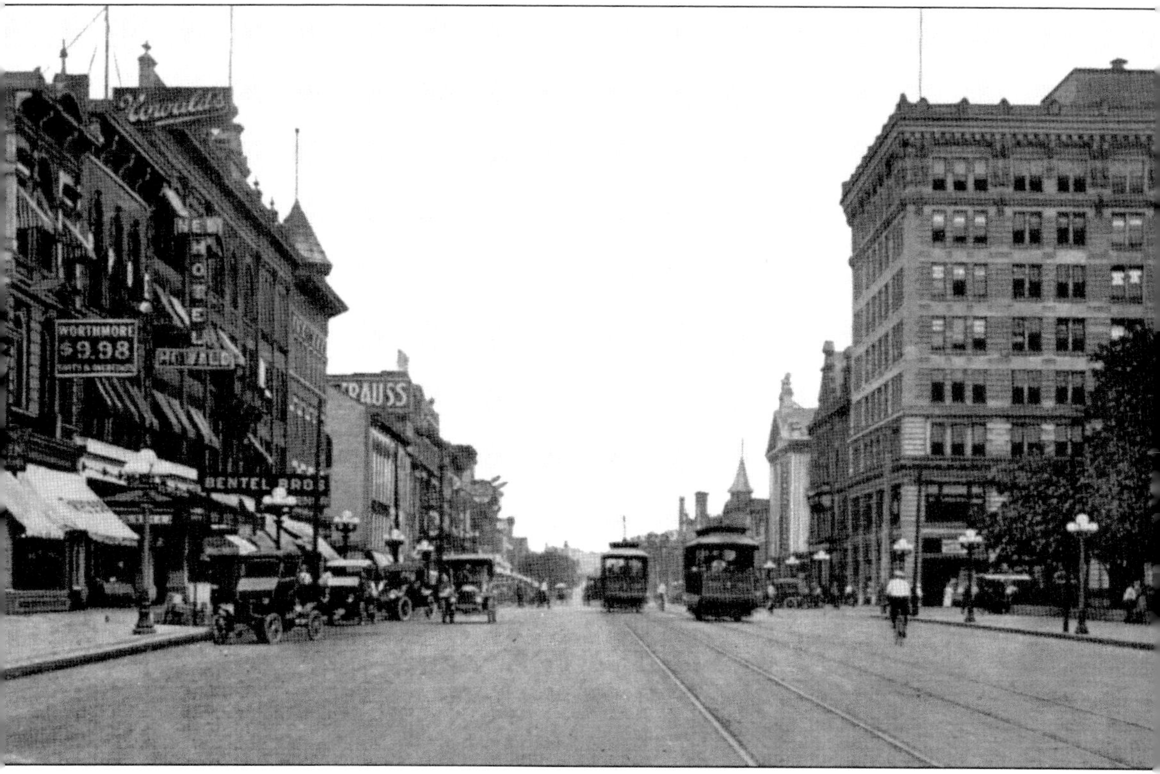

A few years later, the traction cars had become electric and automobiles had replaced horsepower on High Street. This card provides a view looking east from Front Street. Signs on the left side of street read, "Worthmore $9.98 Suits & Overcoats," "Howald's Hotel," "Bentel Brothers," and "Strauss." On the right side is the Rentschler Building, Hamilton's "skyscraper." Construction began in 1903. County entrepreneur George Adam Rentschler built the structure to house the offices of his Citizens Bank. When it opened in 1906, it was Hamilton's tallest building and a desirable business address. In 2003, a brass plaque was added to commemorate its construction.

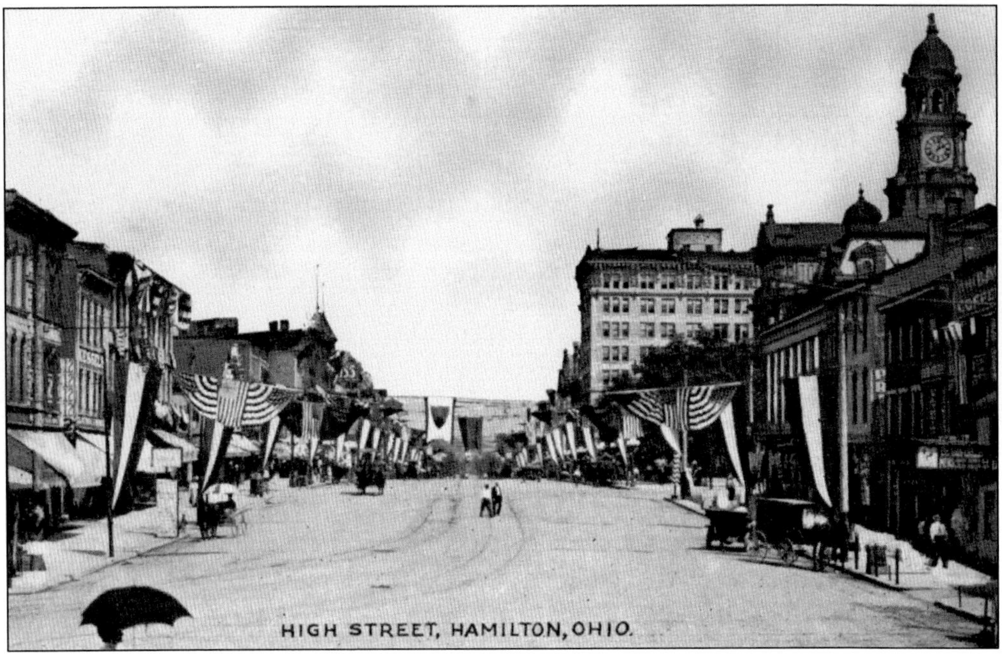

High Street is decorated with bunting, perhaps for the 1906 dedication of the Soldiers, Sailors, and Pioneers Monument. Also visible are the Butler County Courthouse and the Rentschler Building.

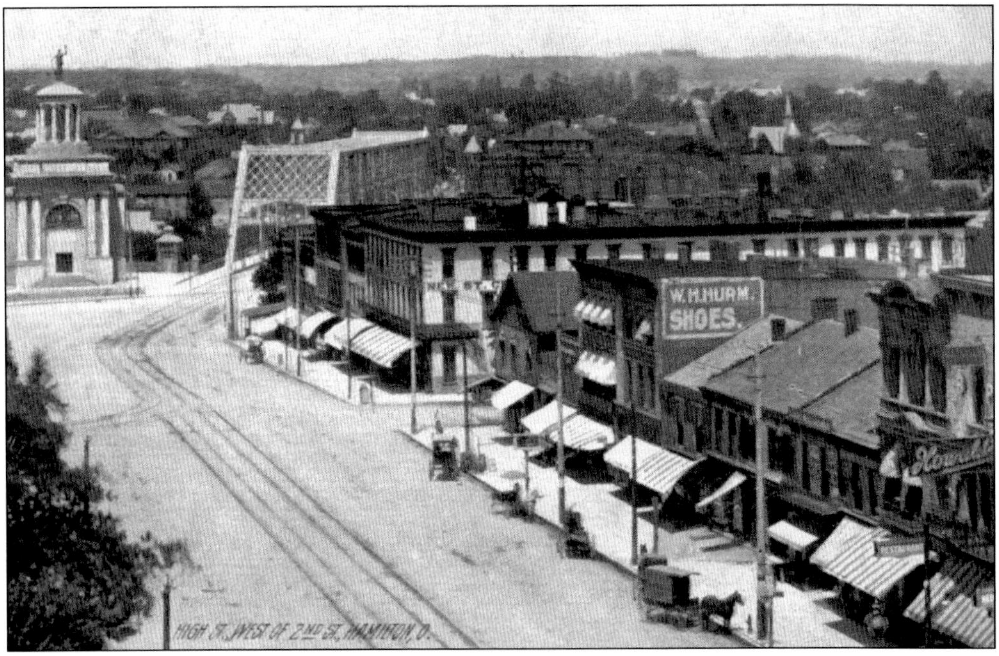

This view shows High Street west of Second Street. Postmarked 1909, the card shows W. H. Hurm Shoes on the right, the High-Main Streets Bridge, and the monument, on the far left. The locally well-known clothier George Krebs also had a store on the street.

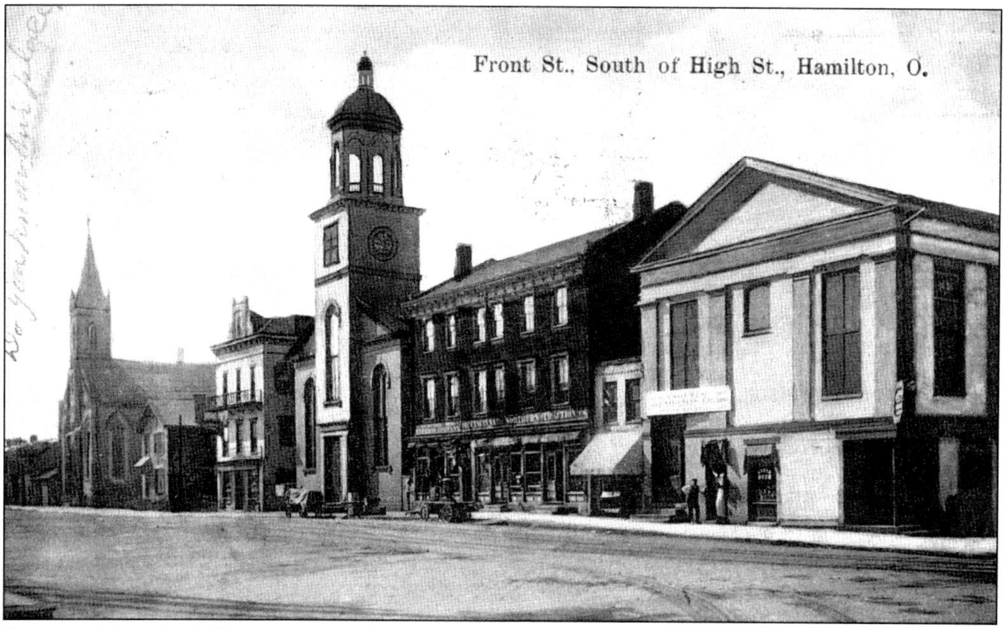

"I am waiting for Milton to come from the shop. He starts work down at Greismer's tomorrow morning and so . . . I will [be] back in old Lindenwald. Cannot begin to tell you how glad I will be," wrote the correspondent, identified only as Ebbie, on this card dated August 1908. The view of Hamilton's Front Street features the First Presbyterian Church in the foreground.

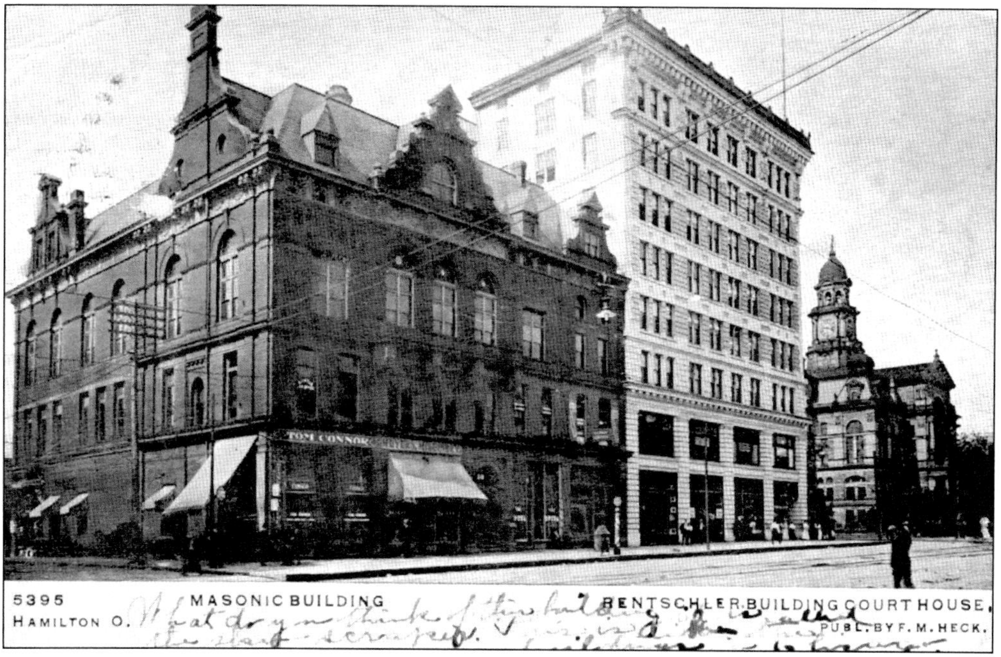

If the magnificent Masonic Building (left) were standing today, Hamilton's historic skyline would have a major boost. The Masonic stood on High Street, east of the Rentschler Building (center) at Journal Square. The sender of this postcard was more enthralled with the new skyscraper, telling a friend, "This is like the buildings in Chicago." Well, almost. The Butler County Courthouse is on the right.

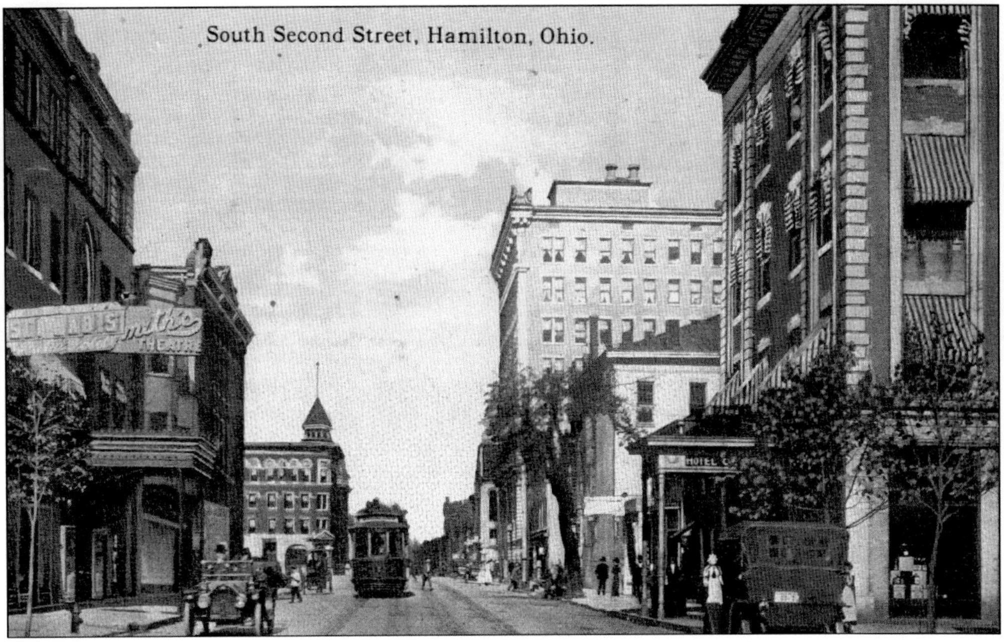

This card, postmarked September 4, 1913, shows South Second Street in Hamilton, with Smith's Theatre on the left, across from the Hotel Connor. Trolleys served the downtown regularly in those days.

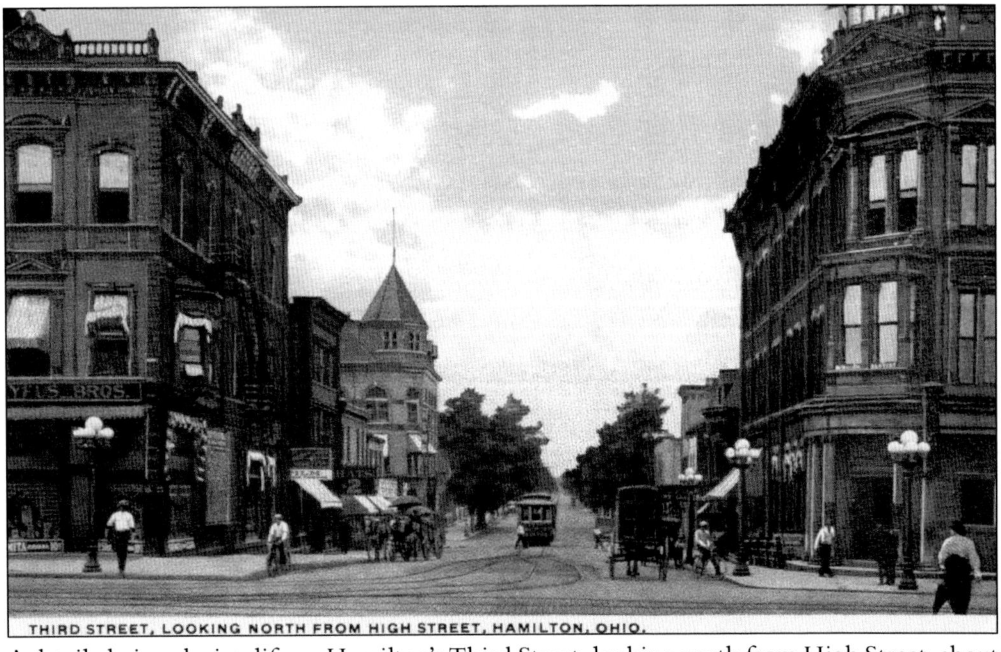

A detailed view depicts life on Hamilton's Third Street, looking north from High Street, about 1910. A small sign at a business on the left reads "film."

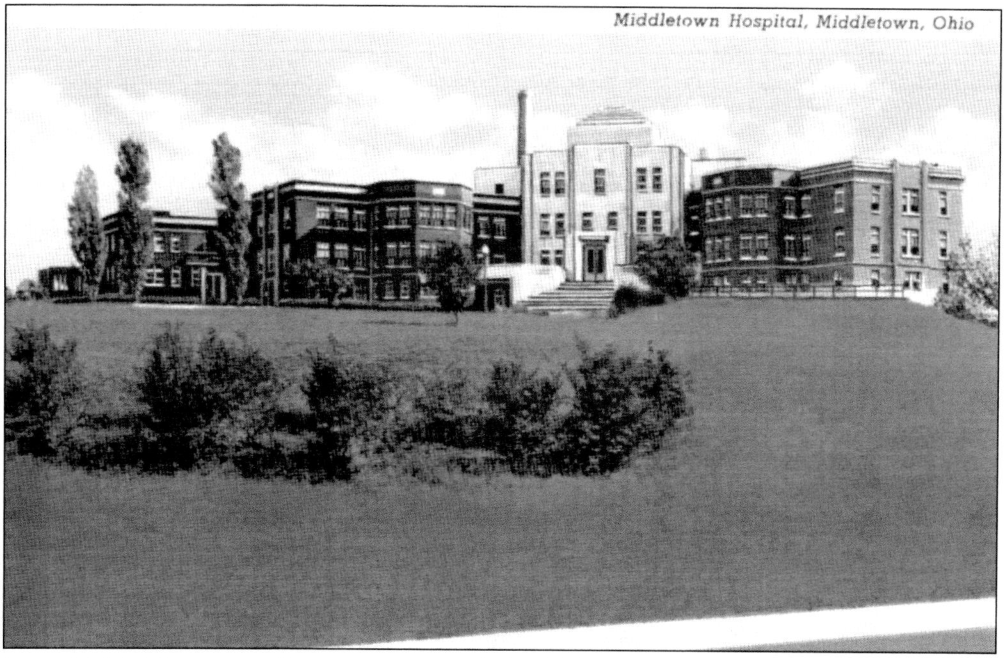

Some 5,000 citizens contributed money to help build the new Middletown Hospital in 1917. A $25,000 bequest by Rachael Magee sparked the building fund. By 1920, the hospital featured separate wards for men and women, in addition to a maternity ward, X-ray room, and special room for tonsillectomies.

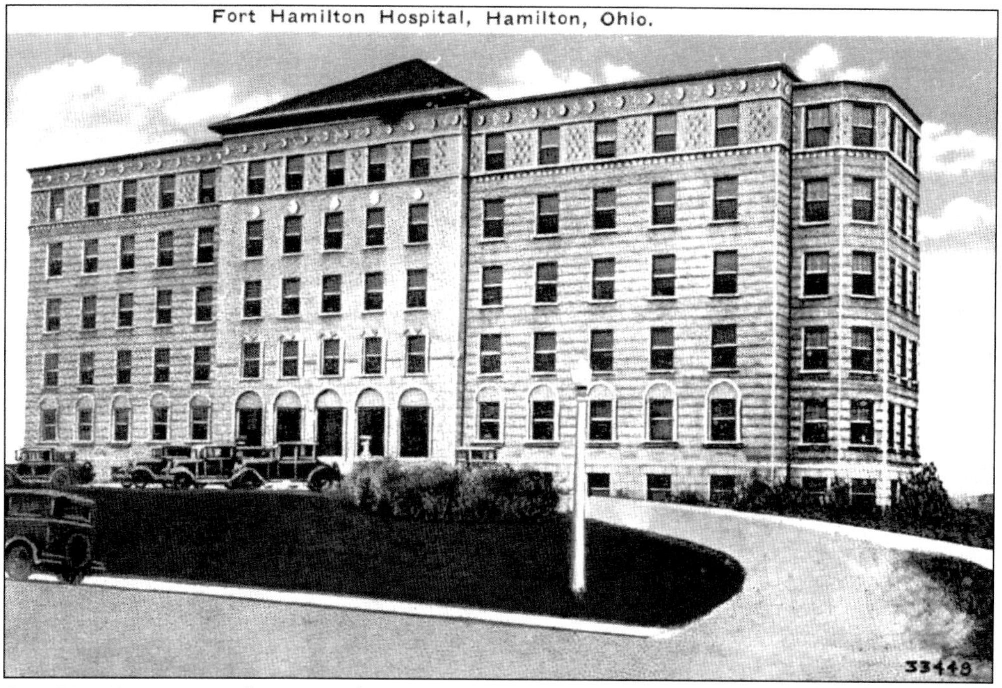

Fort Hamilton Hospital on Hamilton's Park Avenue served the west side of the city when this postcard was issued in the 1930s. It was opened for inspection on April 27, 1929. Since then, the facility has become the sole hospital in Hamilton.

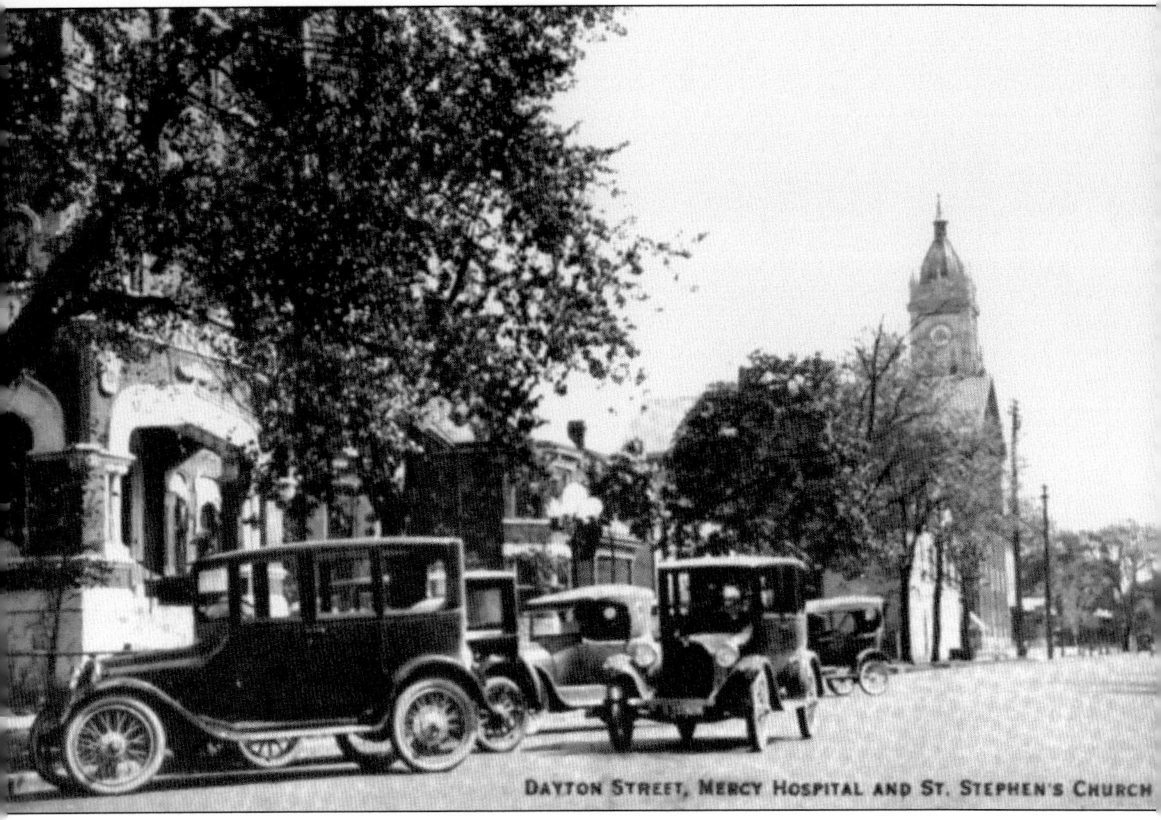

Two Catholic landmarks on Hamilton's Dayton Street are shown in this card from the 1920s. Mercy Hospital, in the foreground, was opened on October 5, 1892, after a committee of city leaders worked out a plan with the Sisters of Mercy religious order to operate the hospital. A new addition was built off Second Street in 1904 at a cost of $50,000. Mercy was closed on June 1, 2001. In the background is St. Stephen's Roman Catholic Church, one of Hamilton's oldest and most beautiful. It dates to 1832, when a brick, Gothic-style church was built that could seat 500 people. A two-story brick school was erected on the same lot in 1848. The Irish and German members of the church parted in the mid-1800s to allow each group to retain its native language. The German congregation stayed at the Dayton Street location, constructing a larger sanctuary there in 1853. After church consolidations, St. Stephen's is now called St. Julie Billiart Church.

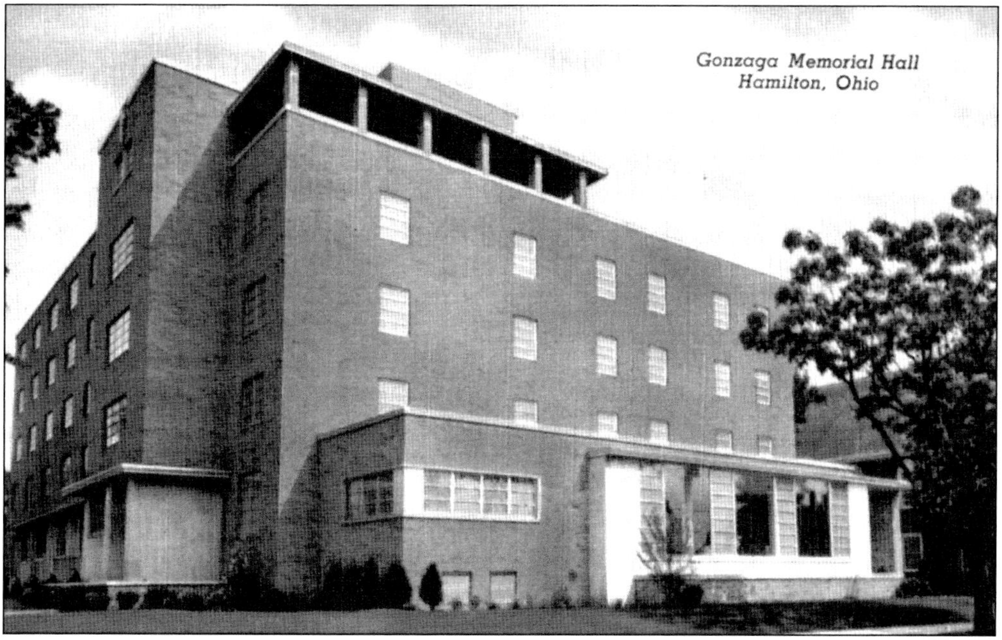

Hamilton once had two hospitals as well as a nursing school. Gonzaga Memorial Hall was dedicated on June 21, 1956, as a nursing school for Mercy Hospital in Hamilton. The brick structure overlooks the Great Miami River just north of downtown.

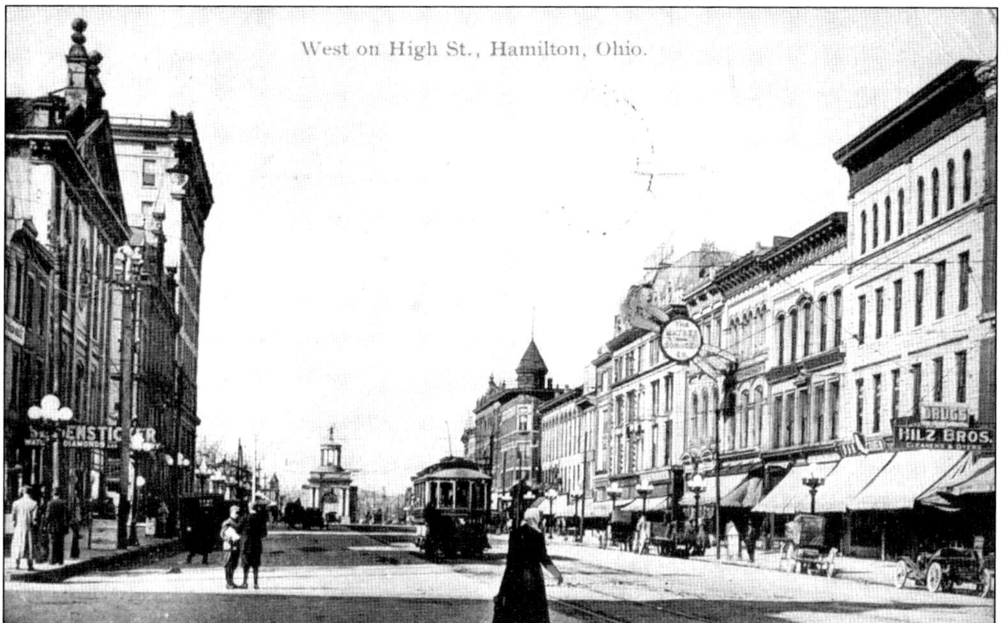

When a man named Carl mailed this real-photo postcard on October 15, 1912, he was "down with malaria for the last week." He could not guess that in five months the flooded Great Miami River would send a wall of water rushing down this road. Note the trolley car in the middle and the old globe lamps along High Street.

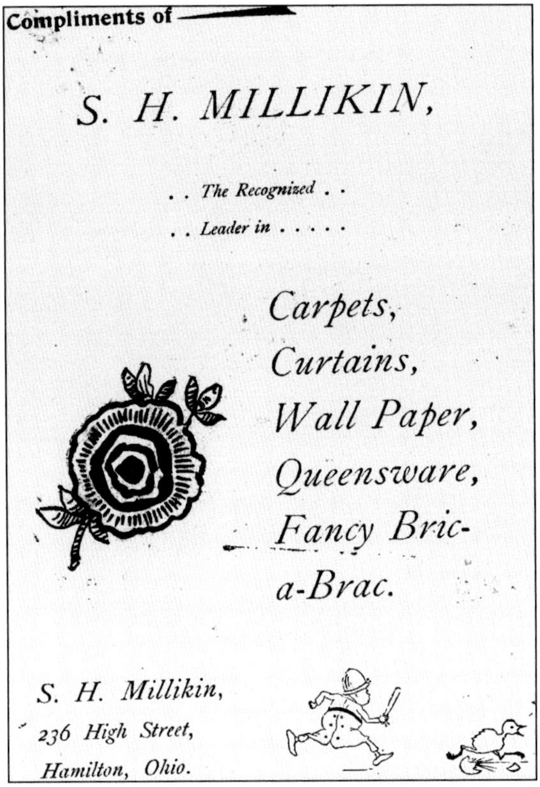

In the years when downtown Hamilton was a busy commercial place, S. H. Millikin sold carpets, curtains, wallpaper, and other items at a store at 236 High Street. The other side of this card features a color painting of flowers, a river, and Romanesque columns in the background, above the words "S. H. Millikin, Leading Carpet House." Back then, a downtown business address meant instant foot traffic.

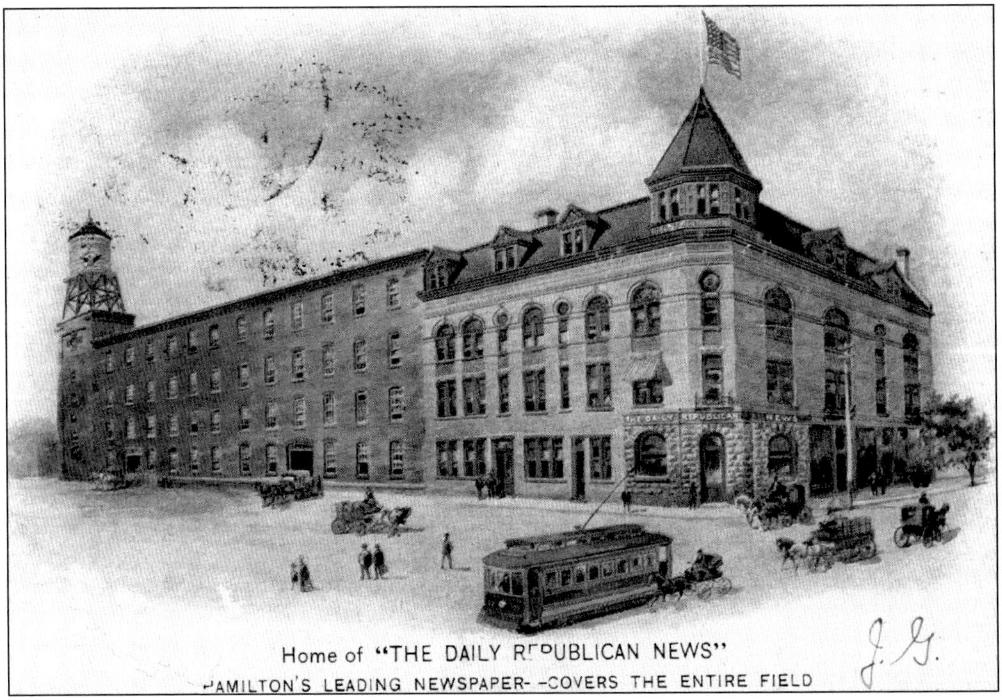

The *Daily Republican News* was both a major Hamilton newspaper and a printing company when this card was mailed in 1907. It survived the 1913 flood and continued to publish new editions.

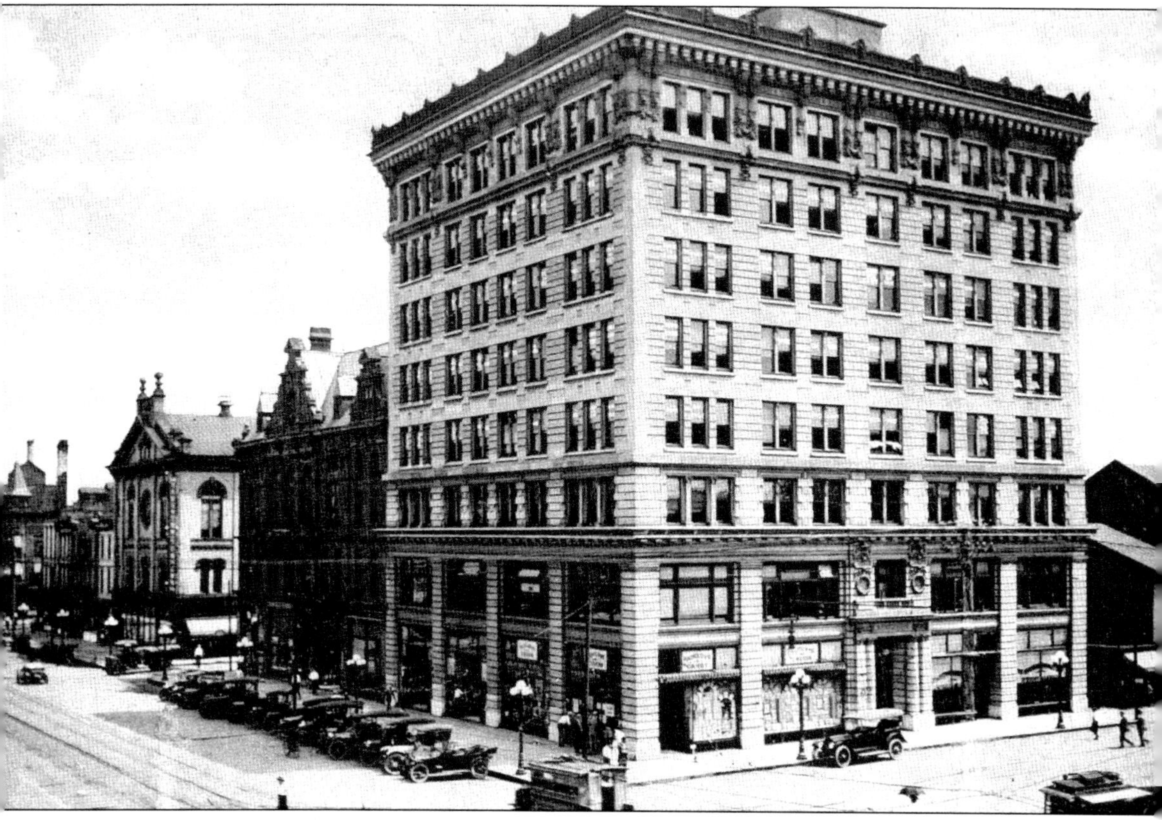

This photograph, taken about 1922, shows cars all backed into their parking spaces along High Street in Hamilton, in front of the impressive Rentschler Building at Second and High Streets. The Globe Opera House, the first building in the next block, has since been restored and is a part of historic Hamilton.

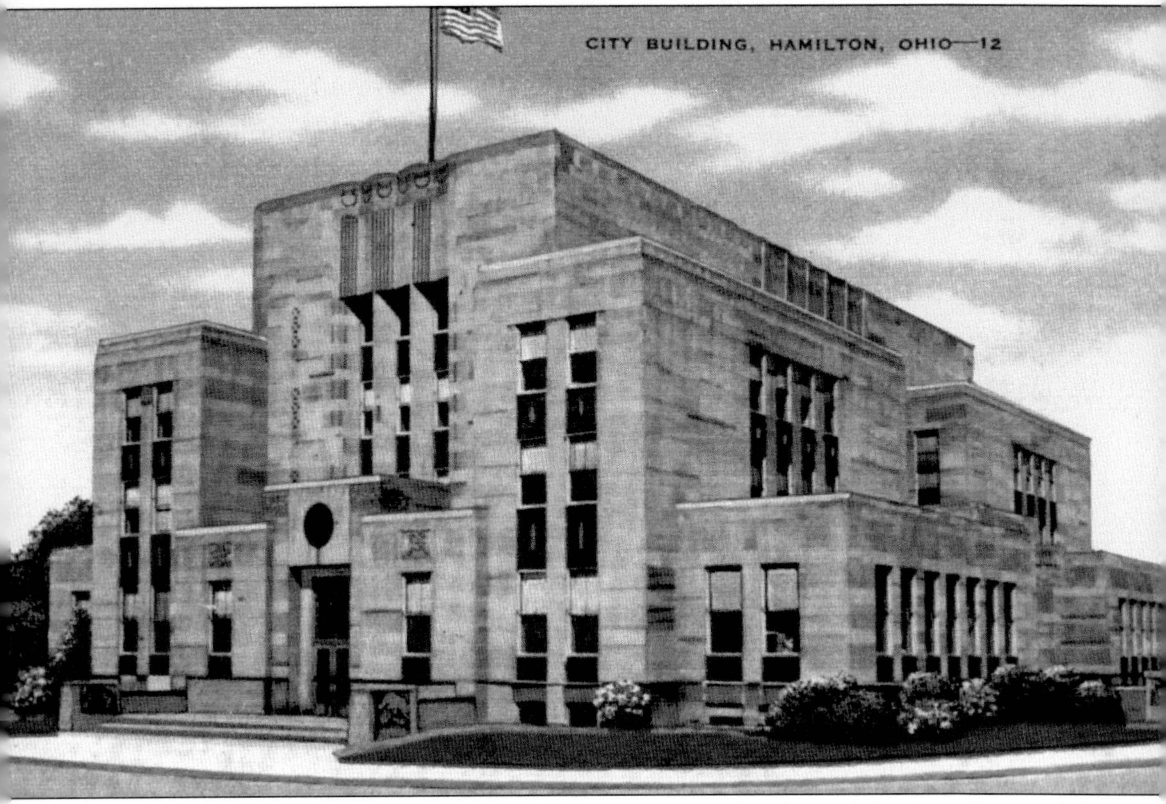

Built during the Great Depression, the Hamilton City Building housed the city offices and the central fire and police departments. This undated card, likely from the 1940s, notes that the city was the home of 70 major industries, including Champion Paper Company, General Machinery Corporation, and American Rolling Mills. Today the building is a city-run business incubator.

When this postcard was mailed in 1908, the United States Hotel was one of several successful lodgings in Middletown. Note the red-and-white awnings and the identification. The owners wanted everyone to know that this was *the* place—the U.S. Hotel. The name is spelled out in at least five places on the front of the building.

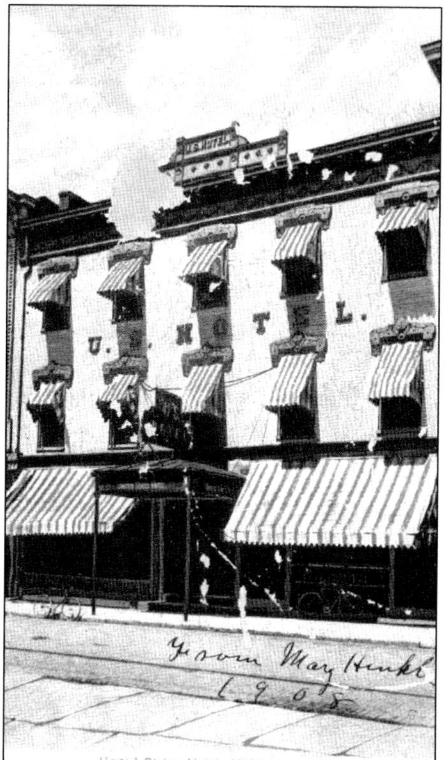

United States Hotel, Middletown, Ohio.

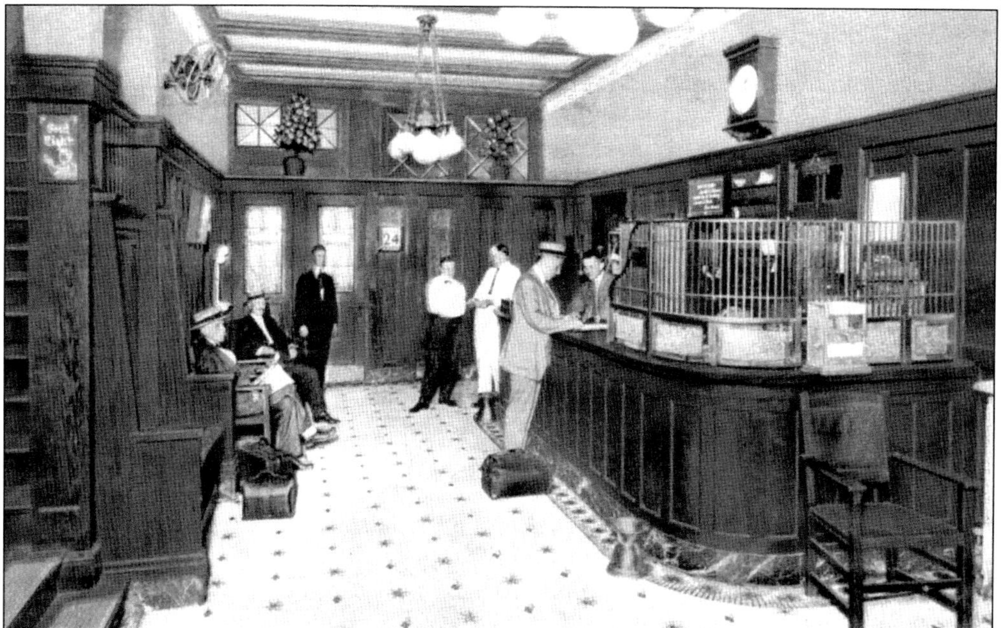

NEW HOWALD HOTEL OFFICE, HAMILTON, OHIO.

Hamilton also had its share of good hotels to accommodate business travelers. The Howald Hotel office featured a brass spittoon in front of the desk. Owner Charles Howald prided himself on quality and convenience for the traveler.

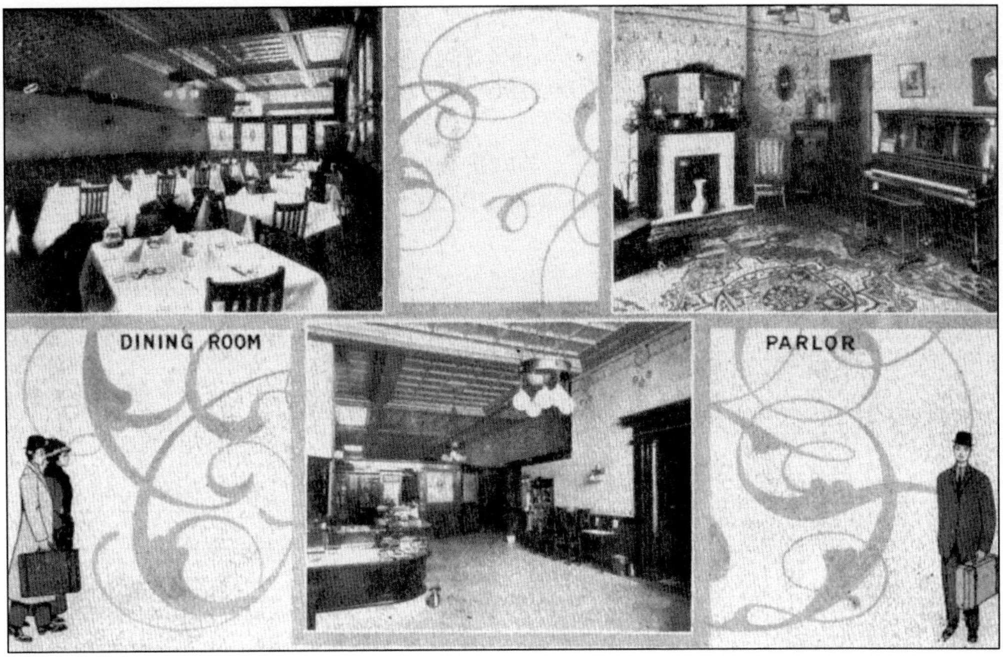

Arthur Mullin sent this postcard to his mother, Mrs. Willie Mullin of Liberty, Indiana, on May 19, 1913. He must have been proud of downtown Hamilton's Hotel Connor, for he wrote, "Mama, here is the dining room office and parlor were [*sic*] I work." Notice the white tablecloths and the piano in the parlor.

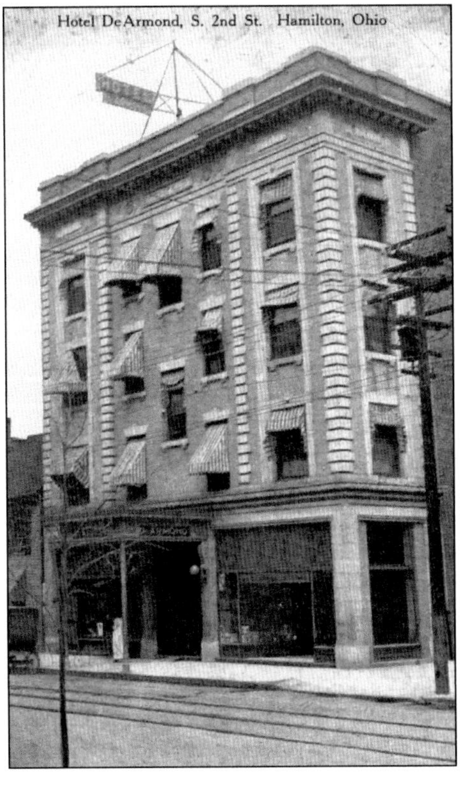

On April 26, 1914, Arthur Mullin wrote to his mother again, telling her of his upcoming visit. He wrote on the back of a postcard from the fancy Hotel DeArmond on South Second Street in Hamilton. At this time, did Mullin work at the DeArmond? Perhaps.

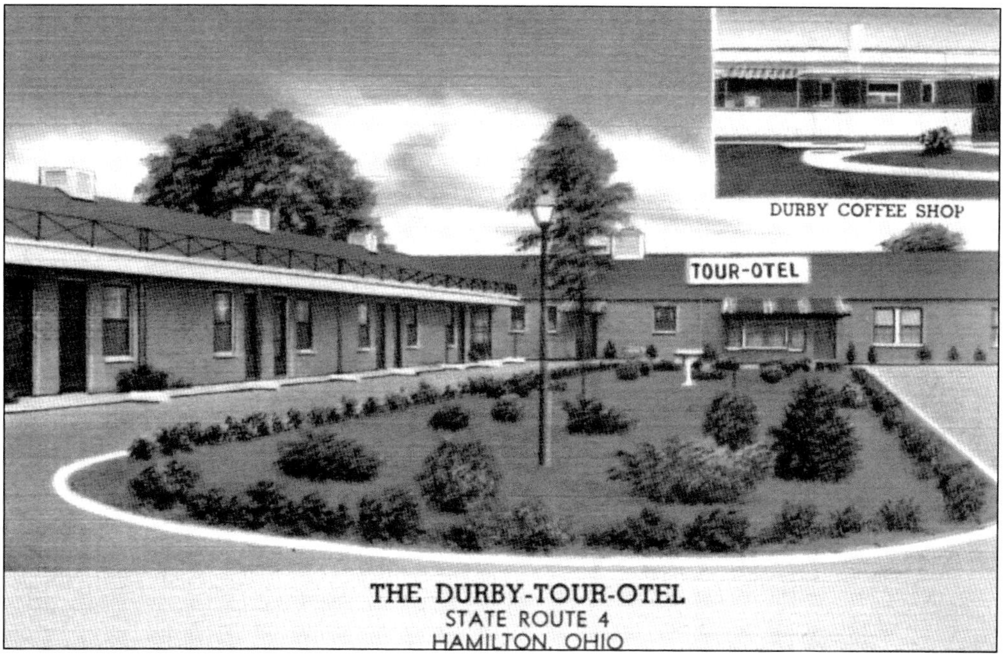

When this card was mailed in 1955, small motels like the Durby-Tour-Otel on State Route 4 in Hamilton were popping up across the country to take advantage of postwar vacationing. Route 4 was a good spot, as it was the main road before the arrival of interstates. The Durby featured a coffee shop too. Unfortunately, the sender did not mention the motel in her message to her family.

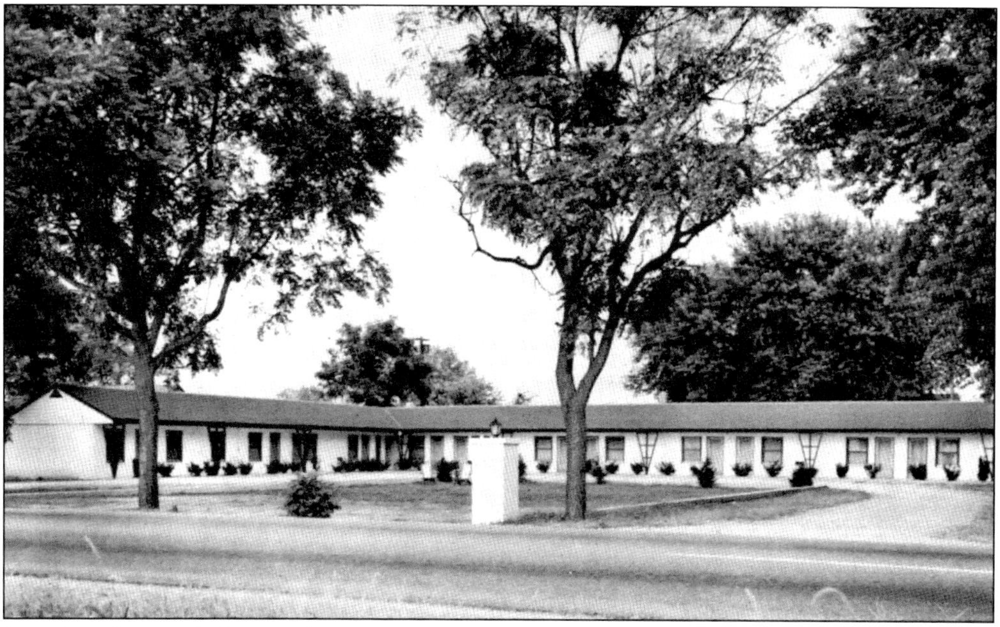

Ross Motel, on U.S. Route 127 in Ross, was owned by John M. Shetter. This *c.* 1957 card comes with some important explanation: the Ross Motel is equipped with air-conditioning, radio and television, and, thankfully, hot-water heat.

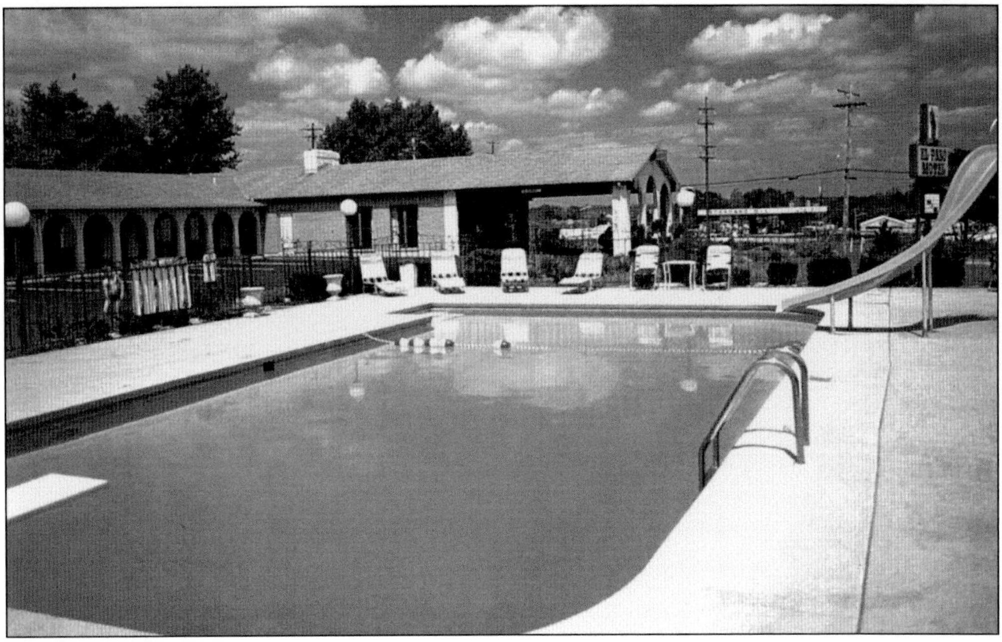

When the El Paso Motel opened in Fairfield in the 1960s, it offered a pool, 25 modern rooms, a bridal suite, direct-dial telephones, individually controlled heaters and air-conditioning, and a feel of the old Southwest. A Standard Oil service station stood across the street.

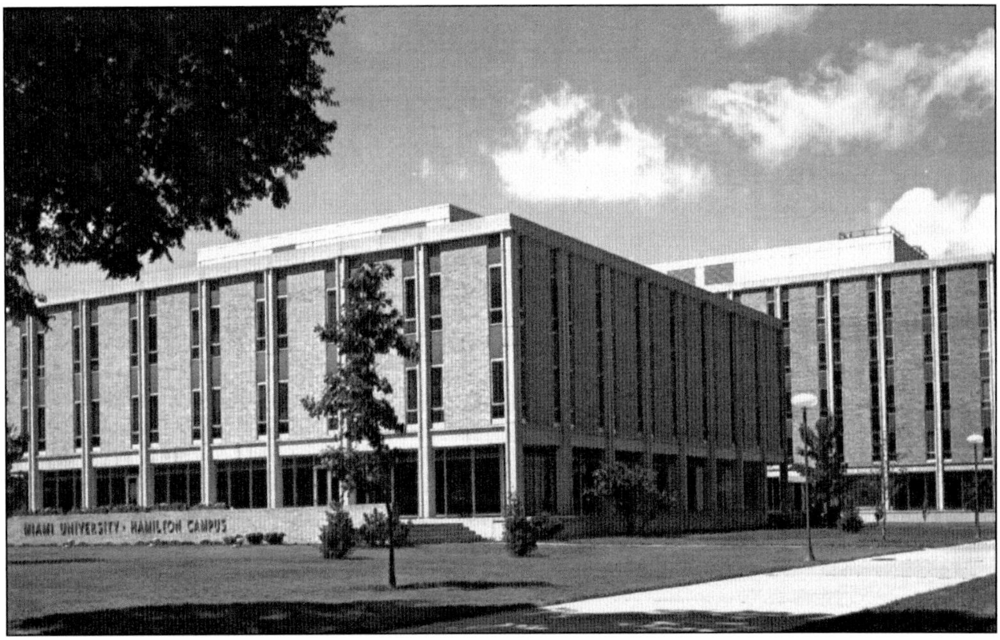

The Hamilton campus of Miami University opened in 1968 to serve nontraditional students, many who worked full-time. In the early 1970s, coauthor Randy McNutt attended the Hamilton campus before moving on to Miami's Oxford campus. This *c.* 1969 postcard shows the main classroom building and, behind it, the library. Today the campus has expanded to include additional buildings and programs.

Nine

THE GREAT FLOOD

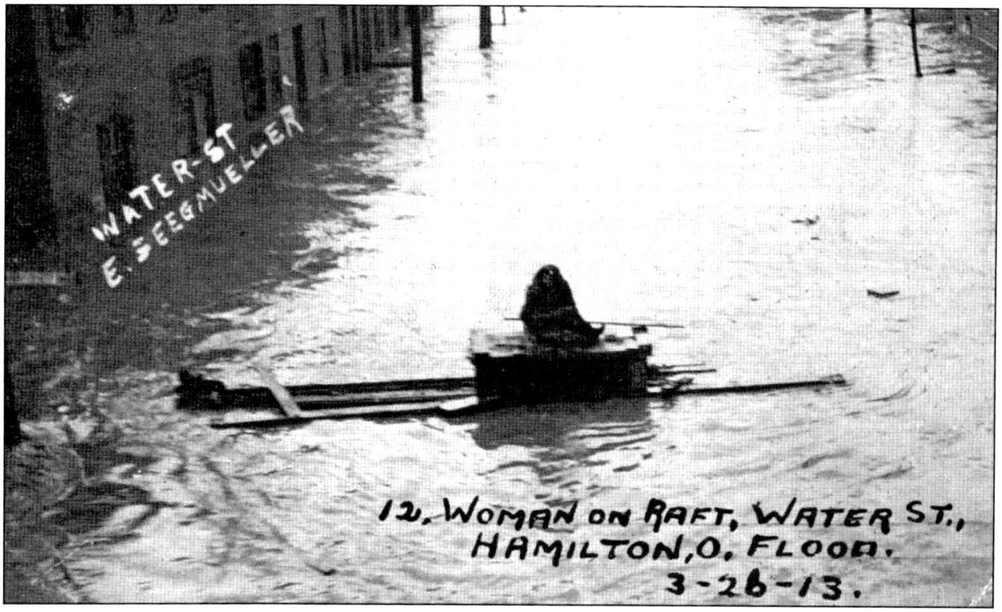

A woman huddles on a makeshift raft, awaiting rescue in downtown Hamilton following the March 1913 flood that ravaged many Miami Valley communities. The storm struck swiftly and violently on March 25, catching many people unaware. Lacking protection, Hamilton flooded as the Great Miami River rose. Butler County residents who lived near the river and its tributaries were as hard hit as many parts of Middletown.

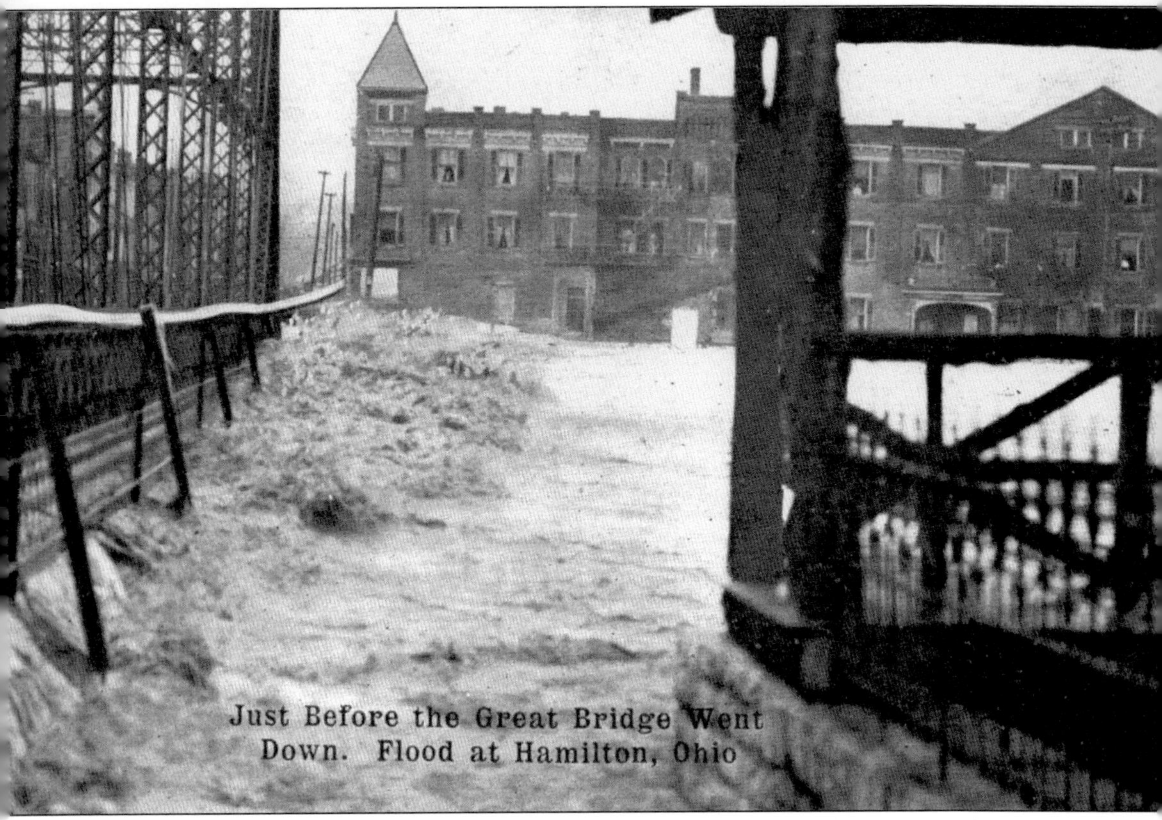

A brave but unidentified photographer stood next to the old Fort Hamilton powder magazine to capture an image of the raging flood as it swirled around the large truss bridge that linked Hamilton's east and west sides when the rains came on March 25, 1913. In the background is A Street in the Rossville neighborhood. Soon the bridge and the historic magazine would be swept away by the fast-moving river, and Hamilton would be helpless. Such floods had caused havoc in Butler County and Hamilton in 1866 and 1898, but 1913 was the biggest disaster of them all—2,300 buildings destroyed, 300 deaths, and 10,000 left homeless in Hamilton alone. The whole Miami Valley looked like a war zone.

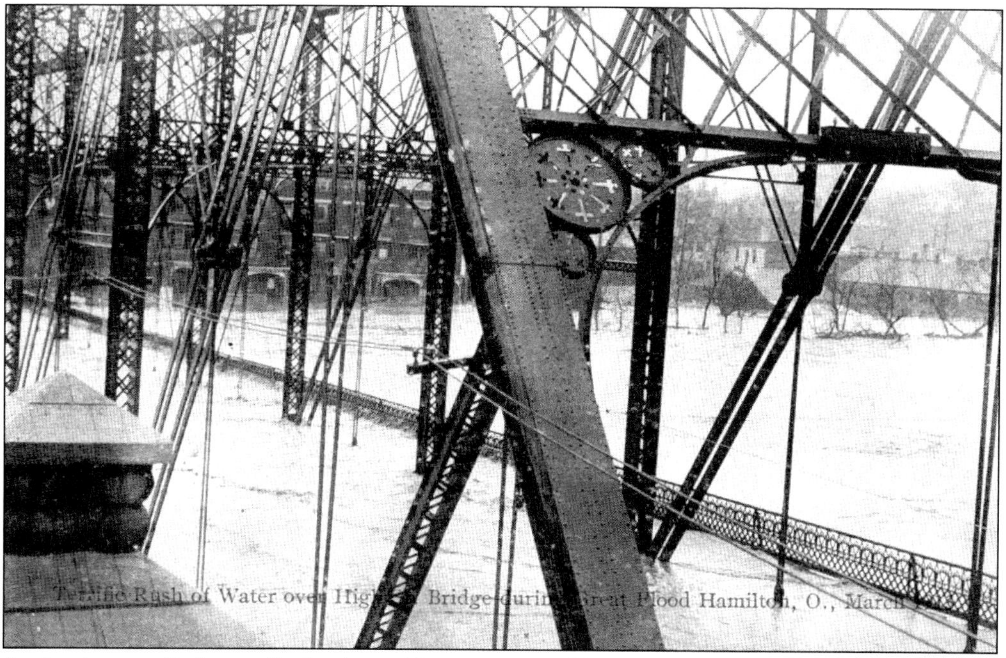

As the river swelled out of its banks, swift current engulfed the iron bridge over the Great Miami River. Notice how the water covered the deck of the bridge just before the collapse occurred.

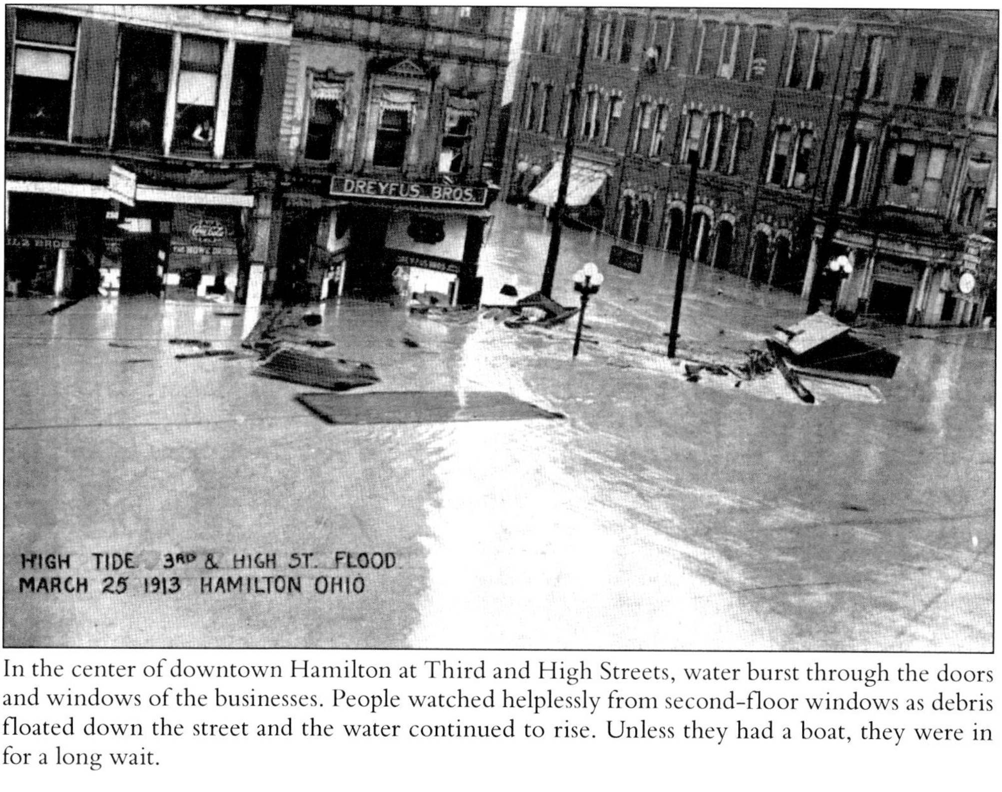

In the center of downtown Hamilton at Third and High Streets, water burst through the doors and windows of the businesses. People watched helplessly from second-floor windows as debris floated down the street and the water continued to rise. Unless they had a boat, they were in for a long wait.

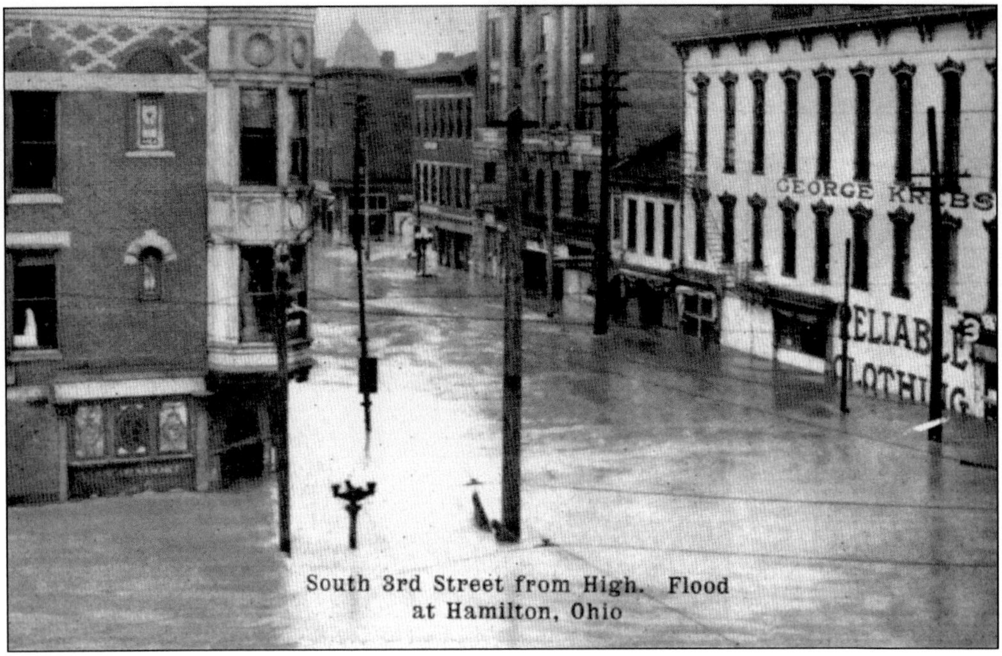

This is another flood view of High Street at South Third Street. The water entered George Krebs's clothing store and every other business in the devastated downtown.

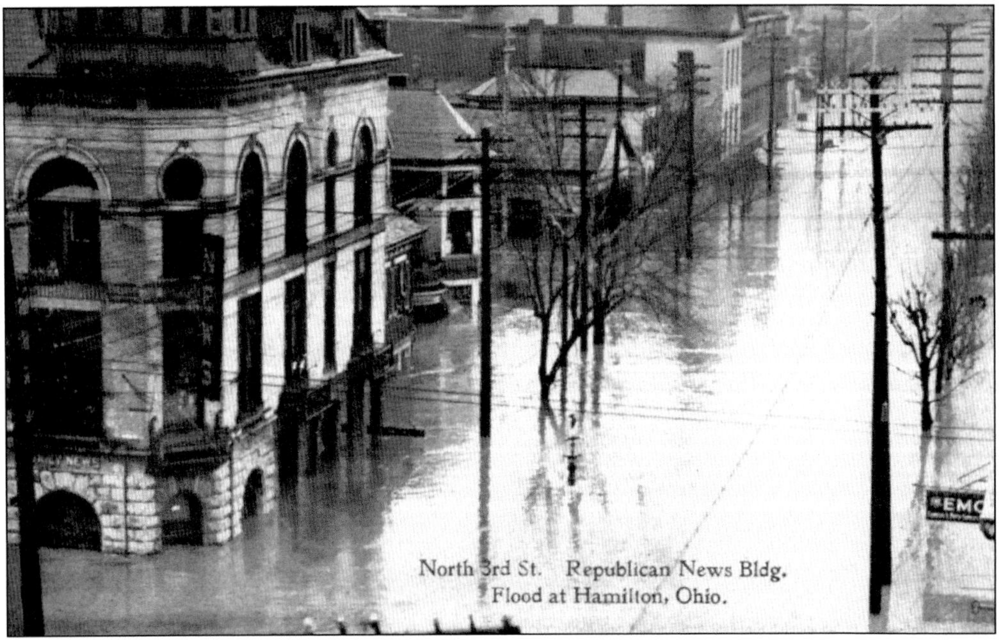

On North Third Street in downtown Hamilton, the water poured into the Republican News Building, but that did not stop the editors from doing their job. Stranded printers retreated to the second floor and printed on a manual press. The water was just one foot below them. The only edition missed was March 26.

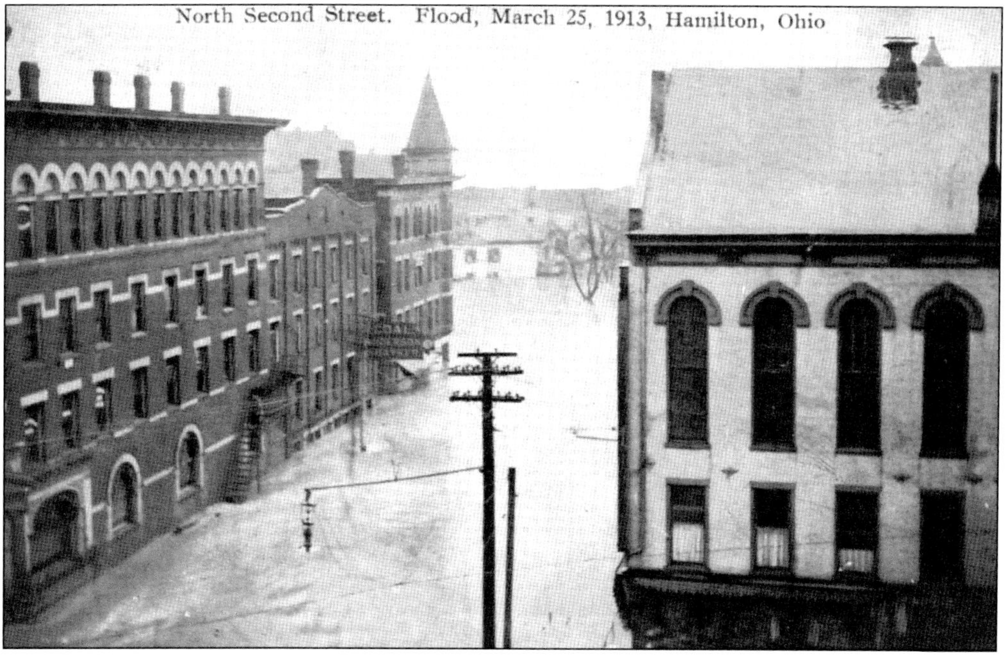

Looking down on North Second Street on March 25, 1913, the unidentified photographer must have thought he was having a nightmare. Water covered all the streets and alleys. The river town's worst scenario had come true—flood!

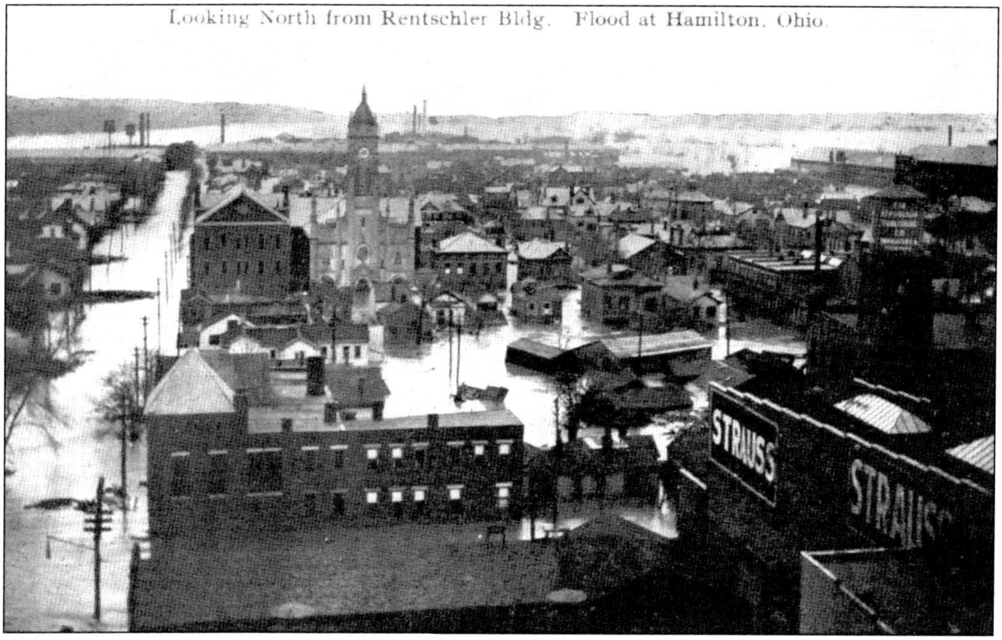

This eerie view was taken from the Rentschler Building, looking north. The expanded river is in the top of the photograph. It appears to roll straight onto the streets of Hamilton, leaving a somber and dark business district.

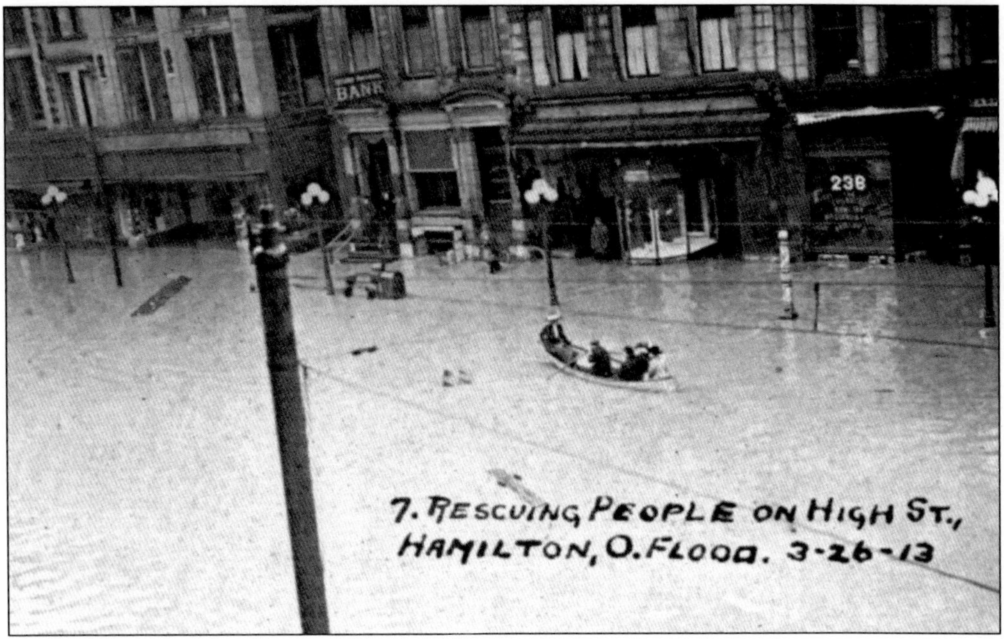

It took days for rescuers to reach all those who were left stranded by the flood. This card shows rescuers in a rowboat on Hamilton's High Street on March 26. Cincinnati city police aided in rescue efforts in Middletown. As the danger subsided, some boat owners started charging to take people on sightseeing tours of the worst areas.

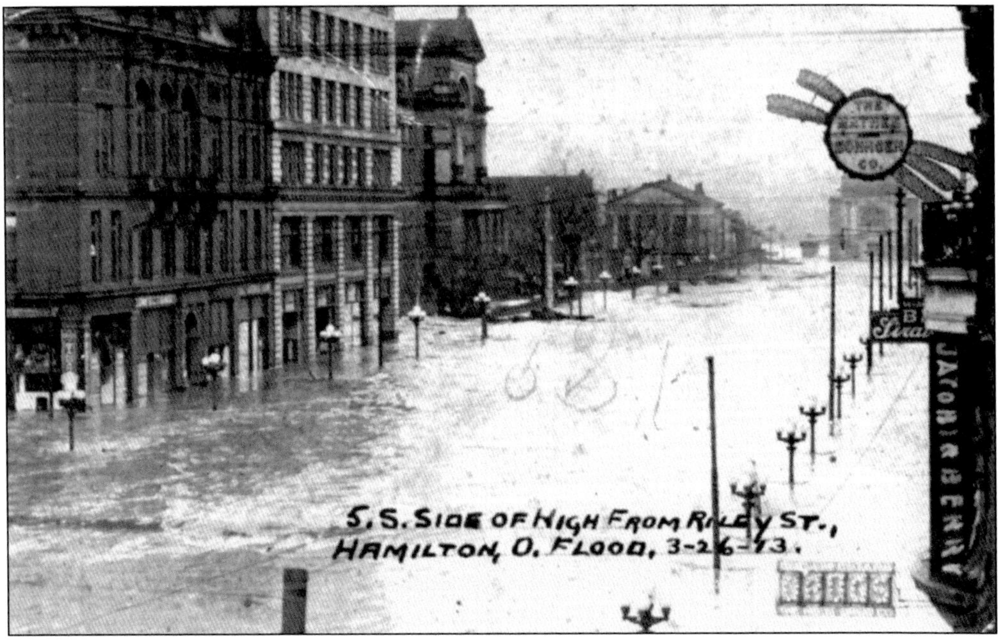

In this view of the south side of Hamilton's High Street, taken from Riley Street on March 26, 1913, the water stands halfway up the lampposts. This shot was produced by Jacobi and Berry, a photography studio operating at 308 High Street. The faded image of the new Soldiers, Sailors and Pioneers Monument can be seen to the far right, partially covered by a sign.

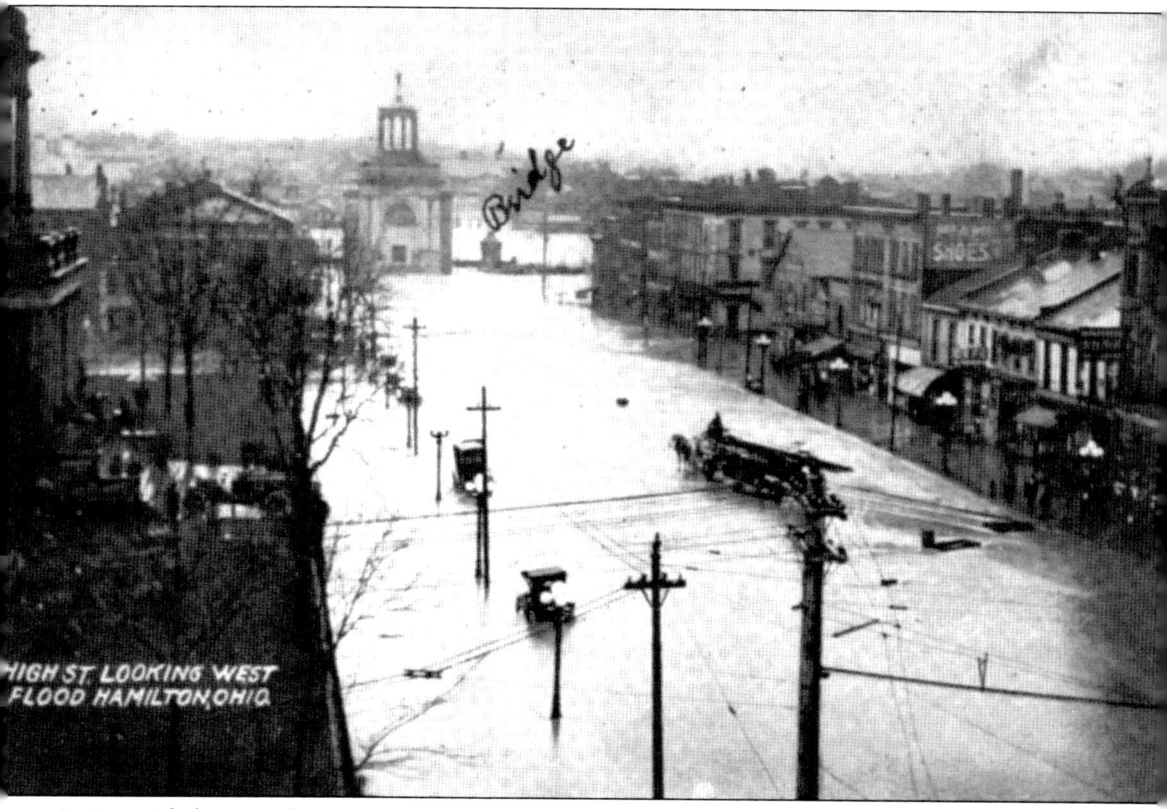

An intrepid photographer stood atop a building to record the receding flood from the west. Cars and a horse-drawn wagon are visible on High Street. The sender of this card wrote the word "bridge" in the spot where the iron span had stood only a few days earlier.

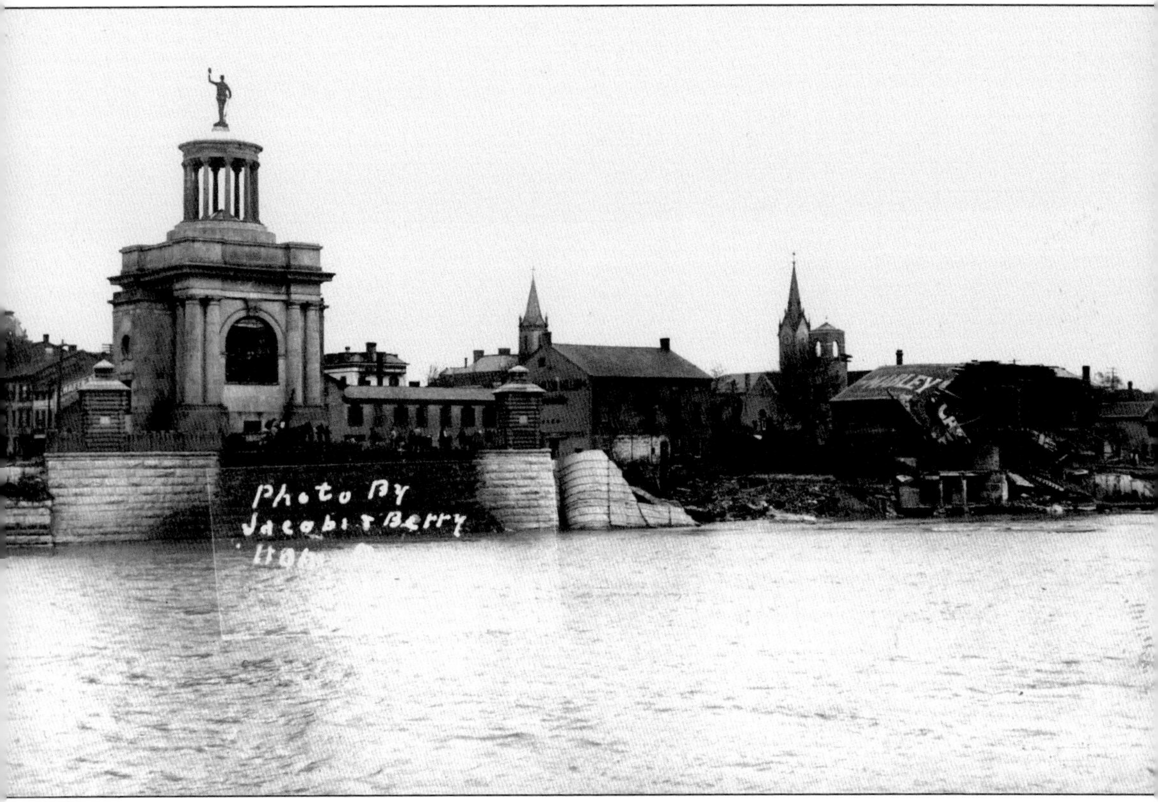

A photographer from the Jacobi and Berry Studio stood along the river on the west side of Hamilton to capture the devastation on the east side. Miraculously, the Soldiers, Sailors, and Pioneers Monument survived the flood with little damage.

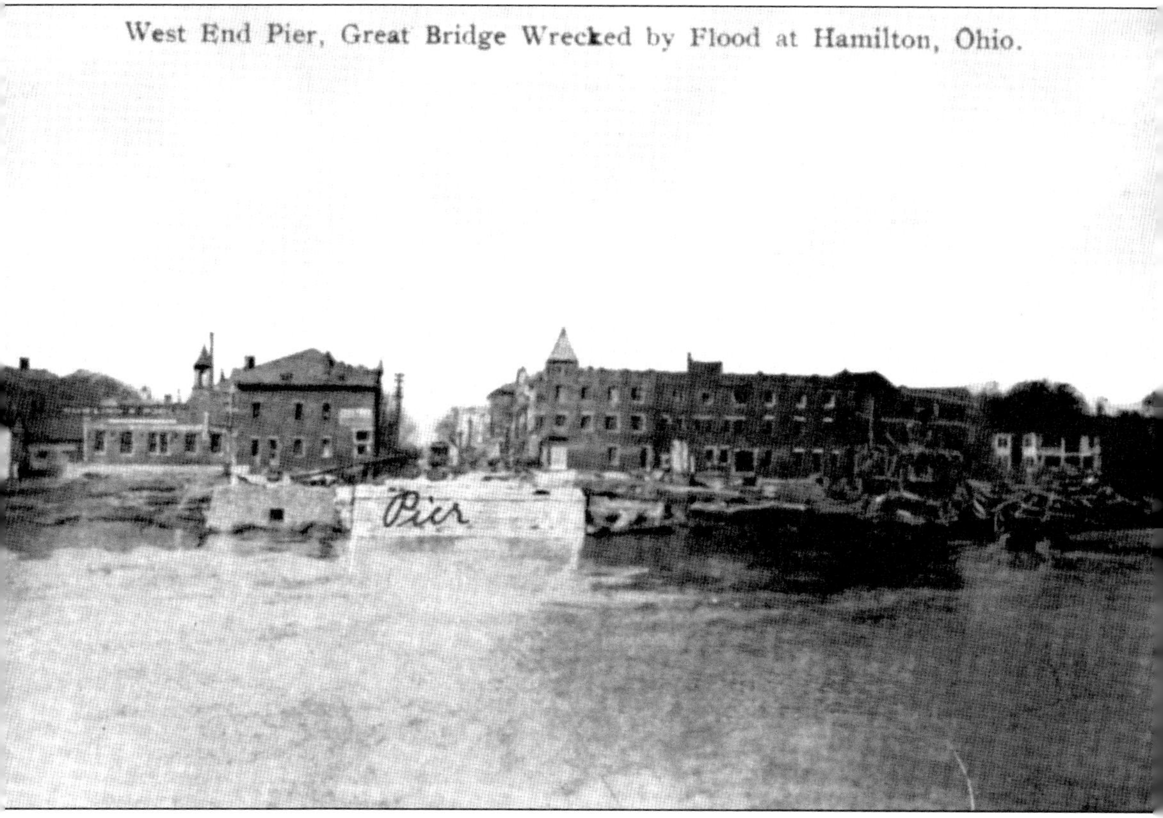

The owner of this card wrote the word "pier" on the stone base where the iron bridge once was. The span was washed away in the March 1913 flood in Hamilton. National Guardsmen built a pontoon bridge to connect the east and west sides and carried supplies across it by hand. The city operated under martial law for a time so that the soldiers could assist flood victims and protect property. It was a welcome sight for thousands of homeless Hamilton residents and others who feared what might happen during the disaster.

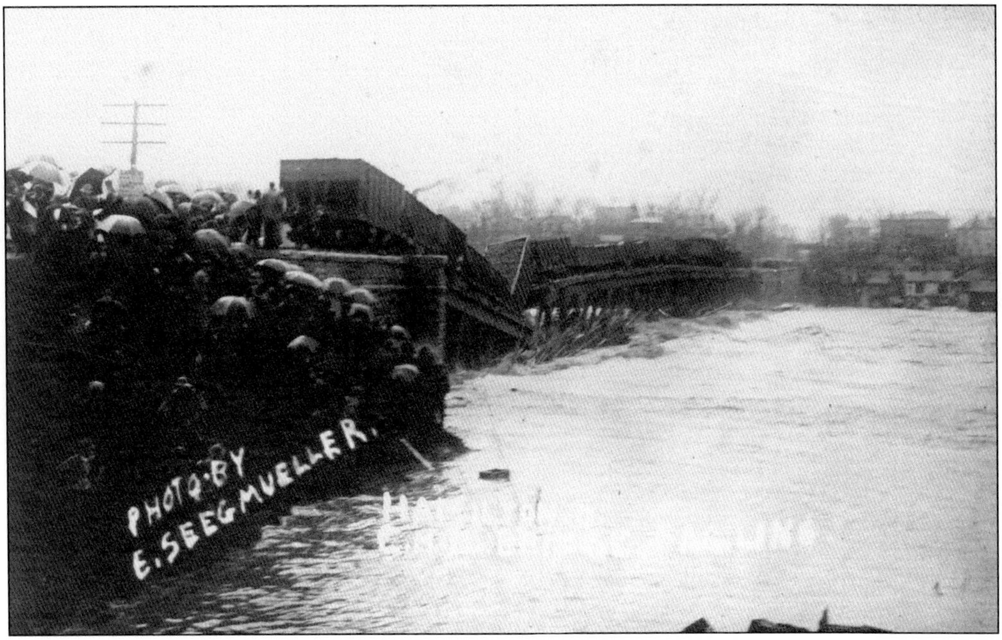

In this dramatic postcard photograph by E. Seegmeuller, rushing water collapses the Cincinnati, Hamilton, and Dayton Railroad bridge while freight cars fall into the river. The river is so deep that the bridge appears to be built close to the waterline. Notice the people, protected by umbrellas but little else, who watch the bridge cave.

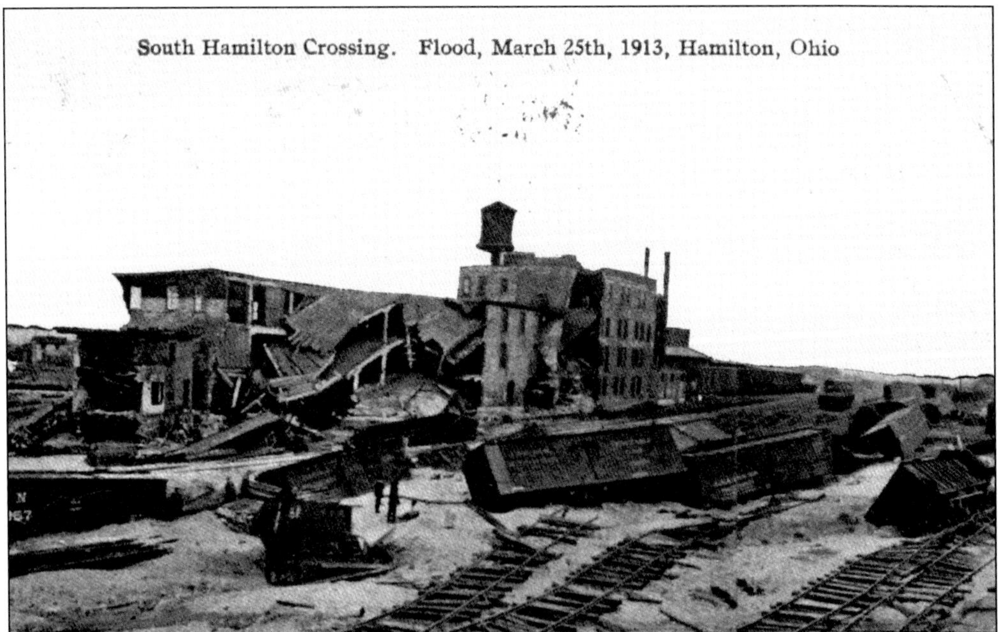

At the South Hamilton railroad crossing, tracks and train cars are twisted and dispersed like children's toys. The flood badly damaged this industrial area. In only 48 hours, the Great Miami River rose from 4.8 to a record 34.6 feet.

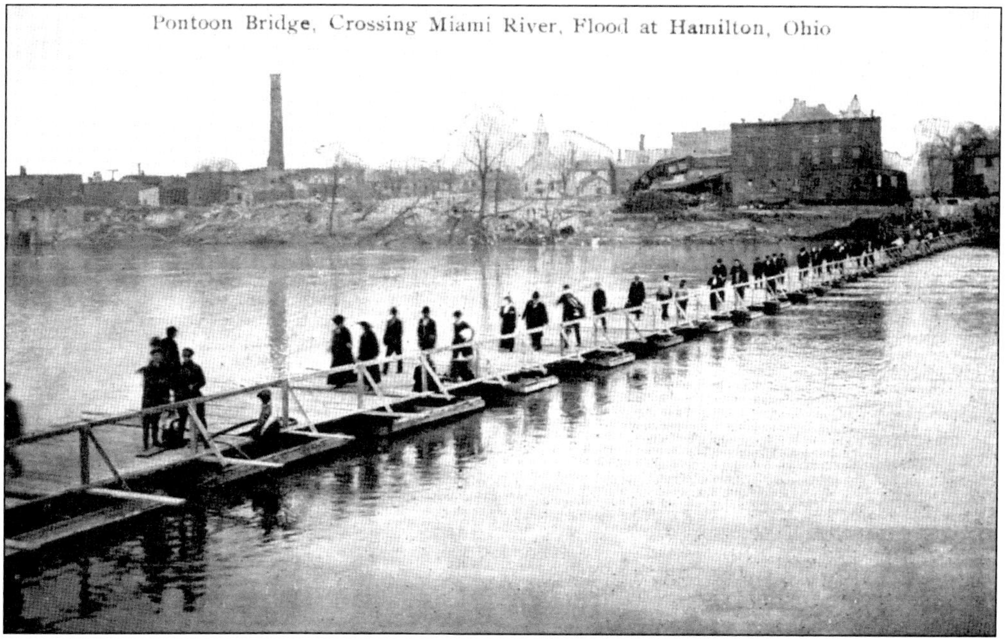

The rain dumped between 9 and 11 inches of rain on Hamilton in only three days. By the time the rain stopped, people started emerging from their hiding places. Some walked across the pontoon bridge to visit the other side of town.

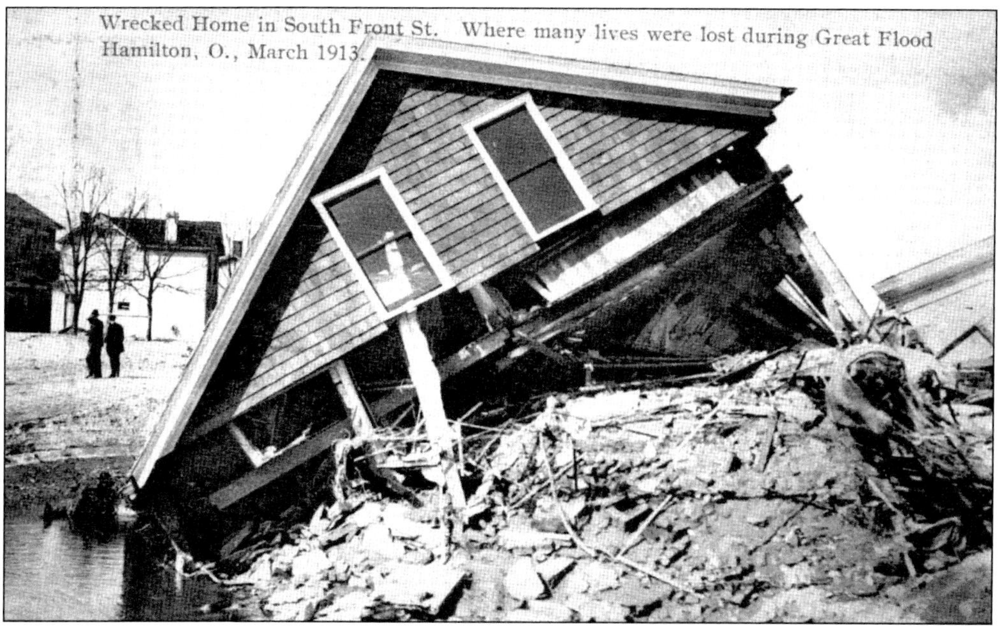

A wrecked home on South Front Street suffered a direct hit from a wall of water during the 1913 flood in Hamilton. Many other houses were similarly destroyed. The caption reads, "Where many lives were lost during the Great Flood."

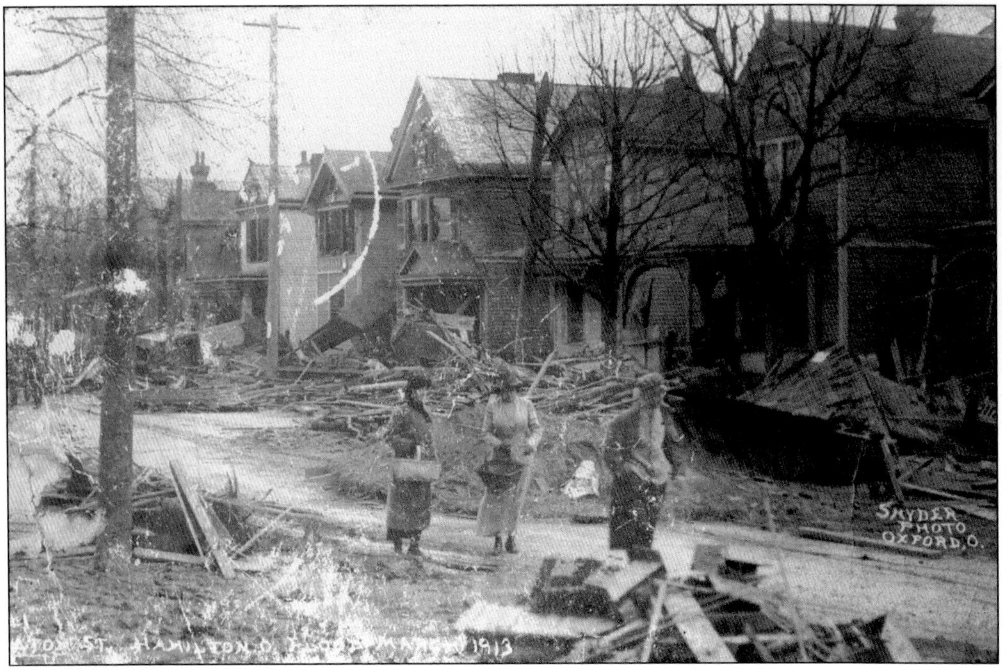

A photographer from Snyder Photography in Oxford captured this grim scene on Hamilton's Heaton Street after the flood. "This is indescribable," a woman named Lena wrote on April 16, 1913. "This is not the worst. High Street is beginning to look right respectable, but my, what work there is yet to be done until they get the streets clean. They still have martial law."

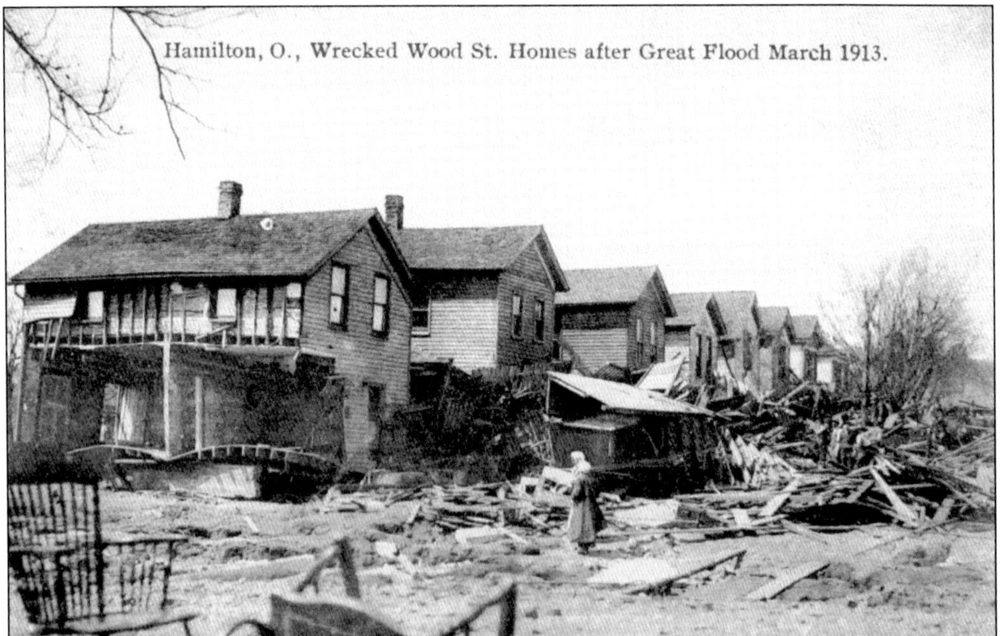

Viewing what is left of her life, a woman stands before a house in Hamilton that has been peeled like an onion. People could not believe the raw power of water until they experienced it first-hand across most parts of their city.

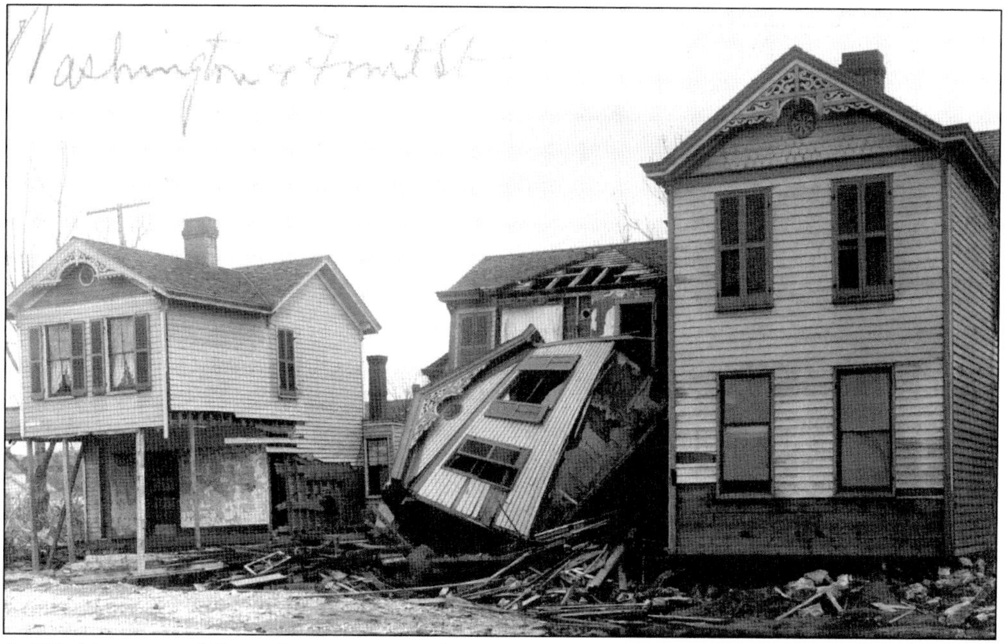

At Washington and Front Streets in Hamilton, houses were stripped and tossed. The one on the right was the "lucky" one. The card buyer wrote, "As I stood selecting these [postcard] views, two women stood by. One suddenly said, 'That is my home!' The sad part is, most of these homes are owned by hardworking people."

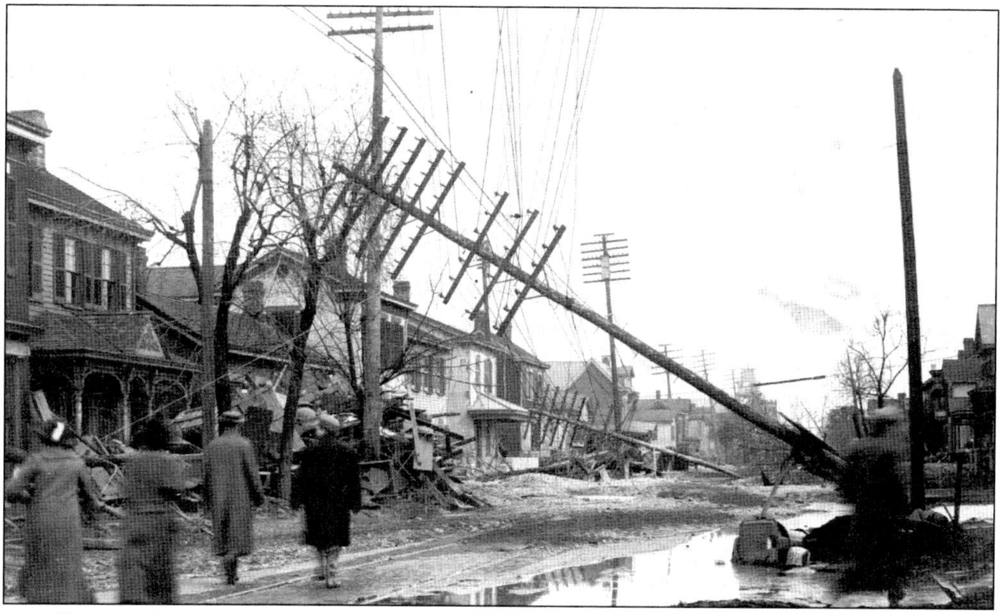

Hamilton residents emerge to inspect the ruins of their city after the 1913 flood. Telephone lines cross the streets like spiderwebs and mud coats everything. It took months to clean up the debris and repair the houses that could be saved. The others had to be torn down.

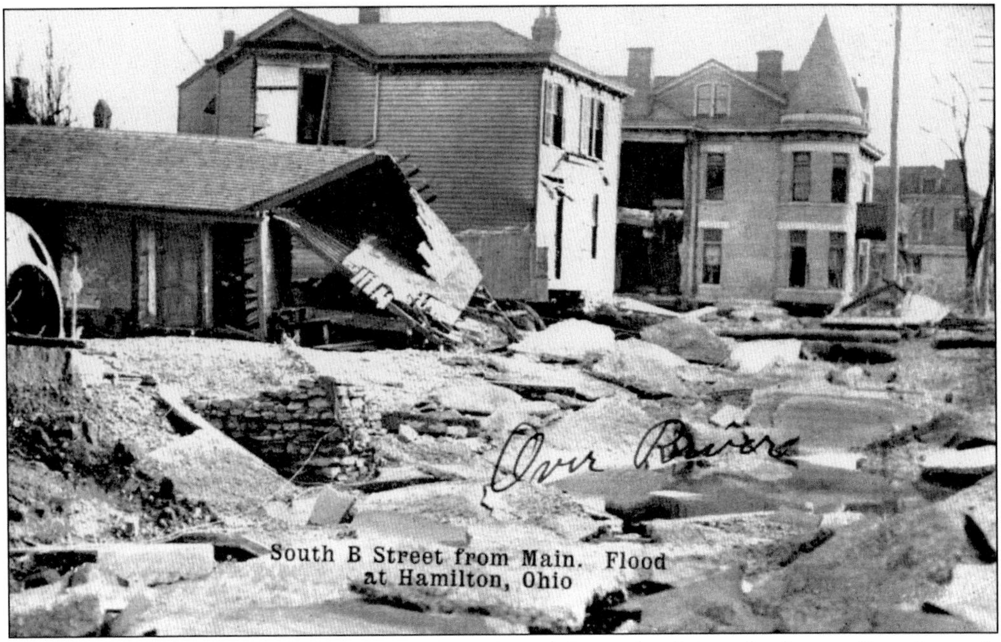

"Our River," noted the unidentified writer, although he or she did not bother sending the card. It remained as a grim reminder of what the city endured in March 1913. This photograph shows damage in the Rossville neighborhood on the west side of Hamilton.

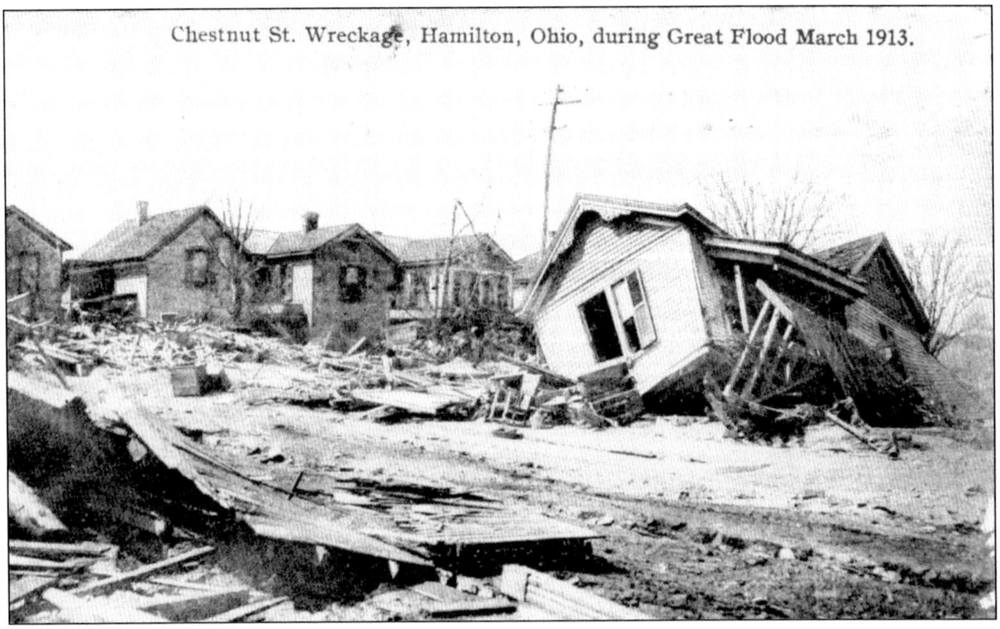

On Chestnut Street on Hamilton's east side, more houses were crumpled by the fast-flowing water and left as debris. The remaining one looks as though it were struck by a tornado.

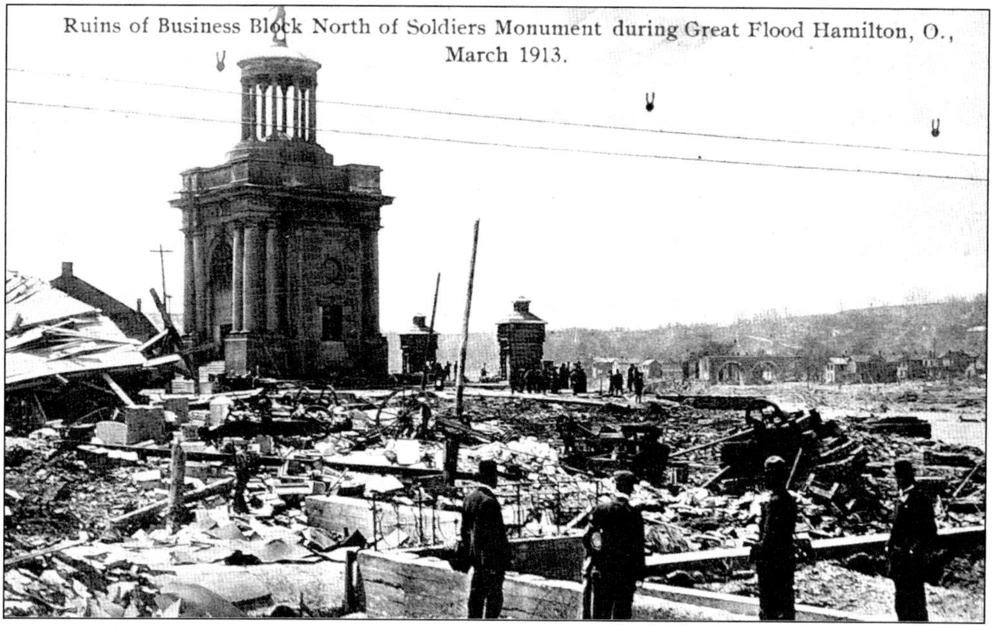

After the flood, a photographer stood near the river to capture the debris around the Butler County Soldiers, Sailors, and Pioneers Monument. The new memorial—dedicated only seven years earlier—somehow avoided heavy damage, even though it stood directly in front of the river. In the distance are the stone railroad viaducts.

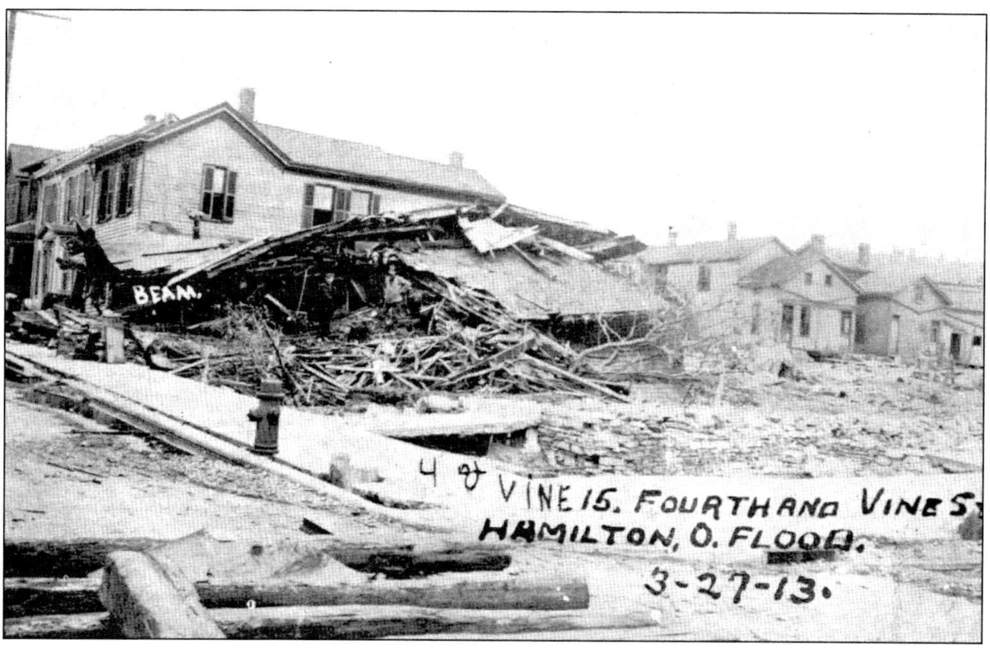

Two days after the flood began, it was gone, although not without leaving its mark in the form of debris. This view shows Fourth and Vine Streets in Hamilton. Look closely to see a man standing in the center of what used to be a house. The name Beam presumably identifies the owner.

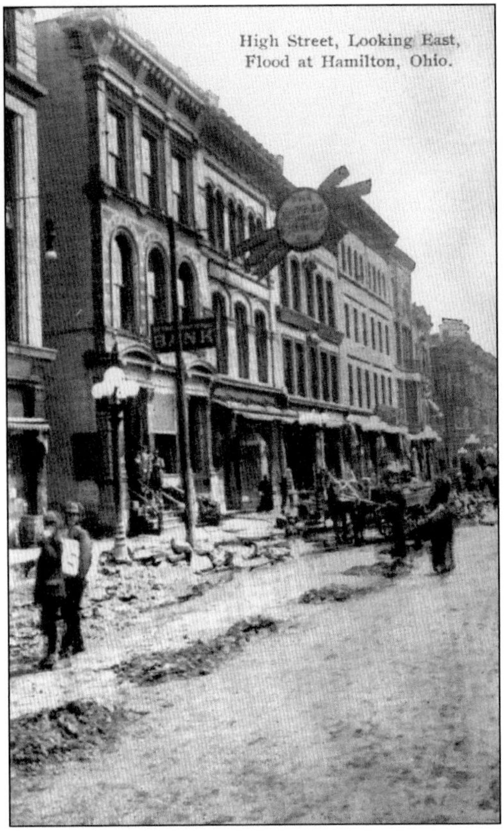

On Hamilton's High Street, a photographer found life returning after the big flood. Gone is the seven-foot wall of water. Boys deliver newspapers. Wagons make deliveries. Commerce is returning to the business district.

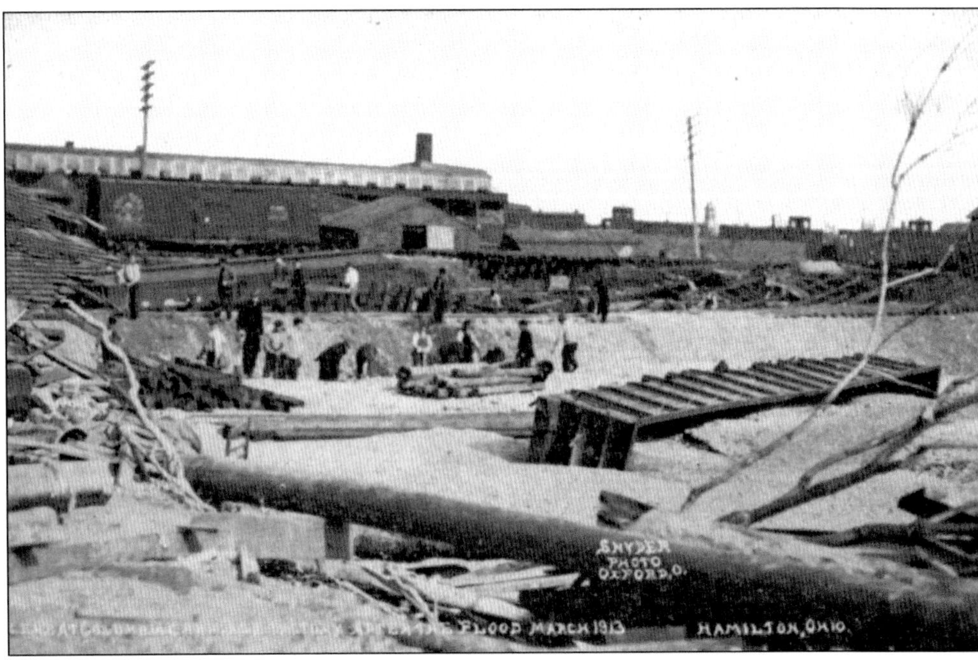

At the Columbia Carriage Company in Hamilton, Snyder Photography of Oxford found workers cleaning up what was left of their loading area near the rail line.

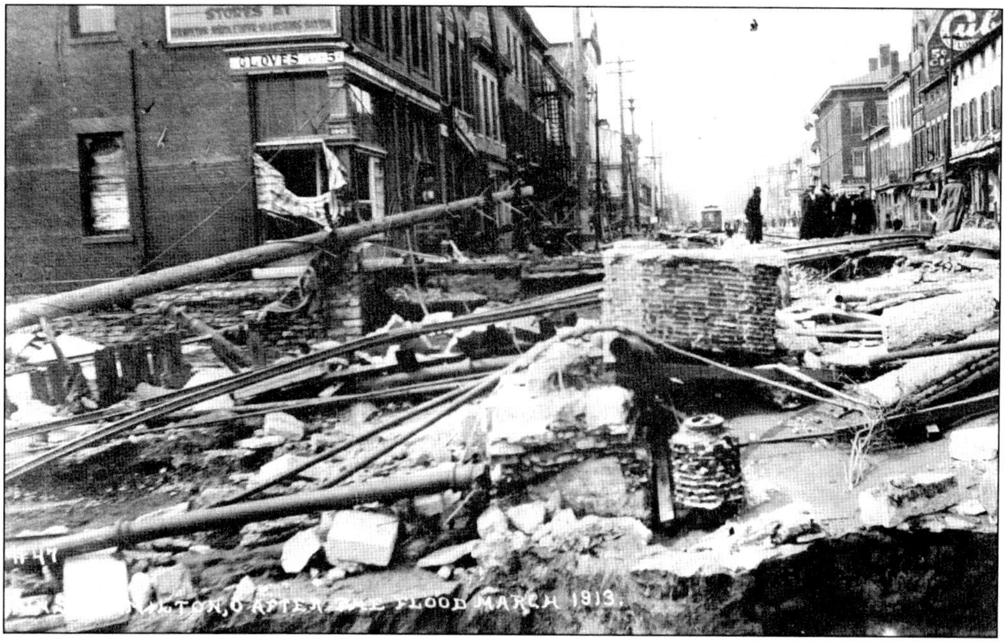

A cold day in March reveals more debris, as Hamilton residents observe the big job that awaits them. The disaster continued to affect some survivors for the rest of their lives.

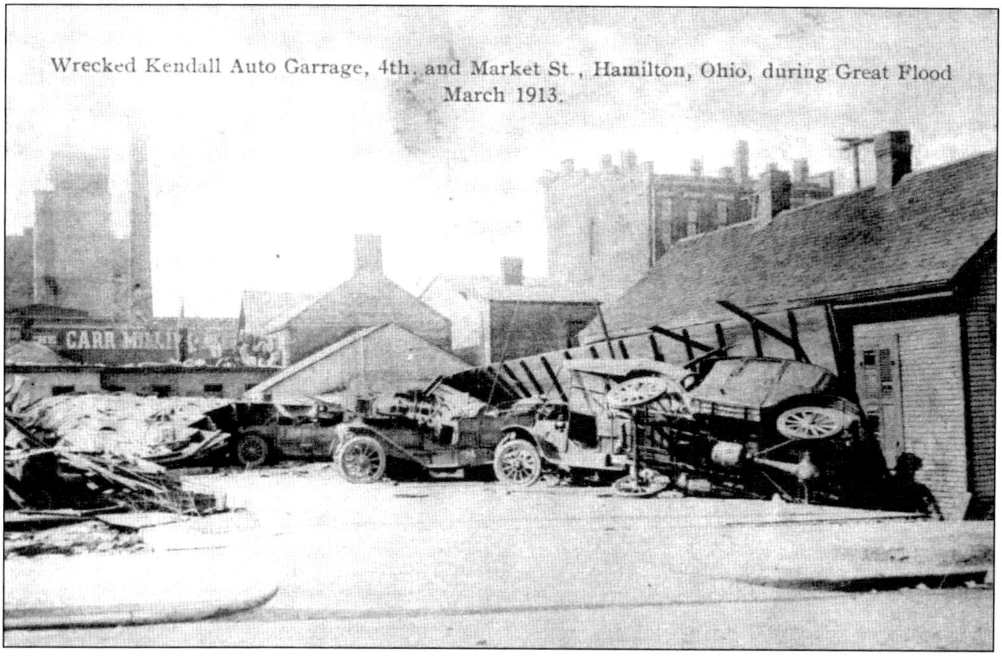

At Fourth and Market Streets in downtown Hamilton, the flood damaged automobiles parked at Kendall Auto Garage. Because of the magnitude of the disaster, it has been referred to in Butler County simply as "the Flood" ever since.

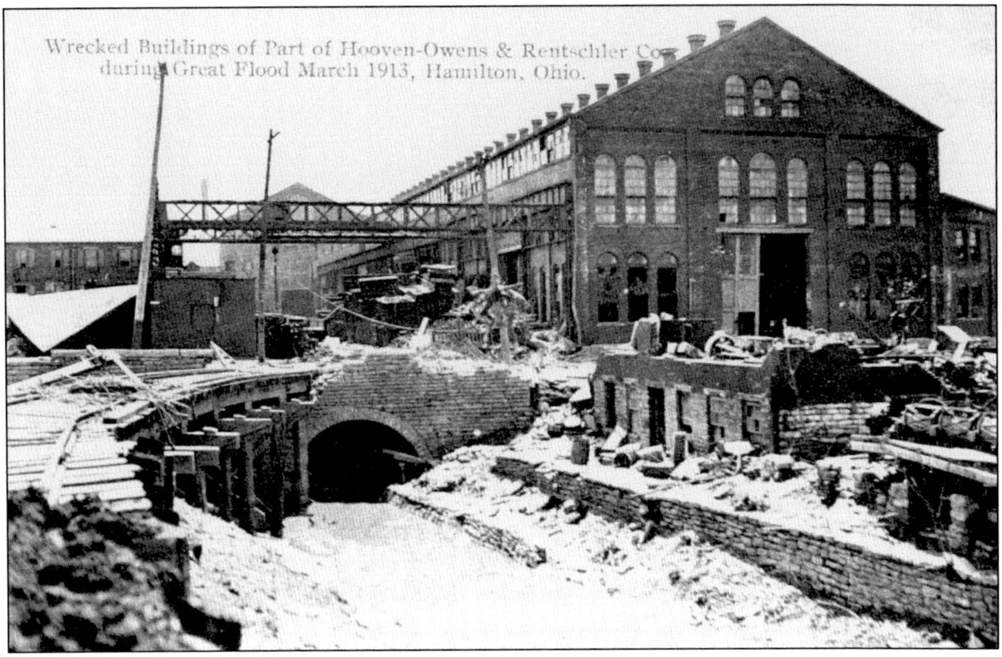

Water destroyed buildings on the lot of the Hooven, Owens, and Rentschler Company factory in Hamilton. Fortunately, the city's industrial base recovered fairly quickly from the flood damage. A group of county governments in the Miami Valley formed the Miami Conservancy District to implement long-range flood control measures that would prevent future disasters.

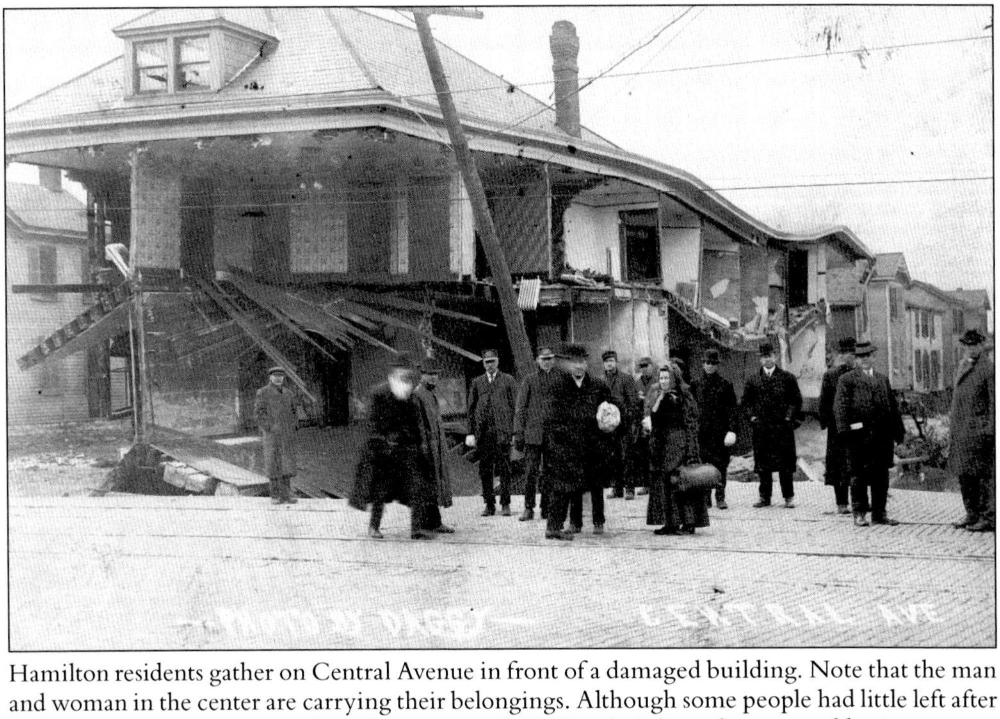

Hamilton residents gather on Central Avenue in front of a damaged building. Note that the man and woman in the center are carrying their belongings. Although some people had little left after the flood, most citizens stayed in the county, rebuilding their lives, homes, and businesses.

Ten

Scenic Views

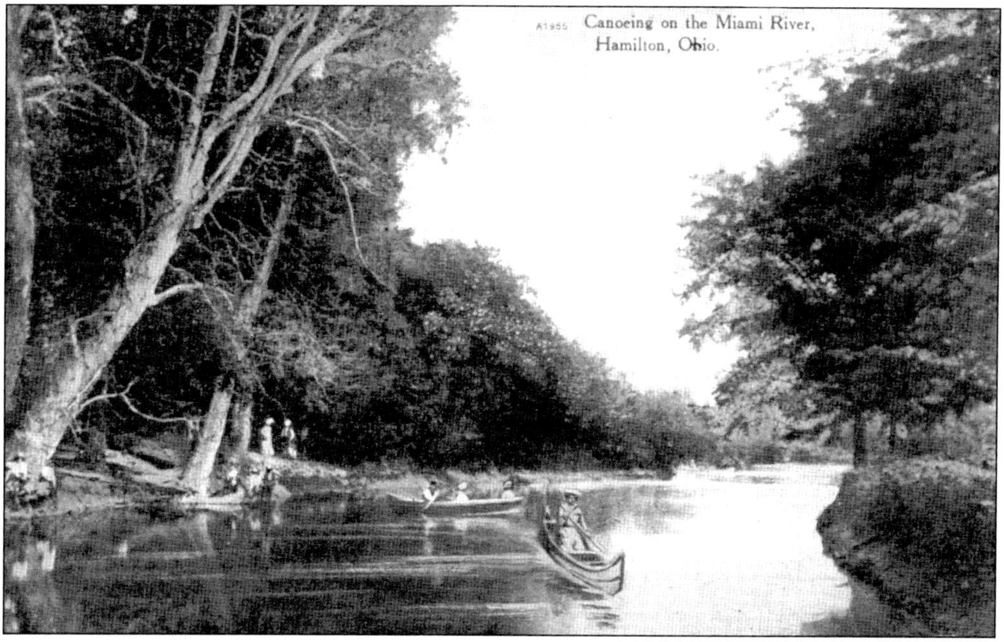

This artist's rendering could be a scene from any river in any community in America. But supposedly it depicts the Great Miami River in Hamilton about 1912. To Butler County residents in those times, the river must have had a split personality of both good and evil. It could turn on them in a matter of hours. The picturesque river could become a raging corridor of water gushing down their streets.

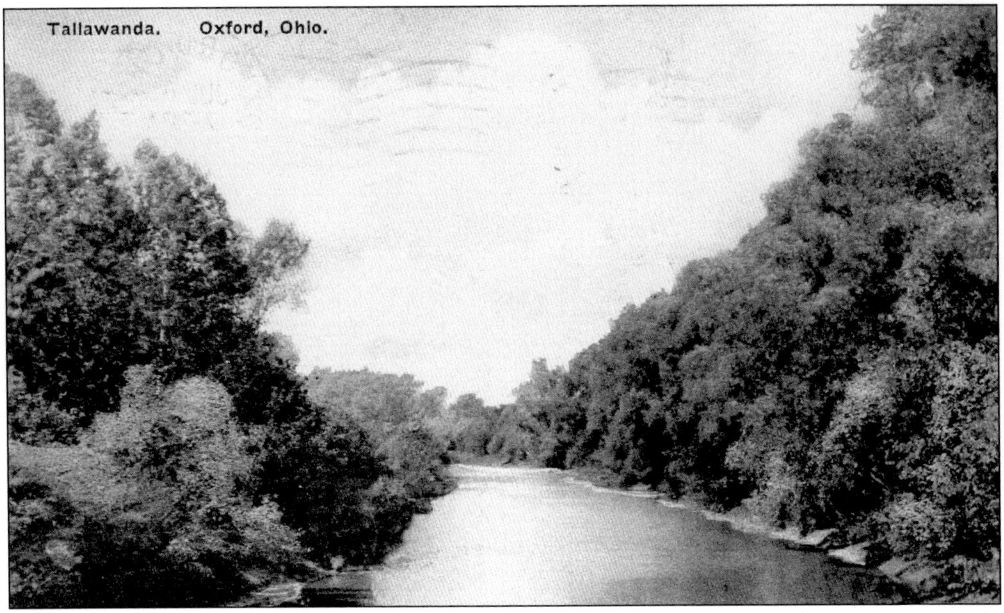

In 1923, someone named Genoa sent a postcard of the beautiful Tallawanda Creek to Myrtle Rhoads in Dayton. The stream is better known as Four Mile Creek.

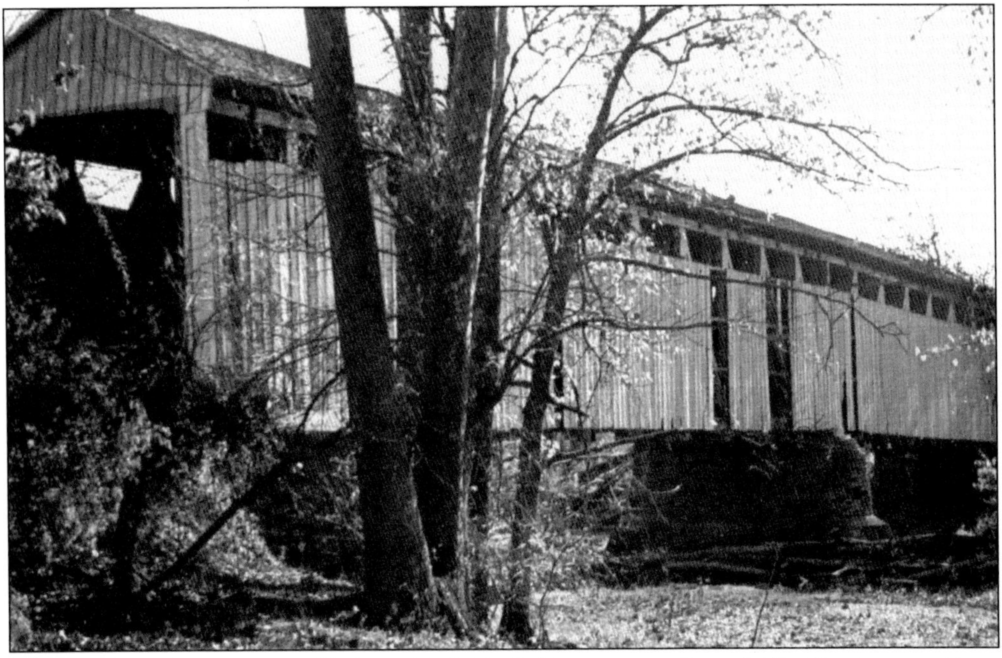

The Black Bridge—once called Pugh's Mill Bridge—spans Four Mile Creek, near State Route 732 north of Oxford. The Oxford Museum Association spent years raising money to restore the 200-foot-long span, the only covered bridge in Butler County remaining in its original location. The original bridge reportedly dates to the 1870s. This postcard shows the bridge before its restoration in the 1980s and 1990s.

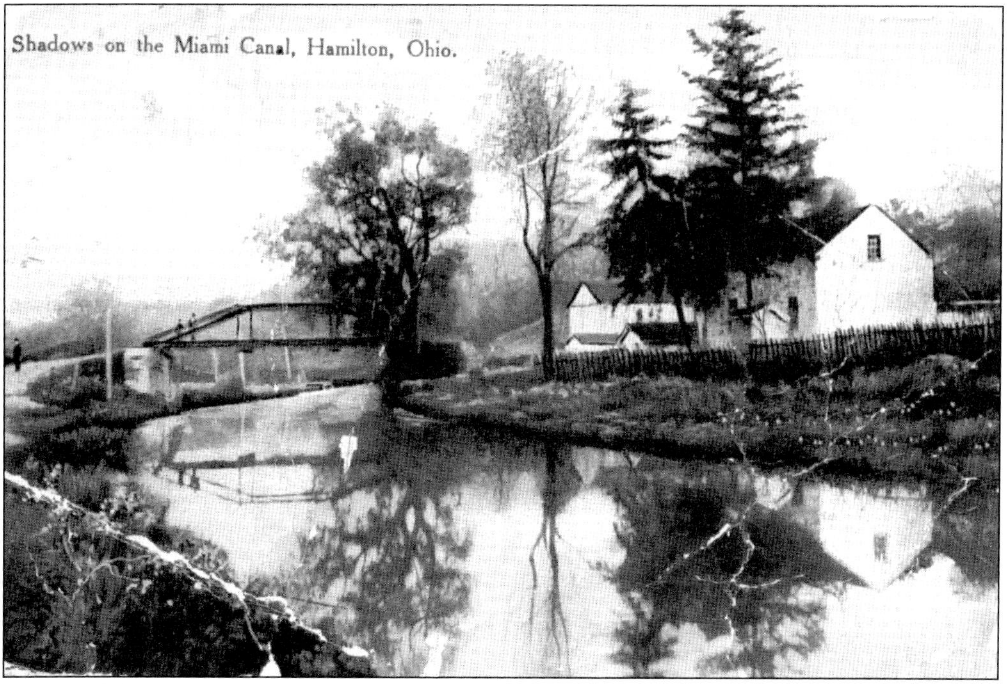

This card displaying an artist's scene, identified as the Miami and Erie Canal in Hamilton, is postmarked July 8, 1911. By then, the canal was used mostly for local boat traffic. It ran down from Middletown and along the present site of State Route 4. In rural areas north of the city, people relaxed along the canal and even swam in it—that is, when it was not infested with mosquitoes.

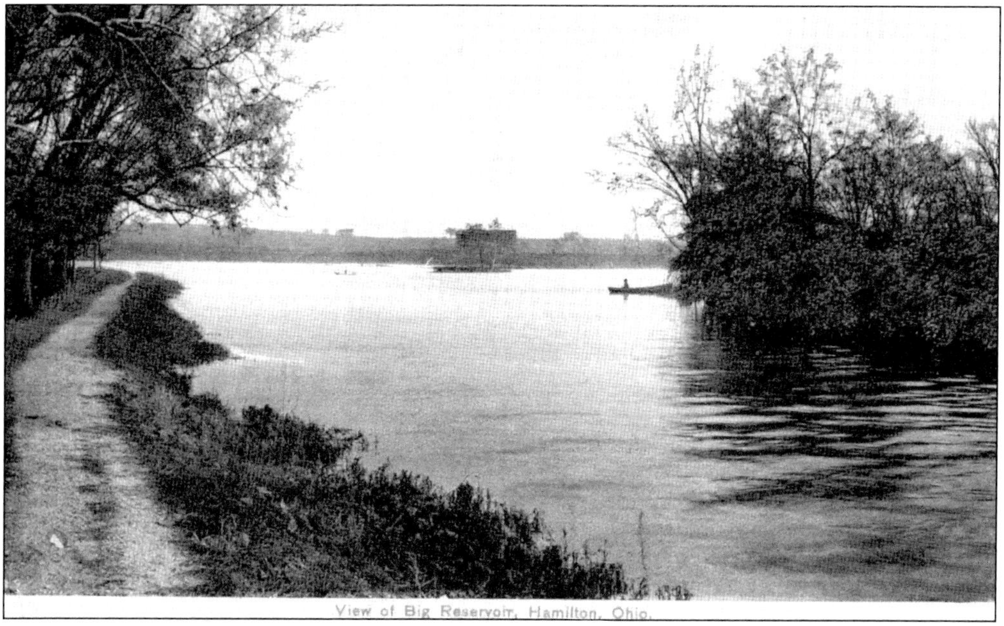

Water was important to Butler County residents in the early 1900s. Canals, hydraulic canals (for old water-powered factories), and small reservoirs still existed, although by then their need had diminished in favor of the railroads and automobiles.

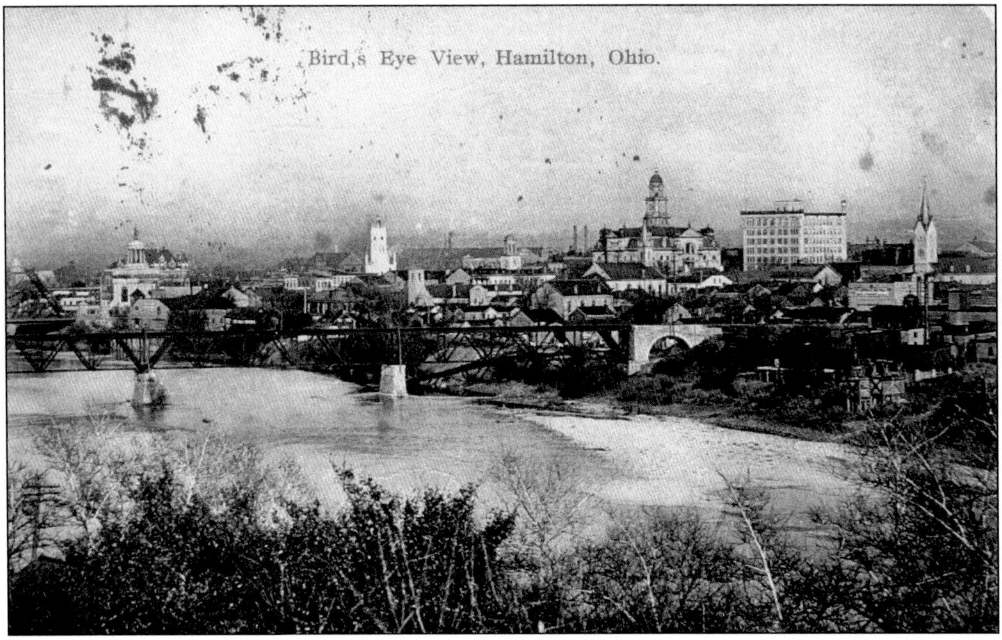

This hilltop view, southwest of downtown, shows Hamilton's skyline and the railroad bridge crossing the Great Miami River. Visible architectural landmarks include the Soldiers, Sailors, and Pioneers Monument (left), the Butler County Courthouse (right), and the Rentschler Building (far right). The card is postmarked 1914.

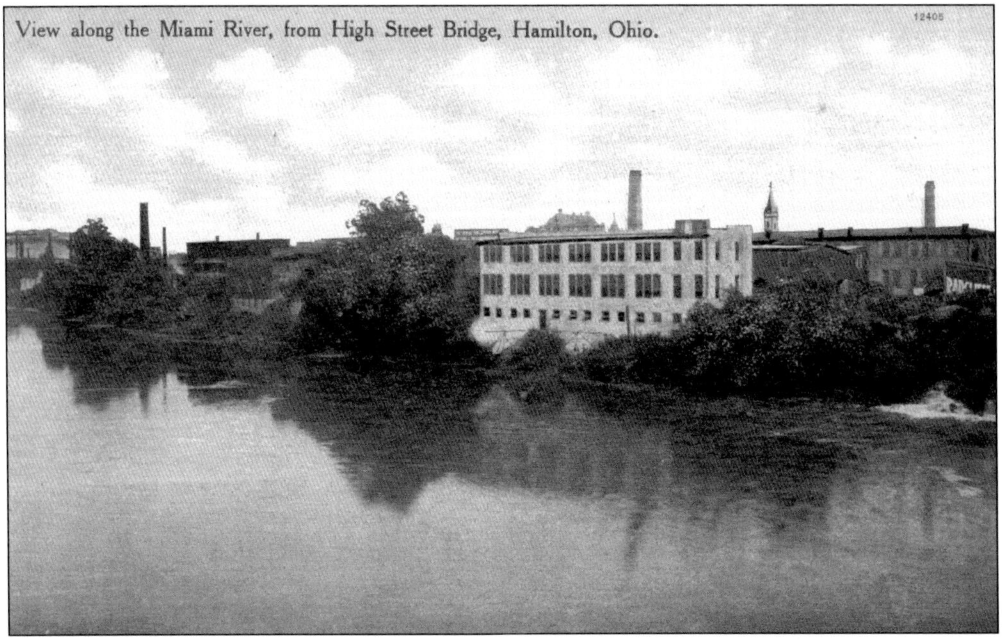

Taken from the High Street Bridge, this river view reveals Hamilton's two sides: scenic river and industrial landscape. This postcard was mailed in 1910, three years before Butler County's destructive flood.

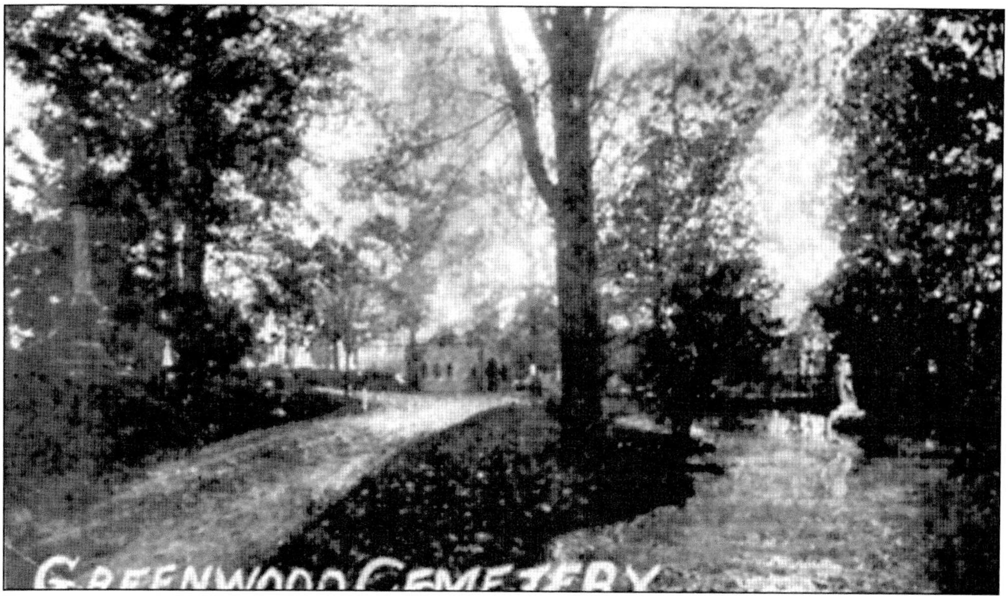

Founded in 1848, Hamilton's historic Greenwood Cemetery embodies the characteristics of the rural cemetery movement, popular in the United States in the mid-19th century. Many of Hamilton's prominent early citizens are buried there. Renowned landscaper Adolph Stauch helped design the grounds. Stauch, former gardener to Austrian emperor Ferdinand I, also landscaped Spring Grove Cemetery in Cincinnati.

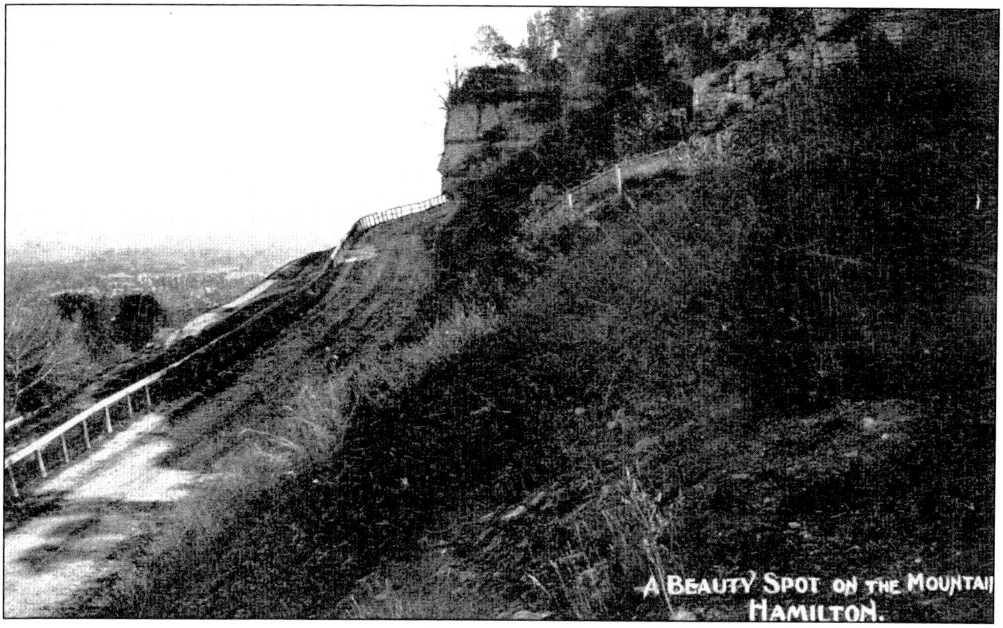

This card supposedly depicts a view from "the mountain," overlooking Hamilton in the early 1900s. In those days, postcard publishers used generic shots for many communities. If this one is genuine, the photographer probably overlooked Hamilton from the hill above Main Street in Hanover Township, or possibly from an east side hill in Fairfield Township.

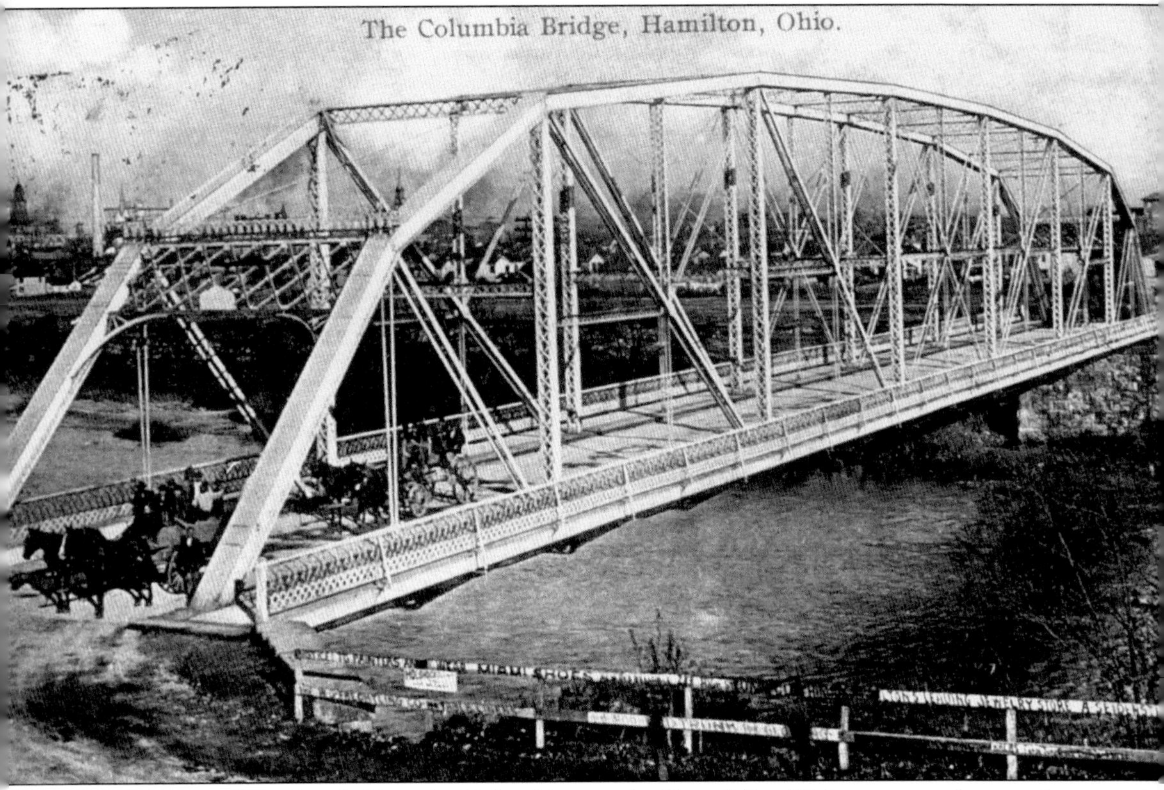

This magnificent iron bridge, the Columbia over the Great Miami River, spanned east and west sides just south of downtown. By reference, today it would stand where the current Columbia Bridge connects Neilan Boulevard with New London Road and State Route 128. Notice the merchants' advertising on the wooden fence to the right of the old span. This sepia-toned postcard was mailed in 1912, one year before the flood would wash away four important bridges—the Columbia, the High Street, the Black Street, and the Cincinnati, Hamilton, and Dayton Railroad. Hamilton's bridge losses from the flood totaled $500,000.

Bibliography

Bartlow, Bert S., and W. H. Todhunter, eds. *Centennial History of Butler County*. Cincinnati: B. F. Bowen, 1905.

Bauer, Cheryl, and Randy McNutt. *Hamilton*. Charleston, SC: Arcadia Publishing, 2005.

Benzing, Esther R. *Historical Gleanings*. Privately published, 1976.

———. *Historical Notes*. Cincinnati: Porter Printing, 1989.

Blount, Jim. *Butler County Biographies*. Hamilton, OH: Past/Present/Press, 2001.

———. *On the Home Front, 1941–1945: Hamilton in World War II*. Hamilton, OH: Past/Present/Press, 1995.

Crout, George C. *Middletown USA: All American City*. Middletown, OH: Perry Printing, 1960.

Elliott, Valerie Edwards. *Oxford*. Charleston, SC: Arcadia Publishing, 2004.

Glos, R. E. *The Buildings of Miami University*. Privately published, 1983.

Greater Middletown: A Dream Come True. Middletown, OH: Middletown Civic Association, 1924.

History and Biographical Cyclopedia of Butler County, Ohio. Cincinnati: Western Biographical Publishing, 1882.

McBride, James. *Notes on Hamilton*. 1831. Reprint, Hamilton, OH: Republican Publishing Company, 1898.

McCoy, Alan H., ed. *Middletown Memories: A Bicentennial Year*. Middletown, OH: Middletown Bicentennial Commission, 1991.

Schwartz, James. *Hamilton, Ohio: Its Architecture and History*. Hamilton, OH: Hamilton City Planning Department, 1986.

Smith, Ophia D. *Old Oxford Houses and the People Who Lived in Them*. Oxford, OH: Oxford Historical Press, 1941.

Discover Thousands of Local History Books Featuring Millions of Vintage Images

Arcadia Publishing, the leading local history publisher in the United States, is committed to making history accessible and meaningful through publishing books that celebrate and preserve the heritage of America's people and places.

Find more books like this at
www.arcadiapublishing.com

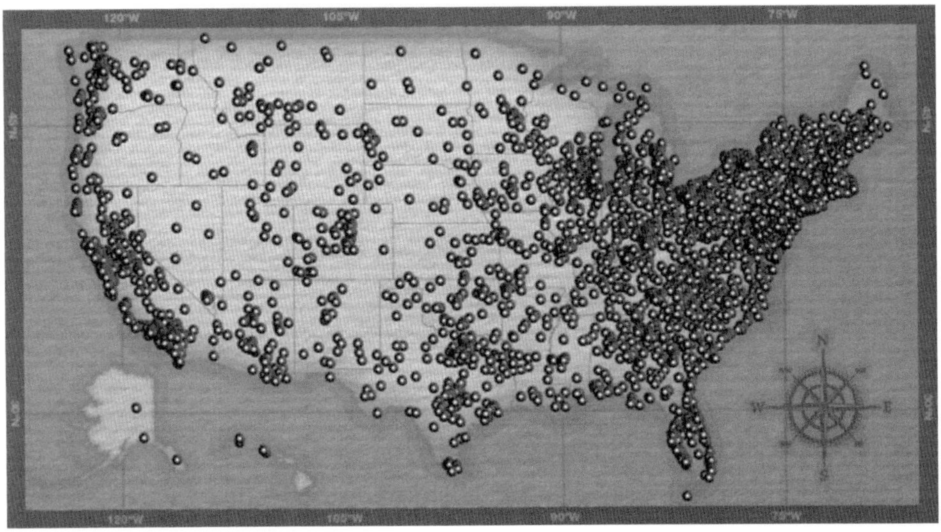

Search for your hometown history, your old stomping grounds, and even your favorite sports team.

Consistent with our mission to preserve history on a local level, this book was printed in South Carolina on American-made paper and manufactured entirely in the United States. Products carrying the accredited Forest Stewardship Council (FSC) label are printed on 100 percent FSC-certified paper.

MADE IN THE USA